Traveling Light

Traveling Light

On the Road with America's Poor

KATH WESTON

Beacon Press, Boston

11549845

Beacon Press
25 Beacon Street
Boston, Massachusetts 02108-2892
www.beacon.org

Beacon Press books
are published under the auspices of
the Unitarian Universalist Association of Congregations.

11 10 09 08 8 7 6 5 4 3 2 1

This book is printed on acid-free paper that meets the uncoated paper
ANSI/NISO specifications for permanence as revised in 1992.

Text design and composition by Susan E. Kelly
at Wilsted & Taylor Publishing Services

Library of Congress Cataloging-in-Publication Data
Weston, Kath
  Traveling light : on the road with America's poor / Kath Weston.
      p. cm.
  Includes bibliographical references.
  ISBN 978-0-8070-4137-6 (acid-free paper) 1. Poor—United States.
2. Poverty—United States. 3. United States—Description and travel.
I. Title.

HV4045.W47 2008
305.5'690973—dc22   2008008214

for Geeta
meri jaan

Contents

Prologue:
Freedom in My Pocket

How far can you get on two tacos (spicy beef), one Dr. Pepper cherry cola (small), and a thin dime held in reserve at a time when ten cents could still buy a phone call? Nine hundred seventy-six miles, come to find out. Somehow these scant provisions had to stretch to cover thirty-eight hours from Albuquerque, New Mexico, to Minneapolis, Minnesota, on the return leg of my first cross-country bus trip. Our bus was delayed, so the first taco disappeared before we ever left the station, with the other soon to follow. At the snack bar in the Amarillo depot, a kindhearted passenger shared half a bowl of chili with me. By the time we reached Tulsa I was lightheaded. By the time we reached the Twin Cities I was starving.

I had climbed aboard courtesy of a government-funded program intended to expand the horizons of city youth by sending us to summer field schools where we would learn a bit about archaeology and environmental science. The scholarship provided us each with a bus ticket and fed us while we were on site but included nothing for meals or lodging along the way. So we rode, and we rode, and we rode, coming from Denver, Indianapolis, Oklahoma City, and D.C. to gather in the small metropolis of Las Cruces, New Mexico.

The year was 1975. Global fallout from the oil crisis had

introduced my generation of graduating high school seniors to something called stagflation, a combination of economic stagnation (good luck finding a job) and an expanding money supply (good luck paying those inflated prices). Still, the United States had yet to experience the right-wing-sponsored campaigns against "big government" that would cut and disband social-service-oriented programs like the one that brought mobility to my world. It wasn't class mobility, not yet, but it was mobility of a sort that made the humiliations of scrambling for money recede. For a time.

On that journey to New Mexico I met—or should I say joined?—an ever-changing band of riders who travel by bus across North America. Not everyone who rides the bus in the United States is poor, of course, by any measure, but if you are living poor and you manage to travel any significant distance by land, the bus is one of the vehicles likely to carry you.

Within hours of my departure, I had struck up conversations with a baby-faced Chippewa recruit reporting for boot camp, a self-proclaimed pimp, a first-generation college student from Bemidji State, and a gray-skinned white girl looking for a place to kick her heroin habit. When the rear axle broke in the middle of the night just outside Iowa City, the gray-skinned girl and I wandered past dark-shingled houses looking for a place to ditch her stash while we debated whether it was possible to make it on the street without selling sex. She had traveled a different path from mine, but we had one thing in common with most of the passengers on that bus: we were living poor in what passed for the wealthiest country in the world. Both of us had had years of practice in the fine art of parleying a little something into a little something more.

I had grown up in a "respectable" working-class family

with a father who held a steady job walking a delivery route for the post office. Yet it had taken only a single, simple twist of fate for me to become homeless after high school ended. Temporarily homeless, as it would turn out, but who ever knows the extent of such a thing except in retrospect? Like most people who end up on the street, I possessed little in the way of material resources. I was far luckier than most in that I had secured financial aid to attend college in the fall, but I did not know how I would pay room and board or how I would bridge the time between the end of the summer program and the beginning of school. I was sixteen. I was alone. And, although I dared not say so, even to myself, I was scared to death.

One thing I was not was deprived. For me, in that situation, the bus ticket in my pocket felt like freedom: freedom to travel, freedom to experience, freedom to try. A shot at something that was mine to want. A chance that could lead to the next chance. This, you see, is the very antithesis of what it feels like to grow up without money, once you understand what money can do.

Once you understand what money can do, especially to people who don't have it, attention has a way of turning to the little matter of getting by. How to survive the indignities required to access the things you need to live. How to hold on to hope in the face of all the things that will never be yours to undertake, or will at best be yours to undertake someday, dreams of "if only" permitting. That ticket in my pocket had its price. A price I could not have paid. Yet every time I touched it, I conjured up a different sort of riches.

I could have spent that trip to Las Cruces impatiently gazing out the bus window, grumbling about how I would have been there already if only I could have afforded the plane. No doubt that complaint crossed my mind long before the thirty-fifth hour. I certainly would have been less exhausted, better fed. Envy is another time-tested way of learning to manage with less. But the more privileged, insulated, convenience-oriented route of air transport would also have taken away the opportunity to learn from people like the gray-skinned girl, companions of necessity whose shadows crossed mine at an impressionable time and who occasionally speak to me still. Coming from Roma—Gypsy—people on my father's side helps me to remember that arrival is not all. Often the road is the thing.

Twenty-five years and a higher education later, I took to the road again by bus to begin the research for this book. As the United States entered a new century, the airwaves were filled with news about a "widening gap" between rich and poor. It sounded ominous enough, but what did this abstraction mean, and what if anything did globalization have to do with it? Was there anything distinctive about living poor and traveling poor in a country where riches are on display all around you?

Rather than hanging out on the corner, searching for a low-paying job, or living under a freeway ramp, I looked where I knew I would find poverty in motion. The bus is a place where extraordinary generosity coexists with pickup lines and scams, where hard-working people resigned to living poor ride beside hard-working people who claim they're just having a run of bad luck, where some folks pass the time complaining about how they've come down in the world while others rap, sketch, and story new worlds into being. The bus is also a place where injustice finds some of its most acute analysts and civic debate thrives. "Poverty" can't begin to describe it.

Step up onto the coach. *Achen devlesa.*

It's a Poor Rat That's Got But One Hole:
An Introduction to Living Poor in a Rich Country

It was late in the day when my neighbor Daniel found out he was getting laid off from his job as a sheet metal installer. He had held that job for years. And how likely was he to get another, an African American man approaching retirement? In fact, retirement may have had something to do with why he got laid off. The company said it was cutting costs, but who's to say? Maybe they didn't want to pay that pension. He was in great shape, wiry and working out, but nobody seemed prepared to hire a black guy going to gray. He'd been out there looking and looking.

Employers sounded enthusiastic when he detailed his credentials on the phone, but then did their best to show him the door as soon as they got a glimpse of him. Daniel voiced all of this and more when I stopped by his house a week later, a month later, a year later to ask him whether he needed food, what he thought about the elections, and how the job search was going. His deepest concern, with winter coming on, was the supplier that had threatened to cut off his mother's source of heating oil. It bothered him that he wasn't in a position to help. Once, when I asked him how the company that laid him off thought he was supposed to manage— a rhetorical question and we both knew it—he told me not to worry. It's a poor rat, he grinned, that's got but one hole.

And that about sums up the art of living poor. Living without ready money is a juggling act. With humor, imagination, cleverness, and more than a little luck, the balls stay up in the air, at least for a time. It's also a continuing education in the skills required to hustle possibilities, forge connections, engage in give-and-take, cultivate resilience, keep your balance, and live to tell your story. Diverse tactics, multiple "holes," allow people to pursue their own visions of living well, in ways that exceed raw purchasing power. Often enough, these stratagems involve travel.

There's the man with joint custody and a tie-dyed T-shirt who took his ten-year-old daughter along with him on the bus whenever school let out for the summer. He was proud of figuring out a way to show her the country, even a little bit of Mexico. They visited historic sites together, gathered edible wild foods, debated current issues with people from all walks of life. In his opinion, the bus provided the best education his daughter was likely to get. The rest of the year he rides until he runs out of money. Then he picks up odd jobs wherever he happens to land until he saves enough to get back on the road again.

There's the exasperated woman who had already ridden twelve hours with two fussy kids on the way to a funeral in Louisiana. Her brother was supposed to meet her en route at the bus terminal in downtown Los Angeles. That man is late, as usual, and he knows I'm tired! she said, trying to brush her teeth with a toddler balanced on one knee. Would you watch my youngest while I call him? We had to pass the hat to get the money for the tickets, but we managed. I'll be damned if my children don't get to see their grandfather buried.

There's the husky young fellow who had hitched his dreams of upward mobility to the sports lottery. I met him when he was traveling to Boston to play a game in the semi-professional New England Football League. He wasn't sure, but he thought his team would be playing a squad from one of the Marine bases. Had I seen the field out by Logan Airport? he wanted to know. The one hemmed in by loop roads, overpasses, and a subway station? That's where they would face off against their opponents. Does anybody come to watch you play? I asked. Yeah, some games we get a lot of people, he said. Mostly because it doesn't cost them an arm and a leg to go.

Then there was the woman with one of the most typical reasons of all for riding: traveling to get to a new job. She had heard they were hiring call center workers in Mississippi. It's not true what they say, that all these jobs are going offshore, she insisted. There's good money to be made right here. ("Here" being a relative concept.) Ten, maybe eleven bucks an hour, if you know how to sweet-talk. At least that's what her cousin told her.

Ten bucks an hour comes to twenty thousand dollars a year. I asked her if she could make it in Mississippi on that. Well, she said, that's what family's for. To help you get by. At least they're *supposed* to help you get by. Now my cousin Denise, she talks big, but when it's time to pay that piper, she has a way of never being around. My sister's son, Trey, he's another story. That child would do anything for you. Did I tell you about the time...?

Folded into the stories in the pages that follow are headlines, observations, and statistics that track the intensification of poverty and inequality as the United States entered a new century. "The enormous wealth gap between white families and black and Hispanic families grew larger after the most recent recession."[1] "Income inequality is growing to levels not seen since the Gilded Age, around the 1880s."[2]

"[In 2003] the poverty rate among households headed by a single woman rose to 28 percent."[3] "The proportion of children living in poverty has risen in a majority of the world's developed economies."[4] "If the United States is so rich, critics ask, how come its poor are poorer than almost anywhere else in the developed world?"[5] Many bus riders' comments echoed this question.

Folded into *these* findings are structural changes in the world's economies that lend nearly every story global dimensions. The man who took to the road with his ten-year-old daughter first started riding the bus after a multinational corporation "ate" the smaller company where he worked. When the multinational trimmed costs to make payments on the debt incurred by the merger, his branch was the first to go. Never would he have imagined that a layoff could lead him to redefine the good life.

Clarice, the mother riding the bus to get to a funeral, had had a different experience of cutbacks. Forced onto workfare in an era when many governments deemed the so-called welfare state "uncompetitive," she worried constantly about what she would do without health insurance if any of her kids got sick. Jason, the aspiring left tackle, had found employment doing something he loved for rock-bottom pay because U.S.-based sports associations had begun to groom talent to allow them to expand their franchises into Europe and Asia. He acknowledged that a serious sports-related injury would be "the end of the line," but said he tried not to think about that.

Shantelle, the woman seeking call center work in Mississippi, found it interesting to hear that unemployed Europeans had migrated to South Asia to work in call centers there. How can that be? she wondered. Those are poor countries! Then she began to laugh at herself. Here I am, she said, talking about how lucky I am to live in a rich country, and I can't even afford to buy my lunch!

For generations that had grown up with nationalist rhetoric about being number one and televised invitations to consumer paradise, the world sometimes seemed to be turning upside down. "Poor nations" had begun lending funds to "rich nations," transforming "rich nations" into debtors. In the United States, "middle-class people" borrowed to maintain their standard of living and "rich people" received bailouts for their hedge funds, while "poor people" failed to share even the paper wealth.

When I started riding the buses for this project in 1999, an economic boom was under way. Not that riders necessarily noticed the difference. Some of the working-class African Americans interviewed by Studs Terkel for his oral history of the Great Depression, *Hard Times,* laughed and told him that every time was like depression times for black folk. Likewise for the uptick. By 1998, hard on the heels of "prosperity," real household income had *fallen* over two decades for the bottom 20 percent, leading critical commentator Doug Henwood to pose the question: "Boom for whom?"[6]

By the time I finished the research for the project in 2006, the country had embarked upon new imperial ventures, racked up a staggering trade deficit, reduced taxes for the very wealthy, borrowed ever greater sums from abroad, and passed stringent new bankruptcy legislation (applicable only to individuals, not to the fictive persons known as corporations). Workers whose wages rose tended to put in longer hours rather than collect higher salaries, especially if they were women. The government took action to abolish time-and-a-half pay for employees in many occupations. Then the Treasury set the printing presses to working overtime in order to pay its own bills.

On the streets, the results looked something like this: A homeless person tapping on car windows for loose change at the end of a highway off-ramp near Reno might have as little to his name, in absolute terms, as a pavement dweller in Calcutta. A single mother in Brownsville trying to stretch a bag of *frijoles* until the end of the month might have more to her name, in absolute terms, yet still have to cope with the indignity of relative poverty: controlling far fewer resources than others around her. It's hard to watch your kids go without when other people's kids don't have to. An elderly homeowner on a fixed income in Raleigh might join a growing number of senior citizens who took out risky second mortgages on their homes to pay off their credit cards. A third-grader in Chicago who calls sugared-up chocolate milk "breakfast" would probably manage to ingest more calories than his counterpart in Niger, yet the inferior quality of his food might well leave him in a similar state of malnutrition. Meanwhile, a child born into the top 1 percent could rest easy. By 2001 this tiny fraction of the population in the United States controlled 33.4 percent of total net worth.[7]

In a cash economy, living poor is all about the money. And then again it's not. Respect, a key demand of people living without resources the world over, can be readily intuited, though it cannot be counted. No one wants to be excluded or treated as a criminal without cause. Yet vagrancy laws, introduced to tackle social "problems" such as begging or "rough sleeping," do just that. So do signs that limit the hours of use for public spaces such as beaches or parks. So do informal restrictions on public transportation that prevent buses and trains from stopping in better-off suburban communities. So do city beautification campaigns that forbid overnight street parking. Someone should do a study of the numbers of Americans who have worked their way through school while sleeping in their cars.

Living poor in a rich country adds a twist to the arts of survival. Five hours waiting to change buses at the terminal in Las Vegas should be enough to convince anyone that poverty in a rich country isn't *all* relative. There are individuals in the wealthiest communities in the world who own as few possessions as individuals in the poorest. But where the poverty *is* relative, living poor requires a special skill. A person has to be able to resist the inevitable grinding comparisons between the things she lacks and the things that somebody across town takes for granted.

This temptation to compare has as much to do with sharing as shopping. Americans of all classes like to teach their children to pass around the bags of fruit or candy they bring to school. Call it sharing. Call it an exercise in redistribution. Call it justice. Yet adults often forget to look for those same convictions in themselves. That's another reason why living poor in a rich country, like living poor period, is all about the money. And then again, it never can be.

How to negotiate the tensions between the want incited by consumerism and the more pressing want that separates you from the things you need to live? Without bitterness, without paralyzing anger? One way is to master not only the arts of survival, but the arts of illusion as well. What was the failed company Enron but a seemingly stable, wealthy employer that turned out to be running a shell game in the back of the bus? What does the future hold for the "wealthy" homeowner, sitting in his fancy house of cards atop a foundation of debt? If a person has nowhere to sleep, is it because he has no money or because the world is set up in such a way as to bar him from even a space at the side of the road? If a person has friends, how poor can she be?

I don't have much by way of possessions, a lady riding the bus to Montgomery once told me. But, she said, I do have lots of belongings. I belong to my family, my people, my church. And they belong to me. With all the mouths I feed, she continued, looking out the window, I won't lie to you— I could use one of them big houses! But don't never, ever let anybody tell you that you're poor. In the eyes of the world, maybe, she said. You just keep looking through your own eyes.

"Rich" and "poor" can be misleading terms. It doesn't matter whether you apply them to a country the size of the United States or to a writer boarding the bus for Montgomery. These are static, homogenizing concepts of the sort that foster misapprehensions. No wonder so many residents of "poor countries" believe that everybody living in a "rich country" like America must be well off, if not rolling in dough. No wonder so many prosperous Americans are surprised to hear that "poor people" in their own country travel.

"Rich" and "poor" also obscure something about the nature of class as a relationship. If your new microwave oven costs ridiculously little and the company that sells it makes a handsome profit, then somebody working on an assembly line may not have enough to eat. If your own paycheck doesn't begin to cover the cost of your groceries, your labor may be underwriting someone else's excess. You may also be caught up in massive structural changes of the sort inadequately described by words such as "globalization." Poverty is never some affliction that mysteriously fastens onto unlucky or unworthy people. A growing disparity has to come from somewhere.

When headlines describe the gap between rich and poor as widening, discussions of poverty or wealth can't begin to tell the story. Why is there a gap? What factors have conspired to widen that gap? What happens in people's lives when the gap becomes a chasm?

I can't answer all these questions, but I can invite you to

ride the buses with people who are willing to hazard an insight and a guess, based upon how the world looks from the less privileged side of the divide. *Traveling Light* is not a book about people living in poverty. Rather, I have tried to write a book about people who are living *out* poverty at a particular historical moment, facing their circumstances with creativity, despair, animosity, analysis, resentment, and panache.

Yes, there will be riders whose stories incorporate many stock elements of the poverty trade: unemployment, prison, bad food, bad housing, illness, gang warfare. Yes, there will be random terror, as riders use limited resources to cope with visitations of the unexpected. Yes, there will be persecution, and even a touch of pathos. One of the challenges facing anyone who writes about living poor is to acknowledge these conditions without falling into the voyeuristic conventions that pervade well-meaning middle-class exposés of "poverty." These conventions often take the form of tacit questions: Can you believe how tough things are for these people? Isn't it a shame how some people have to live? Whereas, of course, if you yourself are living that life, none of these things would come as a revelation.

By riding the buses I hoped to get at aspects of living poor that have eluded community studies of poverty. The bus gave me a way to spend time—lots of time—with a broad range of people of limited means who hailed from here, there, and the other side of everywhere. Regardless of whether they thought of themselves as poor or not, most had ended up riding hour after hour because that was the only way they could travel.

The bus may be one of the last quasi-public spaces in the United States where people talk, fuss, and fight about corporate finance and household budgets without waiting for some pollster to formulate a decent question. To ride is to listen; to listen is to overhear; to overhear is to wonder; to wonder is to join in the debate, often as not. Passengers also encounter a different kind of class mobility than the one that makes the papers. The road trip has become its own American art form, yet few have bothered to chronicle what happens when people without money take to the road.

One MCI G-series over-the-road cruiser can assemble quite a crew: A third-generation homeboy from the barrio. An army recruit gambling that he will come back from a tour in Iraq to take advantage of free college tuition. A demobilized vet in search of a job. A college graduate with no clue about what to do next to survive. A single mother who is escorting her teenage son to stay with relatives in the South in the hope that they can help heal some of the scars of northern racism. A "house poor" widow who has managed to keep her home in a posh neighborhood but has nothing left once she pays the taxes. A recent immigrant who has discovered that what he thinks of as "big money" doesn't go so far in the land of the far-from-free. A country child and a city child, growing up with very different skills for turning a little into a little more.

Of course, not every rider takes the bus because she can't afford to take a plane. Greyhound, ever protective of its corporate image, contends that a third of its passengers have college degrees. That still leaves two-thirds without. Nor does higher education guarantee an income, as any unemployed Ph.D. will testify. The recurrent attempts by bus companies to upscale their passengers in press releases says something in and of itself about whose lives are most valued in North America.[8]

There are European students of modest means who get the shock of the lives once they realize just how big the country is and how long it will take to get to their destinations.

There are upper-middle-class people who set out to ride the bus once, just for the experience (usually concluding that once is enough). There are regular commuters who haunt the corridors on the eastern seaboard. There are writers like me. But on the long runs, poverty is a lot of what you get. At least if you measure wealth in terms of cash money. Which many riders refuse to do.

In a world beholden, the old saying stands revised: It's a poor rat that's got but one route. Connection, now that is the thing. Or so the desert dwellers would tell me.

I.

When the Desert Fails to Bloom:
Albuquerque to Missoula via Vegas

Pennies from Heaven

A fistful of coins went rolling, spinning, all over the cafeteria floor, with a handful of children skittering after. Get them! the children's mother cried. One of her small traveling companions raced toward the wall, where a metal disk had settled into the dust. Another cupped her hands to receive the bounty gathered by a waiting passenger. The youngest emerged from under the table at his mother's feet, a piece of copper displayed triumphantly between his fingers. *Gracias, mijo.* Six pennies in all, some shiny, a few green with age.

Some years ago investigators used a hidden camera to find out whether people would stop to pick up a penny dropped onto a city sidewalk. It turned out that most wouldn't bother. These days, what could anyone buy with a penny? Why go to the effort of stooping down to collect a coin whose purchasing power was almost nil? Inflation and devaluation had eaten away at the currency, the investigators concluded. Perhaps the penny should be retired.

Of course, the investigators did not station their camera in a section of the city where people scramble to put together a life. Nor did they follow the movements of the low-paid workers who keep the city running when they announced that "people" could not be bothered to pick up a penny, even if it fell from the sky. The woman sending her children in hot pursuit in the Albuquerque bus station is not "people." Her name is Dolores, she's about to board a bus for Socorro, and for her this is a game played in earnest. Put those copper coins together with their cousins and someday they might add up to breakfast.

Let's see how many, Dolores says to her son, who is learning to count. One, two, *tres, cuatro* ... The numbers sizzle through the gap where the dentist had to pull a tooth because filling it was too expensive. I know, Mama, I know! her boy cries, surveying the pile of coins. It's six. Six dollars is enough for candy? Not dollars, *mijo,* cents, explains his mother. Six cents. Not enough for candy.

Her son closes his eyes, clings fitfully to the bougainvillea pattern of her sundress. In the course of shepherding their meager assets, his mother has him chasing change of another sort: the transformations wrought by global capital flows in the everyday lives of people without money. When inflation hits because oil prices spike on world markets, Dolores can't pretend that she has the luxury of ignoring coins that come in low denominations. She simply has to work that much harder to amass them. When pennies from heaven drop into her life in the form of an unexpected gift from a brother who has found work offshore, she immediately puts those coins to use. It's not just because the need is so dire. It's also because she does what she can, while she can. In Dolores's experience, the celestial administration isn't particularly concerned about the impact of unemployment or war or currency fluctuations on her small-small life.

Emma Tarlo puts her finger on the operative dynamic here. "Far from standing outside national policies and events, the urban poor often find themselves deeply implicated within them," she writes in her study of the forced relocation of poor communities in India after the suspension of civil liberties during the 1970s Emergency. Why? Because in a cash economy, people without money "lack the political, economic and educational resources with which to build a shield in moments of crisis."[1] In Albuquerque just as in New Delhi.

Be that as it may, most are inclined to do something rather than simply suffer the consequences of events beyond their own making. Dolores won't, can't, pass those pennies by, because for her family even the smallest sums are integral to *getting* by.

Once, at the bus terminal in Mobile, a white kid with a nasty black eye who hadn't eaten for two days asked me for lunch money. He was so hungry he raced through the cafeteria line with the five dollars I gave him, devouring half his fried chicken plate on the way back. Then he settled down to tell me the story of how he got rolled for $184. Not $200. Not $185, mind you. There's no rounding off for auditors of their own lives when every dollar counts. It was his life's savings.

Capital accumulation, accounting, currency arbitrage: in this economy, nearly all market operations have counterparts run by people with few possessions. Farm workers who ride the bus to follow the harvest, then send whatever they save to their families across the border, are masters at leveraging currencies. Even after devaluation, a dollar stretches further in pesos in Oaxaca than it ever would if they had used it to buy property in California. Bus companies understand this well. The backs of ticket envelopes are filled with ads for money-wiring services.

Even more rarified economic transactions find a place on the bus. Later in this trip, during a layover at Idaho Falls, I would watch three friends who had been riding together since Alabama cash a dollar bill in order to get four quarters. After inspecting the quarters, they offered to exchange them for the quarters already in passengers' pockets. It looked innocent enough. Who could object to a one-for-one trade?

The buses were running late that rainy day, so most riders willingly sorted through their loose change to pass the time. What were these young people up to? Their leader, a nineteen-year-old with shaggy auburn hair named Junior, took me aside to explain.

Early in 1999, the government began to issue quarters with a new design that would eventually feature scenes from each of the fifty states on the back. The Treasury Department dedicated the Delaware coin to a man named Caesar Rodney, a delegate to the Continental Congress depicted riding his horse to Independence Hall. Only thing is, said Junior, they misspelled "Caesar" on the back. At least that's what he'd heard.

Oh sure, the feds caught their mistake soon enough. But once they stopped striking the coin, the worth of those flawed "Cesar" quarters naturally skyrocketed until they doubled their face value. Imagine that! Junior's face lit up. Doubling your money! Of course, the gain would only be the difference between twenty-five and fifty cents. No matter. The gleam in his eye at the thought of discovering the grail after an hour of passing coins from hand to hand would match that of any Wall Street trader on a good day.

But of course I'm still in New Mexico, about to board the first of many buses, and I haven't met Junior yet. My journey, like Dolores's, begins in Albuquerque, land of desert light and chile verde, one of the cities I rode through as a girl-child so many years ago. I arrange to spend the night before the trip at the Lorlodge Motel, which occupies the buzzing intersection of the two interstate highways that bisect the city. Despite the one-star rating proudly displayed out front, the motel in many ways is typical of the kinds of accommodations within walking distance of the bus depots of America. Concrete walls topped by razor wire skirt the parking lot.

The towels are clean but threadbare. The phone in the room won't work unless the guest can produce a credit card. Well, at least there's a phone.

On this corner every day brings a new urban drama. Since I checked in, motel guests have been treated to a high-speed police pursuit with shots fired, a Chevy Impala wrapped around the pole that supports the canopy outside the motel office, and the cordoning off of the entire street by the city's Hazmat (hazardous materials) squad when someone sets the vacant motel next door alight. (Probably for the insurance, bystanders whisper.) Each one-act play is directed by patients at the psychiatric hospital across the way, where residents gaze down at the shifting scenes from the dayroom in a building that began life as a sanatorium for workers on the Santa Fe Railroad.

I have time to kill before getting on the bus, so I head for the neighborhoods around Old Town, the original Spanish section of the city, with its adobe bungalows, accordion-gated windows, and tourist traps. When I lived in Albuquerque during the 1980s in the neighborhood called the War Zone, where the real security came from relationships with neighbors, a little thing like the law would never have been enough to prevent people from running an auto repair business out of the garage or keeping chickens. Now the Old Town area, like the rest of the nation, has become a study in contrasts. Glitzy hotels built with out-of-state capital sidle up against yards with tin-roofed sheds. The backyard sheds and tamale stalls are not relics of another era, exactly. They illustrate the kinds of resources that the low-paid workers who service the tourist shops and hotels command. Before long the hoteliers might agitate for the raggedy shacks and sheds to be cleared in an effort to "improve" the neighborhood, without giving much thought to how people displaced from the community would get to work when they had it. Then the local chamber of commerce would have to organize some facsimile of the old New Mexico in the modern register of "quaint," or what would tourists come to see? Imperialist nostalgia, the anthropologist Renato Rosaldo calls it. The process is already well under way.

Near the historic Mission Church, a tourist trades stock tips and complains about what locals call coffee. There's a sprinkling of homegrown yuppies meeting for lunch, *Hispaño* store clerks, people from the Pueblos selling jewelry, and the occasional African American family with a guidebook in hand. Mostly, though, the place is overrun with middle-aged Anglos in slicked-back, sprayed-back hairdos who don't seem particularly interested in the sights. They spend 2.4 seconds absorbing the *retablo* paintings in the church, an hour in the sandwich shop next door. Could this be the national association of bowlers, warmly welcomed with red-white-and-blue signs posted by Old Town's merchants?

At the Western Warehouse on the edge of the square, where I stop to buy a shirt off the clearance rack, the cashier asks me how I'm doing. One of the enduring beauties of working-class life, especially in New Mexico, is that people who give voice to pleasantries often mean what they say. So I read the cashier's nametag and decide to take Leo Chavez at his word by telling him how I am. Not bad, as it turns out. I used to live here, I explain, but today I'm just passing through on the bus. Why'd you leave us? he asks. Let me guess: You left for the money. The only reason people leave us is because they can make better money somewhere else.

He's right. Albuquerque is, in many senses, a military town, heavily dependent on the cash that flows through weapons research laboratories and Kirtland Air Force Base. Yet the influx of funding from elsewhere hasn't done much to

sustain households at the roots. New Mexico has long occupied the bottom rungs in state-by-state comparisons of
income and employment. I want to know if it's still as hard
to make a living here as when I left. Leo says yes indeed,
but his girlfriend, who's been taking care of her mother in
Louisiana, is returning anyway. She can't stand living anywhere else. Welcome back, he smiles, handing me my bag.

When I make my way to the bus station early the next
morning, only folks without a roof to call their own are
awake to see the sun split the peaks of the Sandia and Man-
zano mountains. A line of men waits to get into a shelter on
Central Avenue for breakfast. To one side a Native American
woman leans against the railroad overpass, belongings neatly
piled at her feet, absorbed in a book by Angela Davis. Everybody is layered and shivering in the frosty air. As I pass I offer
one of the men a cigarette from a pack I occasionally carry
just for giveaway since I quit smoking years ago.

Generosity can be another currency. The Old Town
cashier's openhearted inclusion of me in the ranks of hon-
orary New Mexicans turned a passing encounter into much
more than a business transaction. I had energy the rest of the
day. If he had asked me for a favor, I would have seen what
I could do, but that was not the point. What is it they say
about the kindness of strangers?

Still, living according to the old ways under the pressures
of the dog-eat-dog economy ushered in by globalization can
be a struggle. While I wait for my bus at the station, I think
about Yvonne, an Afro-Caribbean woman who rode with me
into New York last year after the Christmas holidays. Like
many border crossers, she described having to rethink the
forms of giving, laboring, and solidarity that she had learned
growing up in the islands. Where I come from, she insisted,
we do not buy a person for favors. You either ask for some-

thing or you get it yourself. That woman I told you about, I sat down and embroidered her a beautiful apron. When she opened it she said, "What is behind this?" "You fool! Nothing is behind it!" That's when I stopped giving presents.

Wasn't there some way, I asked, to keep generosity alive in the United States? In my mind I saw the apron, its border of purple morning glories climbing up the fool's shoulder. Yvonne shook her head sadly. Don't you realize? she said. We are in the darkness yet. We are not in the light.

Final Call for Socorro, Truth or Consequences, Hatch, Las Cruces...

Reveries don't last long for patrons of the bus system. If they do, you'll find yourself with more time on your hands for dreaming than you bargained for as your coach departs without you. While I'm thinking about Yvonne, cities and towns pour out of the loudspeakers, their names scrambled as only words in amplified announcements can be. "Westbound service to Socorro [click], T or C [pause], Hatch, La-a-a-a-s Cruces, and [long pause] Phoenix. With connections to Los Angeles and San Diego. Now departing from Gate 3." Does that give me time to pee? The perennial rider's question.

I duck into the women's restroom, where a vending machine hawks a bright orange plastic keychain with the slogan "A Tisket, a Tasket, A CONDOM OR A CASKET." All set to drop down next to the Swedish Massage Love Oil. Your pick, only $1.50. No time for such choices. I race back outside to find a place on the Phoenix-bound bus. Final call.

The schedule board here resembles the ones in small towns: a single entry for each cardinal direction. Buses don't head for Los Angeles or New York; they go eastbound, westbound, northbound, or southbound, with daily departure times listed. Quite the contrast to the airport-style TV monitors in terminals on the coasts. Although I've lined up for the bus that meanders through the truly small towns of Truth or Consequences and Hatch, once the driver hears "Phoenix" as my destination he points me toward an express bus. My pleas to board the local for the greater good of my writing project ("Your what?") only add to the confusion and make no difference in the end. In the bus system, the driver is a god.

Over in the express line, a Diné woman and her daughter carry a huge, if slightly wilted, stuffed rabbit with purple paws. The mother complains about the slow boarding. Maybe the next time she thinks about visiting relatives in Gallup, she says, she'll stay home. Where are *you* going? she wants to know. All the way to my nephew's high school graduation in Montana, I reply. I always try to have a reason for riding besides writing. This year, since I'm between jobs, I can't afford to fly any more than my seatmates. Besides, it gives me a story to trade.

An African American guy in a natural gets his kids settled near the wheel well. Time to send them back to their mother in L.A. I don't believe in long goodbyes, he says, then has a hard time disembarking. Most of the faces on this bus are *Hispaño*, Mexicano, Native, and black. The scattered Anglos are either very young—that is to say, adolescents—or very old. Hundreds of miles later, when we hit the Phoenix suburbs, this palette will start to shift toward white. In the meantime I imagine the children's father standing sentinel on the loading dock in Albuquerque, willing them back with the power of his longing.

As soon as the bus starts to roll the driver gets on the intercom to emphasize that this trip will be Rated G, which means that we all have to remember the three G's: Goodness,

Greyhound, and . . . I forget the third. Goodness stands for
good language. This is a family bus, he emphasizes. Anybody
who thinks differently can get off now and think it over until
the next coach comes through. There's not a lot of conversation after that fine piece of oratory. People drift into sleep, in
and out, in and out, scarcely distinguishing between day and
night. Many have already been riding for hours. Too old to
wail, "Are we there yet?" they wake up occasionally to in-
quire, "What time is it?" The cry of the bus.

At some point Granola Girl breaks the lull by sitting up.
Her hooded sweatshirt falls back to reveal a shaved or chemo-
crafted head just sprouting into fuzz. An astonishing assort-
ment of Whole Foods yogurt containers emerges from her
pack, each filled with a different soupy concoction. The passengers around her start sniffing discreetly as they get a whiff
of a green substance whose main ingredient seems to be spir-
ulina. That's seaweed to you. I must agree that, seaweed aside,
whatever's in there stinks. Only a white girl would eat this
stuff, somebody whispers. Oh, says another, noting my light
skin: sorry. People close their eyes, trying valiantly to escape
from the smell in the closed metal container that is our
coach, too polite to continue to comment. One guy gives up
the battle and pulls out a can of tuna fish to make a sandwich. Thirty-five cents a can, he boasts. Some of these off-
brand tuna cans, they smell like cat food! He laughs at
himself. Then anyone who has packed a lunch (which seems
to be most everyone) decides to eat. Mercifully the stuff disappears into our bellies and we're once again down for the
count.

Down, that is, until the next rest stop, where we wait in
line amid the boxes in the back of yet another convenience
store to use a toilet that doesn't sway or shake. High atop a
stack of boxes, goopy brown paste coats the inside of what

looks like a used IV bag. "Coca-Cola" reads the writing on the tube that emerges from the bag and disappears into a machine. Gross, isn't it? Granola Girl exclaims. But that's what they make the drinks out of. No wonder they keep it in the back, she says. Decades of counter work surface as privileged knowledge.

We pass billboards advertising Sky City at Acoma Pueblo, the oldest continuously inhabited spot in North America, and the walls of villages where uranium tailings slumber. The Cold War's poisoned gift. A weathered trailer marks the turnoff for one of the Navajo chapter houses as we approach the Checkerboard Reservation. A roadrunner hops into the lower branches of a mesquite tree, then thinks better of it. After every rest stop we rush to climb back onto the coach lest it leave us in the swirling dust. People stow their bags. Somebody begins to snore. Then just when you start thinking you can't imagine how you'll pass the time on this perfectly uneventful ride, the unthinkable happens. The bus is like that.

Everybody Out! Hands Up against the Bus!

The stop that could change your life can't be found on the schedule. Oh yes, company itineraries are quite detailed: 8:50: Grants; 9:55: Gallup. But there are three kinds of bus stops that never appear in these tables: drug inspection checkpoints, passport control, and the periodic raids by *La Migra*. *La Migra* being, of course, the Immigration and Naturalization Service, soon to be swallowed by Homeland Security.

Somewhere between Flagstaff and Camp Verde we're rousted out of sleep by a gravelly FM radio voice that must have taken years to perfect. This one's barking orders: "Get

your ID out now and keep your hands where I can see them."
The minute these words intrude into our dreams
we are criminalized. Each of us cast as a weapon-wielding,
border-jumping threat to the state, until proven otherwise.

If only the proof were in the pudding. We all feel around
for our identification papers, if we have them, and try not to
look the INS officer in the eye. Like the bull you come across
suddenly in a field, whispers the man next to me. Don't pro-
voke him. The officer reserves his harshest glance exclusively
for brown passengers, broadly conceived (though not too
broadly). I could be gray-eyed Argentinean, naturalized Mexican, here legally or no, but they're not interested in me. It's
the age of profiling, and citizens, too, have been known to
spend the night in the aftermath of a raid stranded on the
other side of the border.

How ironic, Laguna author Leslie Marmon Silko observes,
that the continent's original residents should be taken into
custody on their own ancestral land, the shades of sepia,
fawn, and russet in their skin perceived as a marker of belonging elsewhere. Traffic stops have long provided an excuse
to discriminate against particular categories of travelers. In
South Dakota it might be Driving While Indian (DWI); in
New Jersey, Driving While Black (DWB); in Detroit, Driving While Muslim (DWM). (What, you're Lebanese Christian? Who could tell?) Traveling in a beat-up car, sharing a
ride across color lines: these, too, have been enough to bring
a journey to a forced halt. It must be some drug buy, the
thinking goes, or perhaps a terrorist rendezvous. Couldn't
possibly be friendship. They say it's about how you look, but
it's really about how you look to whoever's looking. And
where do those ideas come from?

Riding the bus lends an extra dimension to the profiling
operations carried out by state agencies, because the relative

poverty of the clientele on the buses is precisely what targets them for random inspections. "Police board buses or trains at intermediate stops," writes legal scholar David Cole, "to exploit the fact that the traveler has nowhere to go."[2] He recounts one of the most famous court cases to contest bus sweeps in North America, *Florida v. Bostick.* One fine summer day in 1985 a man named Terrance Bostick fell asleep in the back of a Greyhound bus on a run from Miami to Atlanta. He woke up to the sight of armed officers from the Broward County sheriff's department towering over his seat. They demanded his identification and his ticket, which he duly produced. When they asked to search his bag, he assented. In the bag was a pound of cocaine. Bostick's conservative lawyer, Donald Ayer, argued that no reasonable person in Bostick's place, never mind an African American man who found his way blocked by policemen, would have felt free to refuse to cooperate under the circumstances. "Even if Bostick had been able to push his way around the officers and get off the bus, he would have found himself in the middle of rural Florida, far from his destination, and separated from any luggage he'd checked."[3]

The Florida Supreme Court held the search unconstitutional on Fourth Amendment grounds, but the U.S. Supreme Court reversed the decision, leaving authorities free to continue mounting the type of raid that had me and a busload of passengers nervously awaiting *La Migra*'s verdict in the Arizona desert. "*Dios,* she forgot her license at home!" "They looked at my papers too long." "Are they going to take me?" Across the aisle an old man is praying.

They don't like bus people, a friend explained when I told her about the close scrutiny that passengers had received at the Canadian border on a trip I took to Montreal. What do you mean they don't like bus people? Only low-income people ride the bus, she said, that's what they think. Then they start to believe they can get away with anything. Her husband joined in with a story about the time he brought along a gift box of fancy chocolates on the reverse journey from Canada to America. The customs guy opened the box and ate one, he said. Can you believe it? Right in front of me!

On my Montreal trip, the Vermont Transit driver picked up the microphone to assert that he had no control over what would happen at Canadian customs or how long things would take. After we exited the coach, carrying all our luggage, officials would check the bus inside and out. Sure enough, as soon as we glided to a stop, men with mirrors on long poles appeared to inspect the underside of the carriage. Once inside the little administrative building I watched the passengers shrink back, almost imperceptibly. Someone's got to step up, I thought; it might as well be the light girl with a bit of cash in her wallet. (Traveling to Vancouver in the 1980s I had almost been refused entry because I could not demonstrate that I possessed enough money to last a week.) I took up a position at the head of the queue.

Two immigration officers assumed their posts, gossiping while we waited behind a line painted on the floor. Check-through aisles gave the room the feel of a supermarket, except that we were the only items on display. My heart started pumping, although as far as I knew there was no reason why it should have. I hadn't forged any passports, smuggled any drugs, or laundered any money lately. The longer they left us standing there, the harder my heart had to work. Control by design.

Finally one of the officials motioned me over. The fresh-faced youngster was twenty years younger than me if he was a day. Now commences the theater of interrogation. "How long are you staying in Canada?" A standard question. "Why are you coming here?" To visit a friend. "Where does your friend live?" Montreal. "Do you really have a friend?" What to say to that? "What's your friend's name?" I gave him the name, which he didn't write down, then thought to add, "He teaches at McGill University." As soon as I played this class card, he waved me through.

On that bus, everyone got through. And the accommodations on the Canadian side weren't bad. Beyond the checkpoint, seats had been provided for our use while we waited for our bus to get approval to roll forward fifty feet so that we could reboard. So many questions! I commented to a Québécois woman next to me. The world has changed, she shrugged, so now they have to do this. Especially your country. You think this is bad, wait till you cross to the U.S.

Which I did, two days later. A single-lane road edged with clapboard houses gave way to a strip of generic American highway and presto, before you knew it, there was the border control. From the tidy hut of a building two men emerged with Homeland Security patches silhouetted against the black shirtsleeves of their uniforms. Instead of "Everybody out!" this time it was "Everybody inside!" Easier said than done. A Sri Lankan woman looked for assistance with her huge suitcase, only to discover that there were no porters here, not even carts. An elderly French-Canadian woman folded her cane and gingerly made her way down the bus steps, determined to do it all herself. At these ghost stops it's up to you to manage; if you're smart, you'll turn to an able-bodied passenger and make fast friends.

Inside we realized that they wanted us to form lines. How to do it? There were no aisles, no breathing room, nowhere to stand once your passport was stamped. Toilet facilities? Forget it. And there was a catch: No one could leave this little cube until one of the men finished inspecting the empty bus. Not even to stand patiently waiting at the curb. But the bus inspection hadn't begun because people were still trying to crowd themselves and their luggage *into* the hut.

The delay exasperated the older of the two officials on duty, who grew redder in the face by the minute but made no effort to sort things out. Suddenly he exploded: Turn the damn thing off! No one knew what he was talking about or whom he was addressing. I said, turn the damn thing off! Still no response. I'm not going to say it again. Get off the phone!

Now all was revealed: He wanted a young white man in the back, instantly reconstituted as a security threat, to interrupt the call he was making to his wife to arrange for a pickup at the next station. Fortunately we never discovered what would have happened if the officer *did* have to say it again.

The younger official seemed much more easygoing, so I maneuvered my way into his line. Suspicions confirmed: After a cursory question or two ("American citizen?" "Canadian citizen?") and a look through our bags, he figured he'd done his job. And, I am happy to report, he treated the chocolates my friend gave me with perfect respect.

Not so bad, the Sri Lankan woman whispered as we climbed back on the bus. Ah, I replied, but they're not always that way. She nodded. She knows. These two were like grandfather and grandson, she said, don't you think? Then she and I talked about where we had traveled and why. The same questions an immigration official might ask, with none of the duress.

I explained to her that I had gone to Montreal to open a bank account because at that time things weren't looking so good for the U.S. dollar. Too many horror stories told by friends who had lived through the Mexican peso crisis, I guess. Not that I had so many dollars to play with! Over the phone the bankers had said, No problem: nonresidents open bank accounts in Canada all the time. Even immigrants, the woman on the phone added. Imagine: even immigrants.

By the time I got to Montreal, a hundred U.S. dollars poorer, everything had changed. I arrived at the bank only to be told that nonresidents have to go to a central location to open an account. When I asked the accounts representative to set up an appointment, since I had to hurry back to Boston, she spent twenty minutes on the phone, then set down the receiver in dismay. I'm shocked! she exclaimed, meeting my eyes for the first time. I am ... shocked. In twenty years at Royal Canadian Bank she had never seen anything like it. A bank that wouldn't take people's money!

New rules had taken effect just three weeks earlier. She had understood that the rule change was simply to enhance efficiency, but no. Nonresidents now had to demonstrate proof of employment in Canada, admission to a Canadian educational institution, or ownership of Canadian property before they could open an account. What was the point of all this? I wondered. It's to prevent money laundering, she explained, which involves smaller and smaller sums as tracking regulations tighten. How property ownership was supposed to screen out money launderers and terrorists, neither of us could say.

It got better. If you were lucky enough, as a nonresident, to be permitted to open an account, your funds would be "detained"—that's the precise language used in the memo she showed me—until you showed up to attend classes or to fill the post for which you had been hired. Until that happened, you could make all the deposits you wanted, but no withdrawals. Money in, no money out. If you were like most people riding the bus, it would be high-fee ATMs or check-cashing outlets for you. The poor getting poorer.

So many kinds of detention. There's a game kids play in North America when they're on the road. As the vehicle in which they're traveling crosses a border, they giggle with delight at the notion of being momentarily half in and half out of a state. Even a child can appreciate the absurdity of a body cleaved in two by political territories. The border is, after all, a powerful but imaginary line; the passport, a late-breaking invention. How is it that travel, so symbolic of freedom in this rhetoric-saturated landscape, has become the activity par excellence that opens a person to state surveillance and apprehension?

Back in the Arizona high country we sit still, awaiting *La Migra*'s justice. The air has grown thick with the scent of juniper. Finally the INS man with the gruff and grumpy voice steps back on board. He herds all the passengers without identification papers outside and makes them stand in the globalized posture of the detained, hands up against the bus, while the raiders call for a van to take them away. A sheep shearer in Roper boots, an impeccably attired lady in a sundress, the guy with the tuna sandwich. There are too many to fit into the INS carryall. The woman in the sundress flinches as her hands touch the hot sheet metal of the bus carriage. When they twist her arms behind her back to lock her wrists into plastic restraints, so tight that she can't feel her fingers, she will probably wish her hands were back up against the coach.

None of these riders will have their tickets refunded. They will be transported to a holding facility, then deposited, most of them, a few miles into Mexican territory. They may or may not have a chance to demonstrate residency. If a mistake has been made, it will be up to each individual to arrange her own return. And if she's traveling on her last dime?

The rest of us are supposed to thank our lucky stars that we've gotten off so lightly. Sometimes it's "everybody out!" and the entire bus has to step into the blistering desert to await their fates. When our coach pulls back onto the tarmac, I can't stop thinking about where that poor soul with the thirty-five-cent tuna fish will spend the night. Across the aisle the prayerful old man remains quietly in his seat. He wasn't asking any favors for himself. He was praying for the others.

The Trucker's Lament

Saguaros guard the passes as the bus makes its way down to the explosion of subdivisions that square the desert floor near Phoenix. Most bus stations are caves, but the Phoenix terminal opens out and up, with windows placed high on the walls to admit the quickening light. Signs list *"baños"* first, "toilets" second; the ads offering discounts to military personnel are in Spanish. It will take some time for this newly constructed building to exude the crumbling air of improvisation that marks so many other stops. Who knows: perhaps the bus companies will buck the North American trend toward neglected infrastructure. Instead of letting globalization bite back with budget cuts and deteriorating service, they might start reinvesting in their terminals. Dream on, I think, remembering the broken window glass in Albuquerque.

A man with severely torn jeans emerges from the cafeteria with a supersized cup of coffee. After a few minutes, liquid begins to run down one of his legs, into his boot and onto the floor. At first it's not clear if it's coffee or urine. He moves away, then wanders back to stand in the middle of the puddle. By this point even a family from the Salt River reser-

vation, for whom it's particularly rude to stare, is casting sur-
reptitious glances in his direction. When he joins our rap-
idly growing line at Door 7, a young Anglo turns around in
amazement to exclaim to anyone who cares to hear, Did you
see his sunglasses? They've still got the stickers on them!

He's a loony, replies the portly man in front of me. Didn't
you see how he pushed that guy? Naw, I missed it. Be glad
you didn't see it, the man says. It wasn't a pretty sight.

I take advantage of this break in the ice to introduce myself. Not myself, exactly, but myself by way of my trip: Albuquerque to Phoenix to Flagstaff to Vegas to Salt Lake City
to Butte to Missoula. Whew, says The Trucker, which is what
the portly fellow turns out to be. That's a lot of traveling! He
introduces himself not with a name or an itinerary but with
his occupation. Eighteen years he's been driving trucks. To
bolster his point, he pulls out an identification card embossed
with a drawing of a big rig. I ask why someone like him, who
obviously takes pride in his work, is riding the bus. Shouldn't
you be hauling a truckload of something-or-another to get to
wherever you're going?

As you can see, he says, I don't own my own rig. I drive for
a corporation. They've been good to me; don't get me wrong.
It's just that they make you turn in your truck when you're
going to be out for a spell. Like for surgery.

At the mention of surgery our little section of the line
falls silent. Health is a personal matter, his to explain if he
chooses, and he does not choose. Where are you going, then?
I wonder. Wichita, Kansas, is his destination, and his home,
after a fashion.

I ask him if trucking has changed much since he started
driving. Definitely, he says: worse traffic, better equipment.
One hand brushes his scrappy mustache. Also, there are good
places and bad places to make deliveries. Don't ever go to
Brooklyn. Brooklyn, I respond. What's wrong with Brook-

lyn? The people you have to deal with there, on the docks, he replies. They hate everyone and everything. They make it hard for you. Maybe it's because . . . they hate themselves.

I tell him I don't think I could ever do his job. Sure you could, he snaps back. Nothing to it. See, you don't have to rent a place. No expenses there. You can carry everything around with you in a couple bags like this. (He's shepherding two canvas bags through the line, which makes no progress but has a tendency to inch forward as people move and stretch. One bag weighs about 175 pounds, the other "only" 150. Even for a guy his size, it's obviously a strain to shoulder them.) You know, he says, sketching out my future in earnest now, you might want to set yourself up with a couple of extras, like a little TV or a refrigerator for the cab to keep your drinks cold. A CB radio. Got my CB right in there, he says, pointing to the larger bag.

Is there more pressure these days for truckers to drive fast or keep going around the clock? Not so much, he says. The cops clock you at fifty-five, but you can go sixty-five. That gives you almost too much time. You have to pull over at a truck stop, get something to eat, take a shower. I ask if he has to load and unload. (With my future career as a trucker in mind, of course.) No, they have other ones to do that. Well, once in a while you have to pitch in. Usually no. Just unhook or back up to the dock and let them take the stuff off. What do I haul? Anything and everything. You know the stuff in the Oklahoma City bomb? I've hauled that.

And what about the money? I ask. Is it good money? The Trucker tells me he puts out about $275 a week. That includes bridges and tolls, but then you turn in your receipts and the company gives that back to you. You end up with $225, $275 a week. What you don't spend on food you can put in the bank.

Everything The Trucker tells me fits with what I've read

about the going rates for long-haul trucking. In 2004 less optimistic drivers on the West Coast would stage wildcat strikes to protest the devastating combination of low wages and rising fuel, insurance, and maintenance costs. With drivers paid fifty to two hundred dollars per cargo container, based upon the length of the trip, after-expense income averaged only eight to nine dollars an hour.[4] That meant living on about thirteen hundred dollars per month, if the work was steady. Right around the poverty line. Given the cost of living in North America, with its skyrocketing rents and mortgages, no wonder so many drivers lived out of their cabs. It's a good job if you're single, The Trucker insists.

But he's not single. His wife wants him to come home, so despite his love for the road, he's thinking of doing just that. With the surgery and all, she's put her foot down. What's he supposed to do sitting at home all day, with no money coming in? The wife works too, but not for much. Maybe he can find a job with a company that specializes in short hauls so he can come back to Wichita every night. Only those runs don't pay too good, he says. And you're tied down, so to speak. What do I think he should do? Think about it after the surgery, I suggest.

An hour and a half we've spent waiting in line for the New York through bus that will stop in Flagstaff. When the boarding announcement finally comes, the reboarding passengers, who get preference, practically fill the coach. You can see people's eyes rolling back in their sockets as they wonder whether they've waited all this time for nothing. The next bus comes through in what . . . five more hours? By any count, that's a long time to stand in line.

Although the bus system accepts no reservations, managers try to run a second bus on the same route if needed and available. Luckily in this case Greyhound has rounded up another bus and driver, which probably contributed to the delay. When we do board, the driver accepts The Trucker's ticket, then directs his attention to the antennae sticking out of The Trucker's bags. Are you sure you don't want to carry those on? he asks. They might get banged up some underneath the bus. The two men share a moment, driver to driver. This captain of our coach clearly knows an antenna when he sees one, whereas I, the now-aspiring novice, originally mistook them for sections of a fishing pole.

Once we've finally taken our seats, a voice intones: Sit back, enjoy the ride, and leave the driving to us. It's the age-old Greyhound slogan. Imagine, leaving the driving to somebody else. The Trucker winces.

Keep Your Eyes on the Burrito

"Those of you who will be reboarding here in Flagstaff, this is your lunch stop. You must show your reboarding card, so don't lose it. You have thirty minutes. Listen up: that's thirty minutes. If you want a good meal, there's a Jack in the Box right across from the station." There was a time when bus routes helped support a spider's web of roadside coffee shops, but no longer. Now fast food reigns, often more fast than food.

The twelve-thousand-foot elevations of the San Francisco Peaks recede behind the mini-mallscape wrapped around the bus station. Except for the telltale pine scent of the high country air, we could be anywhere. Most of the cross-country passengers stick close to the depot. If you're African American, especially, you're not going to find a lot of compatriots in this town. I've already eaten my way through the food I brought along from Albuquerque and I'll be riding too long to eat fast food at every meal, so I decide to search for an alternative lunch.

Outside the terminal a Northern Arizona University student staggers to the curb under the weight of a Gateway computer box. An old woman with swollen ankles fishes for spare change with a cup. At the spanking new Barnes & Noble next door, I manage to find a seriously overpriced ham sandwich in the café. On my way through the aisles, I close my eyes to absorb the comfort of books and soak in the irony of these worlds—bus station, bookstore—so close yet infinitely far away. No other passenger has ventured here. The restroom door is open, unkeyed, a telltale sign. If there were a lot of traffic from the bus station, locks and signs proclaiming "For Customers Only" would surely have sprouted.

Where'd you go? The Trucker wants to know when I race back breathless to the station. He himself can't eat corn, which automatically rules out "all the good stuff" on the Jack in the Box menu. Instead, he hazarded two barbecued chicken sandwiches at the station snack counter. Now, he says, patting his stomach, I wish I didn't. Hey, he adds, you missed a lot, running off like that.

What could I have missed in twenty-nine minutes? The cops nearly hauled this guy in, The Trucker explains, gesturing toward a black man in his thirties with a neatly buttoned blue-striped dress shirt and a missing front tooth. I look inquiringly at the guy: Are you all right? The Trucker, an Anglo, speaks for him. A woman in there called the cops on him, The Trucker says. Some white lady. Said something about how he was a witch. (Snorts all round.) She tried to hit him. There he is, ducking and dodging, trying to get away from this nut, and they were going to take *him* in!

That's messed up, I say, catching the man's eye. He introduces himself as T.J. Good thing I had my bus ticket with me, T.J. interjects. Otherwise I'd be sitting in jail right now.

After T.J. showed the cops his bus ticket, The Trucker interceded by telling them that back in Wichita he was in the police reserves. He knew how to spot a troublemaker when he saw one. This guy, he said, meaning T.J., was just minding his own business when the woman went off on him. He'll be out of here in ten minutes, The Trucker told them. Let him get back on the bus.

With a wink The Trucker adds, If it was me they were after, I wouldn't have had to say all that. I could've just shown them my badge. And your skin color, some of us think to add, but don't. After all, he helped save the guy's ass.

So much is happening that I decide to keep riding with T.J. and The Trucker as far as Houck, a trading post on the edge of the Navajo reservation. From there I can get off and backtrack in the direction of Vegas. I'm traveling on an Ameripass, which lets me ride anywhere Greyhound and its affiliates go.

After we clamber back into our seats, a Chicano with a little paunch that tests the pearl snap buttons on his dress shirt makes his way back to where T.J., The Trucker, and I are sitting. In his hands are three foil-wrapped packages. Take them, he says to T.J. My wife made them. Home-cooked burritos. As it turns out, she not only made them; she sent her husband with this care package because she realized that after spending the entire "lunch stop" being searched and interrogated, T.J. couldn't possibly have gotten any lunch.

T.J. accepts the offering and the bearer returns to his seat. Two of the burritos disappear in short order. After T.J. unwinds a thin ribbon of foil on the third, he hesitates. Is this her last one? he wonders out loud. I can't take her last one! He goes to the front of the coach to give it back.

When he returns we get to talking in earnest. T.J., like many passengers, is riding the bus to get to a new job. Wage migration, by any other name. What kind of job? Food processing, somewhere in Oklahoma. It quickly becomes apparent that "food processing" is T.J.'s euphemism for working in a meatpacking plant. I tell him a story about my cousin who worked in a meatpacking plant in Wisconsin. She always said meatpacking is hard work, even if you're strong. Your wrists hurt from doing the same thing at top speed over and over again. Doesn't pay much, either. But, I add, you don't need me to tell you that.

Your cousin still work there? T.J. wants to know. No, I tell him, she passed away. Cancer. Just twenty-eight years old. Worked there five or six years longer than she should have, sick as she was. But she had a young child to support and that was the only work she could get in that small town.

When I ask T.J. if he knows what kind of meat he'll be cutting, he says pork. That's good, I say. Pork is supposed to be easier to handle than chickens. But maybe you should look to the future. Take my cousin's advice: start checking out other jobs.

Outside the window a red-tailed hawk surfs the air high above the currents stirred up by the bus. While we've been talking, the woman who sent the burritos has somehow determined that T.J. hasn't eaten in two days. It's not that he didn't have time to get food while the police were harassing him; he has no money for food at all. So at the next rest stop, she sends her husband on another errand.

We're parked at a circular structure built to echo the form of a Diné hogan. Years ago when I passed through, this was a full-service coffee shop with table service at booths along the perimeter. Now the restaurant has been reincarnated as a Taco Bell Express with a second counter selling burgers, fried chicken, and Navajo tacos. T.J. stays on the bus. The woman's road-weary husband climbs back aboard with a bag full of soft tacos and extends it in T.J.'s direction.

Take them, he says. T.J. hesitates. Take them. They're good! With a kind of battered dignity, T.J. accepts. *Gracias,* he ventures.

In the United States, what happened to T.J. in Flagstaff is an everyday occurrence. The prisons are filled with disproportionate numbers of African American men from communities that the "good times" passed over. What happened to T.J. afterward is not. In a land where people regularly disavow the living legacy of colonization, genocide, and slavery, it's rare to have people rally to one another's assistance across racial lines. Yet it happens. Follow the burrito and you'll find compassion. Follow the trail of people migrating for wages and you'll be led through a forest of irony and critique. It's a rich, rich country that lets the hungry process its food.

Those Fools up at the VA

I need a break, so I decide to join one of the fastest-declining populations in America. It's simple. I buy a newspaper. In recent years newspaper readership has plummeted, at least for the major dailies. When I extract a copy of the *Denver Post* from the beat-up box in front of the restaurant, I begin to understand why. The op-ed pages are filled with middle- and upper-class commentators bewailing the demise of something called "civility" in the United States. Apparently everyone's moving to a gated community. (Well, not everyone: somebody has to be left outside for the gates to ward off.) Everybody's bowling alone. (Could be, but aren't they shooting hoops and skateboarding together?) Everywhere you go, people are in a rage. (Can't argue with that.) Arenas for civic debate are disappearing. (Really? I guess these guys aren't riding the buses.)

If you're looking for some sharp-eyed observation and down-to-earth critique of the health care system, imperialism, the state of the environment, or corporate downsizing, the bus is the place to find it. The conversation might start with tongue clucking directed at the price of gasoline at a service station in rural Maine. Looks like I can't afford to fill her up when I get back, a middle-aged white guy will remark. Why's it keep going higher and higher? It's all this mess we're making in the Middle East, says another. No, you idiot, the oil is running out. Okay, I get your point, but *why's* it running out? You know why: We use too much. We shouldn't have to be over there. Well, says the first guy, we got to use some. Thirty bucks is barely gonna be enough to take me moose hunting. An eight-year-old turns around in his seat to exclaim: You eat moose? For real? Yup, the fellow will reply, that's how we get through the winter.

During our next break, I hang out next to a chunky Anglo with nicotine-stained teeth. Did you see those fires on TV down in Los Alamos? he wants to know. The ones by the nuclear lab. Scary, huh? At least they say the dangerous stuff is buried way underground. I ask him what he thinks will happen when the rains come and start to push contaminated soil down through the eroded canyons into the Rio Grande. Would the government tell people, move people, if their drinking water was irradiated? It would cause a panic, he agrees. They can't do that. He pauses. Water, he says. Water is going to be the end of the world. They used to say it would be oil, but it's water.

Another day, another trip, population growth might catch someone's attention. A remark about a section of suburban Richmond passing outside the window—Just look at all those new houses!—leads into a rollicking debate on China's one-child policy. Let's change the subject, a woman interjects, with a knowing glance toward the back of the coach, where Christian sensibilities have begun to be ruffled. Riding through Vermont, language politics comes to the fore: I'm glad I grew up speaking French, a teenage girl insists. But if your parents speak to you in French and that's all you know, says her companion, finding a job on this side [of the Canadian border] is pretty hopeless. True, the girl admits. True. But I'm still glad.

Even drivers have their say. On a milk run (a local route) through inland California, the driver confesses to having tried his hand at management. The idea, he explains, was to spend more time with his family. Although technically he *was* home—that is to say, driving in and out of his hometown—the long hours on the road meant that he wasn't in his house. Management turned out to mean sixteen-hour days, so he returned to driving. His wife is in the house but she's not home, either, because she runs a daycare operation. Most of what she makes goes to insurance.

Look at the bus you're riding on, he says. It's brand new. Ever stop to think about why they would put a beautiful brand-new bus like this on a pokey old cow-town run? They save the new buses for longer hauls, east–west travel, then use the older ones for casino runs and shorter trips. The only reason you're on this coach today is because I'm transporting it to L.A. And did you know that most of these buses are leased, not owned? It's part of cutting back. The company calls it "streamlining." I call it a hassle. They're always changing buses on us.

Two years and two hundred miles away, where we left our bus in northern Arizona, the military's health care system enters the crossfire. It all starts when T.J., munching his way through his bag of soft tacos, picks up on The Trucker's revelation about belonging to the police reserves. You mean army reserves, right? says T.J. No, replies The Trucker, police reserves. I didn't know they had them, says T.J. You ever in the service, then? Used to be, The Trucker says.

Where were you stationed? T.J. wants to know. Germany, says The Trucker. Panama, offers a man sitting behind us. Oh, you went south, says The Trucker, turning around. Lots of fireworks down there. Want to hear what happened in Germany? Our first night, brand new base, terrorists blew up the motor pool. We had to spend the night on the roof on alert. Didn't sleep for three days!

As The Trucker tells his story, Panama pulls out his wallet. He passes around a piece of red-white-and-blue plastic. It's his new Veterans Administration card, which verifies his military service and authorizes his claim to military benefits.

I got a VA card, but I never use it, says The Trucker. Company insurance? I ask. He nods. Panama still has his card out, admiring his laminated self. But it's not just the insurance, insists The Trucker. You go into those VA hospitals, you come out worse than when you go in. I would never have my surgery there, unless I had to.

It's documented, T.J. agrees: They don't have the best of doctors. Interns, says The Trucker, the ones just starting out. Half those fools up at the VA don't know what they're doing. I knew a guy, says The Trucker, went in there with two good legs, came out with one leg and a stump. They see a black spot on your knee, the whole leg comes off. Then they find out later the leg was good. That ain't health care.

I thought about working at the VA, though, says T.J. You should try it, says The Trucker. Get a job pushing wheelchairs or something. Beats meatpacking.

Who You Calling "Food Stamps"?

There's no VA hospital in Houck, not even an Indian Health Service (IHS) clinic. Just the Taco Express and a convenience store painted with wigwams. Like many rural people, the Diné working the cash register have to drive miles for medical treatment. Like many rural people working minimum-wage jobs, they also live close to the edge financially. A disintegrating Chevy that fails to start, a hospital located in a place without relatives to offer shelter, can mean dropping out of a treatment protocol or worse. It's a life-threatening situation for patients who require something like dialysis.

In the United States, the road to bankruptcy is paved with unpaid medical bills. Although provision of health care to Native Americans constitutes a treaty obligation undertaken by the government as partial compensation for vast tracts of land ceded and seized, the IHS remains radically underfunded. At the time of this trip, IHS per capita spending amounted to only a third of what the average American paid for health care.

When medicine competes with food, eating tends to come first. The Trucker and I follow a mother and her two children into the store. A long counter sells shrink wrap, with sandwiches inserted into the shiny packages almost as an afterthought. The woman's eldest son combs out his natural, sticks the pick into his hair, and wedges it all back underneath his cap, affecting indifference. His sister stares quietly at the pretty aluminum snack packages placed near the door. She knows better than to ask for things they don't need, but her eyes call out, If only...

Outside again, The Trucker exclaims, We Accept Food Stamps! His voice is barely audible above the crunch of tires on gravel in the parking lot. Excuse me? the woman objects. What did you just call me? She pulls her chin back into her neck and casts him a withering look. Her son, instantly alert, takes a step toward The Trucker. Now the child's eyes speak: Who does this white guy think he is, insulting my mother?

The sign, responds The Trucker, the sign! We look up. A notice on the trading post wall proclaims, "Grocery Store—Gift Shop—Indian Jewelry—Ice Cream—We Accept Food Stamps." The children's mother reads along. Oh, I see, she says, "We Accept Food Stamps." As the racial tension diffuses, her face turns dreamy. Food stamps, she says. I wish I had me some. I sure could use it.

I say my goodbyes as the bus pulls out. It's New York via Oklahoma City for them, Missoula via Las Vegas for me. A mourning dove calls. I feel the sharp edge of a stone that has worked its way into my shoe. The little girl presses against the window glass, her left hand clutching a bologna sandwich.

Next Stop, Sin City

Racial tensions diffuse, but they're easily conjured anew in the land of the brave. On the bus to Vegas, the driver sets the tone. *Dos minutos,* he announces at the first rest stop. No *agua,* no McDonald's, no *nada. Hasta la bye-bye.*

Qué? asks the Mexican national next to me. What's he saying? I advise my seatmate to stay close to the bus. This driver will leave without him. Two minutes and a cigarette later, true to his word, the driver closes the doors without searching for stray passengers.

As soon as the wheels touch asphalt, an elderly white woman in the front starts to grumble about the length of the trip. Just two hundred miles out, she's getting tired. The driver interrupts her litany of complaints: Hey, it's not so bad. Think of your forefathers trekking out here with no air conditioning in covered wagons.

At this a Native American in denims looks up sharply, but decides to keep his counsel—that is, until an African American man asks him to pass back a bag. I don't want to reach down there, the Diné guy says, gesturing under the seat. It's dirty. Not the bag on the floor, the first guy explains. I need one of those plastic trash bags. He means the ones stapled to the wall of the bus. Oh, says the Diné guy, no problem. Each one dealing with the accumulated grime of the journey, the history, in his own way.

When new Anglo or black passengers board, the driver instructs them to put hand luggage on their seats to reserve a place during the breaks. If the Europeans at the next stop don't respect that, he says, you report to me and I'll roust them out. We'll help you, promises a skinny towhead from the gang of army recruits just boarding. A ticket to boot camp has extracted an alliance from this mixed group of Anglo and Latino youth. They fall in at the back, where they trade futures in the form of apprehensions.

When we reach Laughlin, a casino town just across the Nevada border, a young German student joins the bus, but he's not interested in commandeering anyone's seat. What he wants to unravel is the mystery of the mobile home. Every few miles a cluster of aluminum boxes hugs the desert floor, some shiny, more patched and rusting. Are there people living in them? the European asks. What are these "wagons" like inside? The good ones can be really good, contends the driver. His uncle owns a triple-wide with a Jacuzzi. But the cheap ones, the driver cautions, they don't hold up. They're not worth it. Of course, if that's all you can afford . . .

Throughout this conversation, there's no mention of the

health risks when the pressboard used extensively in mobile home construction exhales formaldehyde into a sealed container, with a family sealed inside it. No mention, either, of the creativity with which Diné have used trailers to re-create "traditional" ways of living in homesteads scattered across the Navajo Nation. Or, for that matter, of the massive credit expansion underwritten by the Federal Reserve Bank that propelled housing prices ever upward into the twenty-first century, forcing millions to outfit their dream homes with wheels and a cinder block foundation.

The German student wants to talk government, not environment, cultural survival, or prices. Is it true? he asks. You can put the wagons wherever you want? He seems shocked at the lack of state regulation. Sometimes yes, sometimes no, responds the driver. The Hollywood-inspired fantasy of a freewheeling Old West, in which anything goes so long as it doesn't interfere with ranching and resource exploitation, collides with an increasingly regulated New West, in which many things still go, so long as they don't interfere with recreation and resource exploitation.

We're getting close to Vegas now, riding a tailwind of luck and money. What kind of luck, no one can say. A sloe-eyed woman aligns the gold stripe running across her red fingernails with the pattern on her tailored slacks. Blackjack is her game. The last time, she says, I got out of there with six or seven thousand. And the time before? I ask. Ten thousand down, she admits. But that's okay. She's refinanced her house.

The grifter who got on at Kingston doesn't think much of Vegas as a spot to practice his art. Too many con men, too many cameras. Even Phoenix had stiff competition. He's guarded about the details of the games he runs—trade secrets, don't y'know—and about the wife who got busted back in Cruces. The important point is this: after people catch on to the latest con, but before the local authorities master it, it's time to move to another city. The bus is his vehicle of choice. He'll keep riding.

I, on the other hand, am more than ready to disembark. My butt hurts, my head hurts, and I never want to see another bag of Doritos. In the bustling terminal they're hawking miniature feathered dream catchers alongside a new generation of plastic trolls and packages of Sticky Mix, a collection of jelly worms, all displayed at a child's eye level. The only place quiet enough to take some notes on what's been happening on this trip lies past the toilets, down a narrow aisle dedicated to lockers. There are no chairs, of course, or this section would be crowded and noisy too, so I slide down the wall onto the floor.

No sooner have I pulled out my notebook than a six-year-old in a tattered Power Rangers T-shirt wanders over. When I don't look up, he solicits my attention with a battery-powered machine gun that packs a sound to make anyone jump. Marcus is his name and he's reading across race and gender lines. His mission? To find out if I'm a girl. When I assure him that, yes indeedy, this sweaty, comfort-clad ghost of a creature who just crawled off the westbound bus is, in fact, "a girl," he asks me if I'm sure.

So much for writing. I have five hours to kill in Sin City, where buses run infrequently compared to back east. After stowing my pack in a locker, I speak to a ticket agent, who advises me to return early because there are always lines. Vegas, he says, is the real city that never sleeps.

I figure there's plenty of time to step outside for a view of the fabled neon lights, catch a cheap dinner in one of the casinos, and part company with a pocketful of change. All I have to do, literally, is step outside. Unlike most urban North American bus depots, which tend to be located in the

no-man's-land off freeway ramps or in derelict scraps of central cities, the Vegas station in 1999 occupies a prime location at the heart of the downtown circus. Galleries of slot
machines flank the open doorways. The air is thick with
bells, beeps, and buzzers. A block away, a magician attempts
to lure passersby inside to play vertical roulette. He manages
to produce four aces from thin air but can't seem to stop
his top hat from sliding off his head.

There are no hourly exploding volcanoes in this part of
town, no jousting matches or replicas of Venice. That's farther out on the Strip. Downtown, they say, is Vegas as it used
to be, updated with canopies of light and inflated expecta-
tions. With two hours to spare before my scheduled departure for Salt Lake, I reluctantly head back to the terminal.
It's hard to leave behind the fool's gold and the glitter for the
discipline of another queue. Coming back so early, I imagined I was playing a conservative game, but no. The line for
my bus has already snaked across the room and headed out
the front door!

Wait Training

One sultry evening, years ago, I had an epiphany at an A&P
supermarket on Chicago's South Side. There I was behind a
cart piled high with groceries, waiting for my weekly audience with the checkout cashier. I must have made this journey hundreds, thousands of times. For some reason on this
particular Friday in March, when I looked around at the
hardworking people lined up on either side of me, I saw.

The lines turned into a procession of tall people, wrinkled
people, good-natured and crabby people. Despite their su-
perficial differences, they had one thing in common: They

were *tired* people. Bone tired. Crammed into the shopping carts between the toilet paper and the Coco-Puffs were toddlers, bouncing and bubbling in their little seats. The contrast couldn't have been greater. Where does that energy go? I wondered. How do we get from one state to the other in a matter of a few short years? Soon all those lively little youngsters will be slogging along, putting one foot in front of the next, doing whatever they have to do to scrape by. Only if they're very, very lucky will something or someone come along later in life to remind them of what they used to know.

Wait training is everywhere. From grocery stores to bus depots. From the first days of grammar school, when children learn to spend hours seated at their little desks, to the backwash created by globalization, which floats tasks downstream to consumers, who now labor unpaid to accomplish work that used to be performed by businesses before debt-ridden companies cut staff. Advertisements may promote instant gratification, but savvy riders know better.

It's one of the twenty-first century's great contradictions: a service economy in which service itself is on the decline. Endless phone trees sell "customer care" but deliver a time-consuming, interactive form of putting callers on hold. Patients earn their name during the long delays required to obtain health care. Shoddy consumer goods have to be exchanged before they can be used. Frustrated job seekers receive advice to wait for "the economy" to get better.

A very simple equation governs all this wait training: The less money you have, the longer you tend to wait. (My personal record is twelve hours on tenterhooks hoping to get a seat aboard the overnight bus to San Diego.) A first-come, first-served system does have certain advantages when you're living a highly contingent life. If you have to leave town suddenly because your brother falls ill, if you hear rumors of an opening for a handyman in Tuscaloosa, or if your parole officer's on your tail, there are no penalties, no reservations required. Miss one bus and you still have a chance to catch the next. But there is a hidden price to be paid. In the lower reaches of the North American transportation system, passengers, not buses, do the long-term parking.

Watch my bag? asks the woman behind me in Vegas with the smoker's cough and the arm in a sling. Watch my kid? she adds as she heads for the restroom. It's a perfunctory request. Everybody knows there's only one way to accomplish the simple things when you're stuck for hours in a line and that's to forge alliances.

It's a trust born of two parts necessity, one part conversation. Yet who's to say that you haven't met up with an amiable kidnapper or an unusually talkative thief? Snap judgments become the order of the day. Best to have your place in line held regardless, your bag attached to a body, especially in a political climate where the fear of terrorism stalks luggage left unattended.

If the line starts moving before you get back, though, you're pretty much on your own. I'm hoping that the one-armed woman whose place I am holding will get off the pay phone so I can run my own errands. Too much time, not enough time. A yawn travels down the line for Tucson like a wave. With our Salt Lake bus now long overdue, we wait on the unknown.

A pair of brothers in torn jeans and ponytails pulled through their baseball caps ride imaginary Harleys through the crowd, looking like miniatures of their father. A preschooler in a pink ruffled dress and pantaloons stretches her arms into wings. So far, she's the only thing taking off. An African American guy asks an older white guy if he can leave his gym bag to mark his spot in line while he goes to sit down. Okay. The minute he disappears into the snack bar, two men try to cut the queue. Now it's up to the earlier settlers to lay down the law. What the hell do you think you're doing? The end of the line, they shout, pointing out the obvious, is way back there. The challengers back down, but the air sizzles in their wake.

Buses roll and passengers park. But it's only training for the real event. All it takes is the flash of a driver's shirt sleeve, the rustle of a door leading out into the night, to set the games in motion.

The Trash Bag Racer Rally and Other Extreme Sports

Suit up and show up, a wise woman I knew used to say. That's all that's required. Freed from my vigil over my neighbor's eight-year-old, I'm in the bathroom changing out of shorts in preparation for the coach that will take me through the mountains when some indecipherable announcement registers over the loudspeaker. I rush out, just in case the announcement has something to do with Salt Lake, only to discover that the management has decreed new gate numbers for departing buses.

There's no crowd control, no guidance, just absolute and utter pandemonium as passengers realize that their carefully tended positions in line have now become meaningless. Suitcases turn into battering rams. Babies howl for their mothers. Elbows target the occasional throat. A three-year-old secures safe passage for his aunt by biting the leg of a gentleman who now stands between them and Cincinnati.

Here and there throughout the crowd, riders use the extra-large plastic garbage bags in which they've stored their possessions to execute a series of plays unknown to coaches in the National Football League. These are the poorest of the poor, who have managed to scrape up bus fare but can't afford proper gear. They bank and they block, knocking over unsuspecting passengers as they impel the overstuffed black pumpkins toward the doors by hitting their opposition below the knees. Once a hole opens up, fellow travelers slip in behind them.

Like every play in the game book, this tactic is not without risks. I have seen a boy beg for a box in which to put the contents of a trash bag that had ripped open, spilling his clothes onto the parking lot. You can't bring your things on board like that, the driver told him. Put them in something. But there was no box. So the boy just stood there, lost, as his bus pulled out of the station.

To refuse to race, of course, carries risks of its own. There's a good chance you'll spend the greater part of another day watching the hands race round the clock in the depot. If you miss the next bus, no one will guarantee you a spot on the one to follow. In any case, its scheduled arrival comes at dawn, seven hours away. A night sprawled on linoleum in a sea of disgruntled passengers or a night spent in the relative comfort of an air-conditioned vehicle, speeding to your destination. Those are high stakes in any town.

While all this is going on, a new racetrack forms. The children, set in motion by the anxieties of parents, identify gaps in the new lines, which they exploit to circle around and around the station's pillars. Older siblings follow in hot pursuit. Their guardians start to become frustrated, because to chase the children (as they must) jeopardizes a hard-won position and abandons belongings to the desires of strangers.

Over to the left a man in a fedora takes bets. When the dust settles, who will control the first gate? Will it be the three-year-old with jaws of death? Or will it be the men who earlier tried to cut the line, now ruthlessly shoving their way forward? I lose track of the contenders amidst the urgency of locating my luggage. There's nothing left where my green duffel bag once stood but jostling bodies. No boy-child, no sling-wrapped mother.

Anyone who has ever been able to count their possessions without the aid of a calculator knows that moment of panic when it seems you may have lost everything. Even if your situation in life improves, material loss tends to settle in the gut. I've been scanning the crowd madly for my missing bag, beginning with the back where we started. It hasn't yet occurred to me to check farther up toward the gates. When I run out of places to search, I glance halfheartedly toward the front and my panic subsides. Somehow the one-armed woman and her kid have managed to wedge their way into the front of the new line. Like figures in a tableau, they sit silhouetted against a pile of luggage that includes my bag. It's a rare point of stillness in the swirling room. The child must have moved everything.

Now we're five sweet spots from the door. An advantageous position, an encouraging position, but still. No reason at all to think that this will be enough to get us to Salt Lake. Most of the buses going south to north, north to south, have been packed.

Our five-hour wait turns into six, going on eternity, when the incoming bus arrives with room for only three additional passengers. This sport is beginning to look a lot less like football or the Indy 500 and a lot more like a game of musical chairs in which someone has taken *all* the seats away. Not fair! someone shouts. Who told you life was supposed to be fair? clucks the woman who gets six dollars an hour to clean the snack bar.

Fight!

There's only so much discipline a body can absorb. Forced waits can bring out incredible generosity or they can beckon to demons already lurking in the corners. One New Year's Eve in Jamshedpur, India, I watched a platform teeming with passengers explode when our train arrived three hours late without all the carriages. Turn up the heat, fray the fuse, and it doesn't take much to supply the spark.

After the doors to the loading platform close in our face at the Las Vegas station, some people, especially the women, set about making a can't-be-helped situation bearable. They trade kids when they run out of patience, pass around water and vending machine snacks. Elders let their bodies slide to the floor; they don't have the stamina to remain vertical for such a length of time. Farther back in the line, though, people are in a foul mood. Correctly gauging their chances of getting on the next bus as slim, they're doubly irritated because they lost out during the trash bag racer rally even though many of them have waited the longest.

Children bear the brunt of their anger. Get over here! Share that game with your sister! I told you to stop messing around! Don't make me say it again!

That's when it starts. I'm watching the boy-child again while his mother goes in search of provisions. The little boy is restless—who wouldn't be?—and in the course of his fidgeting he throws his coat on the ground. The coat hits the feet of a man who's been yelling at the top of his lungs at his own kids. Don't you throw that at me, the man says. I'm

sorry, the boy responds immediately. He isn't looking for
trouble. Everyone can see he didn't throw the coat as a provo-
cation.

But the grown man won't let it be: What's wrong with
you? Don't you know better? I'm sorry! the little boy says
again, looking scared. He's my responsibility for the moment.
I sigh, take a step forward. Leave him alone, I say. Can't you
see he's only a child? He told you he's sorry.

Really, I didn't mean it! the boy adds for good measure. I
don't care if you mean it or not, declares the man, you want
me to throw things at you? And he does: a piece of a ham-
burger coated with mustard, followed by a paper plate.

The boy's mother, who's been keeping half an eye cocked
in our direction, rushes back from the other side of the terminal. Get off my kid! she shouts, taking in the scene at
a glance. You wrecked his good shirt! she adds in disbelief,
staring at the yellow streak of mustard. Who's gonna pay for
that?

White bitch! sneers the man and holds his ground. The
boy's mother isn't having any of it. She's ready to take him,
one arm or not. I *said,* get off my kid! she repeats, her voice
so low now you just know she means it. *Back off!* Besides,
she declares, *he* ain't white. He's Mexican. Are you blind?

The man takes a second look, but not at the child. What
he sees is a gathering cloud of *vaqueros* in cowboy hats con-
verging on him from different sides of the room. So he does
back off, grumbling all the way back to his place at the end
of the line. When he gets there he yanks his kids from the
laps of two Anglo women who had been sharing their pocket
video games. The kids roll their eyes, then clamber deject-
edly onto the family's cooler.

Nobody disciplines my kid but me, the woman proclaims,
gingerly fingering her surgically repaired arm. I'm his mother.

Turning in my direction, she adds, Thanks for watching him. Mom, I didn't mean to! her boy interrupts plaintively. Now that the drama is over, he looks ready to cry.

Sit down here, she tells her son, motioning with her good hand. Let me explain something. There's no point wasting your energy being mad at that guy. People are different. Black people don't like things touching their feet. That's why he couldn't take it when your coat fell on him.

Don't like things touching their . . . ? The boy-child and I exchange glances, an unanswered question in his eyes, but his mother doesn't pause. Rather than engaging her son's curiosity, she plays the part of culture broker with gusto: Everybody's different, she explains. Did you see those Mexicans behind us in the line? They were ready to jump in. That's why the man backed off. Mexicans don't take no shit. They never take no shit. Just like your father, huh? she adds, tousling her son's hair. He nods.

This is the second fight tonight. On my way into the station, I had already passed two white guys slugging one another over the answer to a quiz show question. Who was responsible for a massacre of Native American villagers in Massachusetts between the Revolutionary War and the War of 1812? Napoleon, says one. Napoleon! exclaims the other. What the hell are you talking about? That was George Washington. (He's right.) Don't you insult my country, the first guy warns. George Washington was a great president. Look, says the second guy, it's my country, too. And it's a free country. I can say whatever I want. The man might have been a great president, but I'm telling you he was a killer, flat-out.

That's when the first fist connects with a face. Physical clashes don't happen often in Buslandia, or at least not nearly as often as the stereotypical association of poverty with violence would lead a middle-class person to suspect. But when brawls do break out, they can acquire a surreal patina. By the time I manage to pull the door open, the same two guys who have come to blows over a repressed piece of the nation's history have called a truce to split a bottle of beer. Demons and generosity. Taken together, taken in turns.

The clock in the terminal strikes 1:00 a.m. when, much to everyone's astonishment, our line starts moving. The sling-wrapped woman, her son, and I finally get on board, but only because some kind soul in the bus company has taken the trouble to locate an extra vehicle and driver. Even with a second coach, there are still many more riders than seats, so we have to force our way to the back. It's a bit of a free-for-all, but not nearly as bad as the one that almost swept us away inside the station.

After we grab three of the last seats, the boy-child's mother sends him back upstream against the current of boarding riders to secure their luggage claim checks from the driver at the side of the bus. What a nuisance this cast is, she says, I'm good for nothing till it comes off. Careful, your little boy could get snatched! someone cautions, so the rest of us collectively watch over him through the windows. When his tousled head finally reappears in the doorway, everyone pitches in by passing his mother's carry-on luggage to us in the back. Demons and generosity.

In an attempt to head off any more nonsense, our driver adopts the bouncer-slash-schoolteacher approach, reciting the longest possible version of company rules into the mike. He saw what happened back in the station. I run a clean bus, he begins, so let me be absolutely clear: There will be no smoking, no fighting, no alcohol, no spitting or cussing on this bus. Do not step across the yellow line while the bus is moving. Do not try to play your music without headphones.

If you have to cuss, let me know and I will set you down at the side of the road where you can cuss all you want.

Damn right! someone whispers into my left ear. And we're off.

You Don't Say

The lights are out. Passengers in the front count their winnings, nurse their hangovers, and try to catch some sleep, but the back is still rocking. Dr. Feelgood just won't quit. He's garnered this sobriquet by philosophizing for the last hour about life's hidden delights and the impermanence of material things: What's that they say about women, wine, and song? A man don't need much more than that. Everything else, he explains, is in my duffle bag. A bag so large we couldn't help but laugh at the sight of him trying to carry it on board, twice his size and balanced on his head. That's your "hand luggage"? a woman queries with amusement. Quick, get it under there! Don't let this driver see it.

Like many riders, Dr. Feelgood hesitates to leave his bag in the compartment under the bus for fear it might be lost or stolen. It's not an unreasonable fear. Passengers collect their luggage at the side of the bus when they reach their destinations, but baggage handlers seldom inspect the tags.

This bag, croons Dr. Feelgood once the bus gets under way, is all I have in this cold, cold world. Got to keep it with me. Hey, a teenager with cornrows objects, I thought you said material things aren't important! Hell no, he replies, of course they ain't. They don't bring you happiness. They don't bring you love. Women . . . well, all right, maybe. Material things ain't important. That don't mean you got to hand over what little you got, though. He sits with the massive bag under his feet, knees almost touching his chin where a five-day stubble edges into beard.

A billboard promoting a restaurant in Elko, Nevada, catches the headlights. Shortly afterward, we're treated to the sound of a falsetto. "Long as I know how to love, I know I will survive..." Oh yes, the doctor is definitely feeling good. "Papa's got a brand new bag..." Another African American rider chuckles at his clever use of the old James Brown song to create double entendres about life, ladies, and luggage. "Life is a cabaret, my friend..." God help us, he's finished with the disco era and the *Billboard* charts of his youth, and started in on Vegas show tunes. By this point even the folks in the back have had it. One by one they drop out, stop singing along. Like a guttering candle, Dr. Feelgood's verses flicker, a phrase here, a glissando there, until finally blessed silence.

The roads are filled with talented, foolish, mediocre, and brilliant people who don't know when to shut up. Everybody has had an experience with a bigmouth of a seatmate, just like everybody wishes they had a rich uncle. Big Mouth might be charming or annoying, a dreadful storyteller or an engaging raconteur. You only have to hope he has a good singing voice and a tolerable sense of timing.

These chatterboxes share the thoroughfares with another group of riders: the ones without papers, the ones without easy access to the dominant language, who talk among themselves but otherwise won't, or can't, pipe up. While Dr. Feelgood entertains us, the Mexican nationals in the back of the bus are quiet as can be. They exchange a few simple words with one another—*con permiso, sentado*—while searching for a place in the overhead rack where the men's cowboy hats won't be crushed. Best, perhaps, to keep a low profile. No one wants to be challenged to produce documents they don't possess.

A common language is not nearly as essential to communication, good times, and trust as English-only advocates would have you think. My seatmate is a young woman traveling alone who started out in Mazatlán. She speaks almost no English; I speak only the scraps of Spanish I've picked up from living in the Southwest. Cheyenne, she says. I take it as her destination.

Whenever the coach slows down Marisa worries that she might have to change buses. She's found other passengers to talk to in Spanish, but they don't understand the long-winded, speaker-distorted announcements of the driver either. Every twenty, forty, or sixty minutes, as the bus slows down, they whip themselves into a collective frenzy by convincing one another that *this* must be the stop where someone needs to disembark. Once Marisa realizes that we're miles from Cheyenne and that most of the stops are small-town interludes, she worries that she won't know what time to return to the bus before it leaves. Plus, she doesn't own a watch.

I decide to take my six words of Spanish out for a test drive. When we stop for a break with instructions to return at 3:15 a.m. Mountain Time, I struggle with the translation. What would "mountain time" be in Spanish, my sleep-addled brain wonders. *El tiempo de montañas?* Nah, that can't be right. I can't always convey the information Marisa needs, but at least I can get her to relax a little with a grin at my willingness to take a linguistic dive.

By the time dawn slithers across the arid flats we've become traveling companions of a sort the bus often creates: I make sure Marisa doesn't get left behind, mistaking a suburb for a city. We share snacks. At a roadside cafe in Winslow, she plunks her bag of soft tacos down on my table with a wink, knowing I'll watch them for her while she disappears into the restroom.

A hundred miles later, I wake up nauseous, with a bad case of diarrhea to boot. Something I ate back at the casino? Pesticides in the food? Whatever the case, this is definitely not the state you want to be in on an all-night bus. The hours crawl. I hardly sleep. A single pothole is enough to roil my stomach. Never was I so thankful for the quiet comfort of a not-quite-stranger next to me, curled into dreams of her own.

When I emerge during a rest stop to puke, it's clear that there's no way to be private about it with fifty-four riders stuffed into a coffee shack in the middle of nowhere at 5 a.m. The sling-wrapped woman whose child I watched back in Vegas now pretends she doesn't know me. Marisa helps me on and off the bus. This had better not turn into a new verse in one of Dr. Feelgood's songs, I think grimly to myself.

It takes everything I have to make it to Salt Lake. Because I'm very sick I start to feel vulnerable. I don't know anybody here. Marisa has to transfer to another bus. I call my sister in Missoula collect from a pay phone, tell her I'm going to look for a hotel, and apologize to my nephew for missing his graduation. Then I head shakily for the doors.

A quick look around brings faster relief than the antacid tablets I've been swallowing. I've landed at Temple Square in the heart of Salt Lake City, complete with tabernacle, a statue to commemorate the seagulls that saved the settlers' crops from a plague of crickets, and Mormon tour guides completing their missionary service. The entire plaza is ringed by hotels. If this were one of the newfangled stops off the freeway on the outskirts of town, finding a hotel in my condition would have been tough. If I hadn't had a credit card in my pocket, it would have been impossible. Any working fool would say I'd be a fool not to use the plastic.

I crawl to the Best Western a block down, pull out my MasterCard, and convince the manager to let me check in

early. Class saves me. There is no room service. It will be
twenty-four hours before I can wobble out in search of plain
boiled rice. But I'm not complaining.

On the floor of the station, Dr. Feelgood cradles his head
on his duffel, waiting for his ride to kingdom come. Except
that he's already arrived. The world is in his bag, not somewhere down some road, and he knows it.

Already Got a Job and a Lot of Good It Done Me

Two days later, I make it as far as Idaho Falls, where I have
to change buses for the old mining town of Butte ("Butt,
Montana," the Missoula kids call it). Rain spills from a lowering sky. That's a good thing for the beavertail cactus and a
bad thing for transferring passengers, since the Idaho Falls
station is nothing but a two-room shack. A few chairs, a
counter staffed by irascible old men, and plenty of room if
you step outside.

For all the glitz that a rider might encounter in a spanking new bus terminal like the one in Boston, it's also common to find stations crumbling, especially in smaller towns.
Shards of glass hanging from broken windows, toilets that
overflow, cockroaches scuttling across the tiles. Signs sten-
ciled on plywood to mark the routes, sometimes touchingly
misspelled. ("This way to Newport, Lnydonville, St. Johns-
bury.") Black-and-white pay televisions from another century bolted onto the arms of molded plastic seats. Empty
vending machines next to an Internet terminal that nobody
touches. A floor so filthy mothers forbid their children to
play on it, even as the women protest to the management:
Somebody ought to put a mop to this linoleum.

They just don't keep these places up, observes a well-coiffed woman as I light her cigarette under the shelter of a dripping eave. Look around! she exclaims, gesturing toward the boarded-over window to our left. People with money, they don't care to put their money here. After all, why should they? They can just fly right over the whole mess, can't they? Her wrist uncoils like a 737 taking off.

No matter how much rain pours down, bringing out the green, the desert doesn't seem to bloom for everyone. Not even during the good times of the 1990s, when the numbers of working poor in the United States skyrocketed right along with the economy. According to the Economic Policy Institute, 13 percent of the workforce in the richest country on earth fell into the "low wage" category in 2003. While the economic boom of the 1990s was under way, more than *a third* of Americans in their forties spent a year or more living below the poverty line. The phenomenon was so striking that a mainstream publication like *Business Week* took note, with a cover story headlined "Working... and Poor," which started out: "In today's cutthroat job market, the bottom rung is as high as most workers will ever get. But the political will to help them seems a long way off."[5]

Indeed. To work yet remain poor is to live out a topsy-turvy version of trickle-down economics. In the standard version, government promises that income returned to the pockets of the wealthy will work its way down through the economic system eventually, creating employment and improving the lives of people dwelling at the bottom. In the updated version, the sweat of the working poor trickles down to water the pleasures of the relatively wealthy.

So much for the time-honored advice of working parents to their ambitious youngsters: keep your head down, work hard, and you'll be all right. The very phrase "working poor" flies in the face of the individualist creed that a person who applies herself can make something of herself. Give your best energies to a working-class occupation in the twenty-first century and you may have to get by on two jobs, little sleep, no benefits. Welcome to what Doug Henwood calls "the workhouse economy." It's a lesson in global economics that starts right here in rural Idaho.

Working poor is what you get when corporations, pleading worldwide competition, decline to raise wages in any meaningful way while awarding productivity gains to investors. Rural economies suffered when the logs ran out, the water ran out, or agribusiness moved in. Jobs in tourism that were supposed to replace mining and ranching paid so little that employees couldn't afford to reside in the communities where they worked. Investors in the pig farms and ski resorts scattered across the New West also tended to live elsewhere. What would they know about the mortgage defaults and badly clothed children of the folks who keep those ventures running?

So much for another piece of time-honored advice: get used to the poor, because they will always be with you. Exponential growth in the ranks of people who work hard for a pittance cannot be explained away using platitudes. Quite the contrary: the point is that the poor no longer *are* with you, at least if "you" are better off. After 2000, poorly paid jobs combined with a credit-fueled real estate bubble to segregate low-income people ever deeper into shelters, slums, and shantytowns. Serving by day, escorted from the grounds by nightfall. They might be the ones to empty the trash cans at LAX, but if they need to travel to a funeral, their limited means guarantee that they'll have to find a less expensive way to get there. Not that the better-offs would notice; "they can just fly right over the whole mess." My chain-smoking companion under the eaves in Idaho Falls recognizes airports for what they are: the gated communities of the transportation system.

It occurs to me then that those crotchety characters working the desk inside the bus shack may have good reason to feel irascible. Although most people here have never been well-to-do, the balding fellow with the raspy voice tells me he's on his last nerve. Working here, working there, he hasn't seen his family in days.

This is the scenario the social critic Teresa Brennan had in mind when she wrote about the "terrors" of globalization visiting themselves upon the countries that had spawned the entire process.[6] From Bangkok to Boise, a traveler drifts through a land of contrasts: food banks located in the shadow of multinational banks, homeless encampments at the base of billboards advertising the latest mobile phone technology, mutual fund schemes peddled by people who can't afford them. A global reorganization of labor and capital has narrowed differences between the poorer countries and the so-called Western world through a certain kind of immiseration. The problems faced by the grumpy old men are western, all right, but mainly because Idaho happens to lie left of the Mississippi.

So why am I surprised when the northbound bus finally pulls out and I find myself sitting next to a woman making eighteen thousand dollars per year? (A fortune in Tanzania, but barely enough to cover her rent.) Because she's a teacher, that's why. Not a security guard, not a janitor, not a nurse's aide, not some Wal-Mart Employee of the Month. Brenda has taken up a classically middle-class occupation. She adores the boy with the ponytail in the front row of her fourth-grade class who reads Spiderman comic books under his desk when he thinks she isn't watching. She believes in the redemptive powers of education. But on this salary, she's not making it.

The open textbook on Brenda's lap catches the light from the coach's touring windows. "Curriculum Development: Guide to Practice" splashes across the glass, a translucent headline that washes over volunteer fire departments, nibbling cattle, and thirty-five-acre ranchettes. Later, as we wind through the bottomlands in silence, mist swaddles the coach. A few towns over the border into Montana we emerge without warning to see junipers drizzled onto the top of the hills like candy.

Seventy miles on, I'm still pondering that textbook. Do teachers really read this stuff? I go right to the source with my question. Brenda says she started out in special ed, but she's trying to improve her financial situation. That means she needs to earn a teaching credential. Thus the textbook. Some of these rural school districts are so desperate for instructors, she says, they let you teach without certification as long as you have a B.A. That's what I've been doing. You take a pay cut, though.

Besides, she says, laughing, what could I ever do with a degree in anthropology? I tell Brenda I know the feeling. Anthropology has been my own hard road through higher education.

You're looking at a natural-born teacher, Brenda insists. But it's a paper world. That's all people care about. Eventually I figured, why not take the money the school district shells out, work my way toward an education degree, and make myself official?

In the meantime Brenda is on her way to pick up her car, a 1986 Alliance that left her standing on the side of the interstate two weeks back. Wouldn't you know, it was the transmission. She says she doesn't even want to think about how long it will take to pay that bill off.

Sometimes, she says, I wonder if I'm really made for working day after day after day. Even though I love the kids. What about you? How do you get time off to go see your sister? If my nephew was graduating, he'd have to go up on that stage without me. Which makes me feel bad. What kind of job have you got? Maybe, she says, I can get a job like yours.

You mean job, as in the kind you get paid for? I reply. Because for the most part, writing books is a labor of love. Yeah, she says, the paid kind. I tell her for me right now it's a job called unemployment.

The thing about working poor, or not, is that it takes so very little to upset the entire apple cart. David Shipler, the author of *The Working Poor: Invisible in America,* calls this chain of want and circumstance "the interlocking deficits of poverty." Many of the people he interviewed had experienced a sort of domino effect that impeded their attempts to overcome hardships. Shipler explains how it works: "An interest rate can be determined by the condition of an apartment, which in turn can generate illness and medical bills, which may then translate into a poor credit rating, which limits the quality of an automobile that can be purchased, which jeopardizes a worker's reliability in getting to work, which limits promotions and restricts the wage, which confines a family to the dilapidated apartment."[7] In each of these interlocking scenarios, public policy and institutions (the bank, the car dealership, the employer, an inadequate public transportation system, a restricted stock of affordable housing) come into play in ways that individual effort alone cannot counter.

Remember those teenagers from Alabama with the brisk interest in currency trading? The ones I promised we would meet in the vicinity of Idaho Falls? They're in the back of this coach now, trying to hustle a ride to a campground. A few states back, one of the young women in their party broke her leg getting off the bus in the middle of the night at a rest stop. Her friends took her to the hospital in whatever town they were passing through, but of course the bus went on without them.

When they tried to resume their journey the next day, the bus company didn't want to let them ride. It's not our responsibility to pick you up when you get off at an unauthorized stop, said the manager. Your little town's not on our route.

Now that really pissed me off, says the girl in the cast. So I told him, look, it's your responsibility. It's your bus I fell off of when you tried to set us down in the dark. Do you think we wanted to get off in the middle of nowhere? Do you think I enjoyed breaking my leg? Okay, then guess what this guy says. You won't believe it! He tries to insinuate that I broke my leg on purpose to sue them! That was the final straw. Now you know why I tell everyone I meet: Don't ever ride the bus if you can help it.

But of course this girl and her friends can't help it. Especially now that they've spent their last bit of savings on a taxi to take them to a bus stop that appeared on the company schedule. Even more so, now that the same bus company that refused to pick them up has lost all their luggage.

How are we supposed to find jobs when all we've got is the clothes on our back? asks her friend Junior. I can't go to an interview looking like this! The best plan they can think of in the wake of recent events is to apply for public assistance, but none of them knows how to deal with Montana residency requirements. Do they even have welfare in Montana? Will the government accept a campground as a temporary address?

It all seems too overwhelming, so they go back to shaking down passengers for misstruck "Cesar Rodney" quarters.

Finding none, they fill their pockets with the conviction afforded to white youth, at least, that something, somehow, will work out. Might work out. And they go to sleep.

The Singing Bus

I can't sleep, because I have to change buses. Again. With a little luck, I imagine I might still make it in time to root for my nephew when he holds out his hand to receive that diploma. Later my sister will ask, Why didn't you call me? I would have come picked you up in Butte! For a minute I won't know what to say. When the answer comes, it will go like this: Ah, but if I'd called you, I would have missed the singing bus.

To get to Missoula from eastern Montana, a passenger has to catch the Seattle through coach. Even in my sleep-rationed state, I can tell I'm going to like this ride. A family that started out in Virginia has transformed the front of the bus into a living room. Veterans of cross-country travel, they've supplied themselves with cushions and a battery-powered television set. The little TV doesn't work because the mountains block the signal, but no matter. Time for more of that chicken, fried in a real kitchen back home.

Are they tired? Hell, yes. Are they about to let it get them down? Let's see. Some people have a spirit so joyful, so infectious, it can't be dampened by a little thing like a broken-down car or a busted credit rating. The Dalai Lama has it. Celia Cruz, the salsa diva, had it. These folks have it. They make a place for me where there is no space, offer me a pillow, help me put my luggage up. Then they go back to the serious business of celebrating.

Not that there's anything in particular to celebrate. Just

life. And life is good, even when it's not being particularly good to you.

The father of this merry band keeps up a steady patter with the driver. Their shared passion for fishing creates a bridge between city and country, east and west, parchment-colored and cherry-colored skin. "Does he always talk this much?" I ask his wife with amusement. It's just his way, she says. Forty-seven hours on the bus and he's been going the whole time! The couple's children, who wouldn't know a rainbow trout from a muskie, pop, snap, and rap into imaginary microphones. And they're good. We wrote that one ourselves, they confess, suddenly bashful when the rest of the bus applauds.

A brief stop outside the gloomy old territorial prison in Deer Lodge doesn't make anyone miss a beat. From underneath the coach the driver offloads great cartons of supplies. The prison's steep walls, built with convict labor in the nineteenth century, sketch out the contours of a fairytale castle. Without the happy ending, one suspects. Inside the decommissioned turrets, self-guided tours of "historic interest" have replaced the sound of roll call. Today there are no tourists in sight, only the receding pile of freight as we circle back to the highway. Pop. Snap. Rap.

By the time we get to Drummond, inspiration, having already struck, strikes twice, though not exactly in the same place. A middle-aged man in middlebrow clothes in the middle of the bus rises up out of his seat. With one hand on the luggage rack for balance, he tosses out a challenge. I've memorized the entire screenplay to *Forrest Gump,* he announces. Give me any line you can remember from the movie and I'll tell you what comes next. Pride animates his face. Any line, he says.

Forrest Gump? objects a low-pitched voice from the back.

Aw, c'mon. That's *history.* Yeah, it is, says the man. So try me. You got something better to do to pass the time?

The kids have stopped their singing now. Silence drifts down over the coach. All right, says a scrawny woman with cat's-eye glasses. What about that part where he's there when Kennedy gets shot?

True to his word, the middle-aged man in the middlebrow clothes can cite chapter and verse for every piece of the plot thrown his way. We follow Forrest through the episodes of school-taught American history: the civil rights movement, desegregation, Vietnam, and . . . what's the name of that hotel? With Nixon and all? Right, Watergate. We cheer when little Forrest, "slow" to everyone but his mama, outwits and outruns his tormenters. We cheer when grown-up Forrest heroically intervenes in ways that put history on a subtly different course. We go wild when he battles the forces of evil (an incestuous father) and poverty (no explanation needed) to protect the girl he loves.

It's a potted history organized by scandal, Big Men, and war. Yet there's also another side: Forrest as griot. Forrest as traveler. Forrest sitting at the bus stop with his briefcase on his knees, determined to tell his story no matter how many riders come and go.

What makes the entire performance uncanny is the fact that the middle-aged man in the middlebrow clothes looks a little like Forrest Gump. More than a little, whispers the mother from Virginia. Did you see his ears?

Which came first? The resemblance? Or did the character creep gently into his bones?

Ten minutes to Missoula, intones the driver. Fire-blackened slopes testify to one of the hottest summers on record. Our chorus director brings us careening through the last of the mountain passes with his favorite cinematic refrain:

Mama always said
(go Forrest!)
I say Mama always said
(said what?)
there's an awful lot you can tell
(mm-hmmm)
about a person by their shoes
(oh yeah)

where they've gone
(gone)
where they been
(been)
I've worn lots of shoes
(LOTS of shoes)

And I bet
if I think about it re-e-e-al hard
(go on!)
I could remember
(go on!)
my first pair of shoes

Mama said
(what'd she say?)
they'd take me anywhere
(take you where?)
anywhere!
(where?)
anywhere!
(what else she say?)
she said
they was my magic shoes . . .

Our bus arrives late. I miss the graduation after all. But it's never too late to celebrate: I have it on the authority of some of the finest teachers the street has to offer. My sister pulls out a slice of graduation cake from the freezer. My nephew wants to know where I've been. If these shoes could talk.

II.

Leaving the City of Cranes:
Boston to Milwaukee in Two Alimentary Acts

Awash in a Great Green Sea

Strangely enough, our next journey begins with cake. A three-tier layer cake, to be exact, with chocolate sprinkles on top that spell "Diana." My seatmate, a rawboned woman with an easy smile and a limp, has sifted three cups of flour with her own hands, added milk, sugar, eggs, a hint of vanilla. Real vanilla, don't you know, not that artificial stuff. The imprint of a butter knife swirled into the frosting. And now, in an act of heroism never seen on TV, she has resolved to stay awake for the forty-four hours it will take her to get to Oklahoma by bus. Lest the cake slide off her lap. Lest she store it in the overhead rack and return to find it crushed. I should have made them something more sensible, she tells me. But I said to myself, why not cake? It's about time my niece had a real birthday.

She tucks the cake safely back into its cardboard box. Outside the city of Boston swims past, held at a slight remove by the pounding of jackhammers. Plywood walls screen the trenches where excavation continues into the night on the Central Artery Project. The Big Dig: the most expensive feat of public engineering in United States history. A project that will sink the freeway deep into the ground, beneath stores and hotels and the offices of financial corporations. A project that will sink the public deeper into debt. Just decades ago, a vital neighborhood called the West End was destroyed to make way for the freeway overpass now judged obsolete, doomed to be replaced by a tunnel. A poor neighborhood it was, the West End. A neighborhood of immigrants. The kind of neighborhood too often considered expendable.

When you wrench people away from a neighborhood that has nurtured them, something profound happens. Root shock, psychiatrist Mindy Thompson Fullilove calls it.[1] During the 1960s, a state-sponsored program called urban renewal leveled churches, homes, schools, and clubs, dispersing the jazz musicians along with the undertakers, preachers, and everyday folk. The effects of dislocation can linger for generations.

Root shock doesn't always arrive in the guise of Big Digs, officially sponsored "improvements," or city planning. By slowly withdrawing municipal services—garbage collection, snow removal, fire response—authorities can, if they wait long enough, declare an area "blighted" and turn it over to government-subsidized developers. Not surprisingly, the people left to pick themselves up in the aftermath have tended to be poor, immigrants, black, brown. In Massachusetts the descendents of West Enders, now dispersed, will pay to bury the road that buried the homes of their grandparents.

As our bus heads in search of the turnpike, we pass backhoes, steamrollers, stacks of highway dividers and discarded pieces of tarmac. A thermos. A spray-painted sign directing crews to Glory Hole 56. We can't quite grasp it, sealed into the sheet metal of the bus, but the labor must have its own rhythm. Bore, winch, lift, unearth. Spend, bill, borrow, collect.

Cranes are everywhere, levering their loads skyward on leveraged funds. Near the airport and the waterfront, mammoth equipment grazes on concrete like some rare species of robotic wildlife. Below the street the unfinished tunnels creep seaward, already weeping.

There's work here! exclaims a middle-aged white guy in

the front of the bus to no one in particular. Where commuters see a traffic tie-up, where government officials see a
financial debacle, where onetime residents see eviction, where
drifters see a chance to hide away amidst the debris and pass
the night undisturbed, this man, an unemployed man, sees
jobs. I see a city of cranes, laid out by giant hands wielding
an old-fashioned erector set.

From the vision to the need, or was it vice versa? Philoso-
phers used to ask whether the farmer and the artist ever saw
the same field. What would they say about the laid-off welder
and the economist?

Even to practiced eyes, what looked like work in the
United States was changing. By the twenty-first century, the
shifts laid at the door of a mysterious phenomenon called
"globalization" had acquired the force of a litany: Manufac-
turing had fled the industrialized countries. Companies tried
to generate profits by downsizing their workforces and un-
loading a hefty portion of the work they used to perform
onto customers. So-called service jobs—long on hours, short
on customer service—proliferated, but they didn't pay nearly
as much as the unionized jobs in the old factories. Employees, now holding down two jobs or doing the work formerly
done by two coworkers, or both, were getting tired. New
forms of consumer credit encouraged many to go into debt.
The wealthier few engaged in equally debt-laden albeit more
respectable transactions, such as financial speculation and
hedge-fund derivatives. All of which raised some new philo-
sophical puzzles. Flipping burgers, flipping condos: was this
work, in the time-honored sense, or did it just amount to
employment?

In the neighborhoods that ringed Boston Harbor, the rising economic tide of the 1990s had promised to lift all boats.
Yet the trade policies associated with globalization seemed to

have brought more inequality, not less, in their wake. To paraphrase Richard Freeman and Joel Rogers, the New Economy raised the yachts, but it also did a fine job of sinking the dinghies.[2] Real wages declined for working families. Aggressive monetary policies on the part of the Federal Reserve pumped easy credit into markets, first stocks, then housing. In a reversal of the white flight of the 1960s, urban neighborhoods gentrified, forcing poorer people out. Economic "recoveries" stopped generating the anticipated numbers of jobs.

For Americans like Diana's aunt, who lived poor during these years, the boom meant money, money everywhere, with scarcely a drop to drink. Granted, during this roaring decade even very poor people could access limited sources of credit, albeit at merchant of misery prices. Buy a chrome kitchen set for no money down, only 24.9 percent interest! Pawn your car title for a loan, risk losing the only way you have to get to work, and walk away with a fistful of cash! Shady mortgage deals lured borrowers to make payments on houses they could never afford. Big-name mortgage brokers slotted black and brown families that should have qualified for conventional loans into the "subprime" category, saddling them with higher interest rates that increased the chances of default. With every hiccup in the economy, negative amortization schemes pushed even middle-class families further down the road to foreclosure. Their less capitalized cousins turned to rent-to-own stores that demanded twice, even hundreds of times the going market price for a couch or DVD player by the time a customer finished paying off the charges. In the meantime these items could always be repossessed. Rent-to-repo stores, some of the bus riders called them.

A person can drown in a sea of plenty.

But all that's supposed to be neither here nor there, because it's a new century, right? And it's dinnertime. A person's got to eat, regardless. No wonder the lady across the aisle with her hair in twists has fixed her stare on my companion's cardboard box. You gonna pass that around? she asks, loud enough to turn heads. Diana's aunt panics. Tell her, she whispers, I baked it special for my niece.

I can't resist the desperate appeal of a woman raised to share. Let her be! I say, summoning up my best FM radio voice. It's a cake she made for her niece's birthday! The other passengers turn obligingly back to their windows. Birthdays *are* special. Food made from scratch even more so. In these days of processed food and endless work, things homemade are not to be treated lightly.

Two blocks ahead lies the ramp that leads to a thread of asphalt that will take us to the suburbs. Two seats up sits a man in a cable-knit sweater who hugs a computer case with a copy of *Investor's Business Daily* tucked into its pocket. This bus is a different sort of lifeline for him than it is for a woman traveling to Oklahoma on the fumes of determination. A commuter run for him, that's all it is: he'll be gone by Worcester.

For the time being we're stuck at a stoplight in the shadow of Boston's scaled-down versions of skyscrapers. When steel-framed buildings first began to tempt the clouds, their reach was critiqued as presumptuous. There's no less arrogance, I suppose, injected into this high-tech hole they call the Big Dig, innovative and leaking.

The light is still red and already I'm drifting. Only—only! —twenty-five hours to my hometown, Chicago, if you count "home" as the place you were born and the staging ground for your favorite sports teams. The bus shifts into gear. The cake wobbles gently on my companion's knees. The ghosts of West Enders peer through the misted windows looking for housing.

The great oral historian Studs Terkel once did an interview with a man who had been part of U.S. forces sent into Germany at the end of World War II. The man could pinpoint the exact moment, he said, when he understood that Europe was going to come back from the war's devastation. Was it when soldiers liberated the concentration camps? No. Was it when governments announced the Marshall Plan, which provided money to rebuild? No. In the cellar of a bombed-out building, the man had come across a table laid for a dinner that hardly existed. Food was still incredibly scarce. In the center of the table stood a wildflower in a bottle. When he saw that flower, he knew.

As we pass the last of the Big Dig's excavations, Diana's aunt leans over in her seat, the glow of a thousand halogen work lights emanating from her eyes. I'm thinking about that queen, she says. Huh? You know, she says. From France, I think she was. The one who said, "Let them eat cake" when they were running out of bread. Marie Antoinette? I venture. I'm not sure she really said that, though. And she came to a bad end. Her subjects guillotined her. Ooh, that's too bad, Diana's aunt responds. But still, don't you think that lady was on to something? I mean, a body can't just survive. We're here to enjoy.

Master and Commander

By the time we pull into Albany for a scheduled rest break, Diana's aunt has to use the facilities. That means she needs to find a minder for the cake. In my time riding buses I have stood guard over infants, kept an eye on garbage bags filled with underwear, hoisted a guitar out of the path of a runaway freight cart, and shepherded the hand luggage of assorted strangers onto connecting runs, but never before have I been called upon to babysit dessert. I must look like a trustworthy sort. It's one thing to fend off the stares of hungry riders; it's quite another to fend off the derrieres of newly boarding passengers rushing to claim a seat. I consider moving the box onto my lap, but I'm mortified at the thought that I might lapse into a dream, allowing the sprinkle-dusted confection to slide to the floor in a sticky heap.

While I'm busy counting bulldozers backwards to stay awake, the driver climbs back on and begins to glower in my direction. Okay, so I don't look like such a trustworthy sort. When I don't respond to his cryptic signals, he strides over to make sure I get the message. Move that box! he orders, towering over me. You're only entitled to one seat. Everybody on this bus gets a seat, but only the one they paid for.

This strikes me as harassment of a sort, because the coach is half empty. It's not uncommon for passengers to spread out when the route is lightly traveled. I open my mouth to explain that the box belongs to another passenger, another *paying* passenger, I might add, but the driver is back in the front, testing the theory of optics by using his mirrors to keep me in sight as he takes tickets and gives directions. I adopt the path of least resistance by pulling the cake up onto my lap. Diana's aunt will be back soon. Won't she?

Above the front windshield, a placard reads, "Your Operator," followed by a blank slot where a name can be inserted but isn't. After the blank comes a pledge: "Safe–Reliable–Courteous." Right.

To be fair, drivers are working folk too. They have to deal with all sorts of nonsense, which they confront in various ways, but generally with authority. While the bus is rolling, they are gods. They have the power to stop in the middle of a sun-baked salt desert flat, pull over to the side of the road, and unload your uppity attitude along with the sum total of your belongings. It's a power more often invoked than exercised, but exercise it they will, if pushed.

I've seen it all, one driver told me: homicides, suicides, you name it. Greyhound put me through seven weeks of training, but driving turned out to be the least of it. First and foremost, he claimed, they want you to have people skills. City skills, you might call them. He estimated that only twenty-five of the two hundred people in his class ever made it to full-time. Getting trained didn't mean getting hired.

If they passed the Department of Transportation–mandated physical examination, aspiring "hounds" committed to two weeks of classroom and computer instruction plus another two weeks behind the wheel, followed by three weeks of on-the-job training. Course topics included navigation, ticketing, baggage, the components of a bus, handling emergencies, and, of course, the operation of different vehicle models. The minority of candidates who made it through the program in 2006 started at $16.20 per hour.

Keep in mind that different schedules pay different, another driver explained. Some guys go for the money, some for the hours, some for the runs where the passengers are more settled and give us less mouth. That can be a good tradeoff for a little less pay. But we can't control the route, because we get assigned according to seniority. The first few years, he said, a new driver typically works off the "extra board." He— or she, I guess I should say—stays on call 24/7, ready to go anytime, anywhere the company sends its fleet.

Most drivers let you know who's in charge the minute they take control of the bus. Almost every route begins with a monologue, delivered over the microphone. There will be no drinking. No marijuana, no loud music, no smoking of any kind. Apparently the entire might of the U.S. government stands ready to back them up. Federal law states...Law enforcement will be summoned...The personas that drivers adopt for this little performance run the gamut: schoolteacher, drill sergeant, standup comedian, the fatherly disciplinarian you always loved to hate.

Over the intercom on a bus headed for Tampa: Anyone who chooses not to abide by these regulations will not make it to his destination. Outside Cleveland: There is positively, definitely no smoking on this bus. If you do so, it can and will have you exited with police assistance. En route to Alabama: For your convenience, a restroom is provided in the back of the bus. If you try to light up in there, I will know it.

Just in case you didn't get it the first time, the captain of the coach will gladly supply you with a definition. "No smoking" means absolutely none. When I say private listening devices only, "private" does not mean putting your headphones on full blast. "Private" means you do not disturb your fellow passengers with your music. If you should decide to strike up a conversation, keep your voices to a minimum. Loud, boisterous talking and laughter will not be tolerated at all.

Somewhere along the line, safety became a North American mantra. Although the rules serve the driver as well as the rider, the phrasing often implies that some powers that be have created restrictions with only one thing in mind: protecting the passenger. As in: For your security, while the coach is moving, no one is allowed to cross the yellow line. As in: There is no medical technician on this bus. If you have an emergency situation, holler out. I will pull over and deal with your emergency. As in: Keep the aisles clear but you may safely use the aisles to travel to and from the restroom at the back of the coach. (Have you seen the condition of that bathroom? asked a woman behind me in low tones. Now *that* would be taking your life in your hands.) Even the Amalgamated Transit Union (ATU), to which drivers belong, has adopted as its motto "Moving the U.S. and Canada Safely."

Some of the passengers are grateful for these rules; most can't stand them. The ones who object often see them as imposing white ideas on riders who have honed their politics with hip-hop lyrics, imposing "stuck-up" (i.e., upper-class) standards on riders who draw strength from exchanges above sixty decibels. So, of course, the rules are violated regularly. And, of course, not all drivers stretch the rules as far as they can go. Only the racist or the misanthrope adds a "no laughter" rule to the "no smoking" rule mandated by law. Otherwise there would have been no singing bus. We would have finished rapping our way through *Forrest Gump* with our luggage stacked around us in some desolate parking lot.

There are even drivers who would rather be appearing on Comedy Central. On a Trailways bus leaving Idaho Falls, the driver satisfied the requirement to announce the route this way: You're headed northbound, he declared, with connections in Butte to Missoula, Spokane, Seattle, Honolulu, and all points west. After a pause calculated to secure a giggle from his captive audience, he asked, What are the chances of rain today? He knew that we knew that he knew we had been standing outside the crowded station in a downpour for hours. Any smokers on board? he continued, over a chorus of groans. A few passengers raised their hands where he could see them in his rearview mirror. Well, he responded, feel free to smoke anytime. Another pause. Really? someone piped up in a hopeful voice, giving the driver just the opening he sought. Yep, the driver replied. All I ask is that, while the coach is rolling, you step outside to do it.

Once, on my way to Washington, D.C., a driver tried irony. The restroom is provided with a wastebasket, he informed us. Feel free to use it.

Some drivers go out of their way to accommodate passenger requests. Some can't be bothered. Driver, turn on the heat? requested a thin man whose arms were covered with goose bumps on a winter run. The driver glanced over his shoulder, holding the speedometer steady. You don't got no clothes on, that's what's the problem, he exclaimed, nothing but a white T-shirt! No words for the man's jacket, soaked through while he had waited for the bus in the rain. No words for the state of the heater, in disrepair, which was set as high as it would go. And what if a white T-shirt was all the man had? Another passenger threw the man a sweater.

Compare this callous treatment to the care taken by the driver who patiently sorted out five screaming children and three worried mothers who had become separated in the rush to board a Portland bus without nearly enough seats. Or the driver in St. Louis who made sure, before he resumed his route, that a homeless passenger received directions to a shelter. Let me handle things, brother, he said. Or the driver in Georgia who offered to recharge a passenger's dying portable music player during his rest break. That's a long way from trying to stop the music.

Every so often, drivers attempt to establish common ground by reminding their passengers that they are there to do a job. We're not really gods after all, they imply, just tired and overworked like everybody else. I realize we're late, admits a soft-spoken driver whose voice belies his military haircut. He's licking the last crumbs of Colonel Sanders's secret recipe off his fingers before he pulls into traffic. I'll get you there just as fast as I can, he says, but remember, this is rush hour. Remember, this is two-lane driving. Remember, there are places where it's impossible to pass. Another driver might promise to phone ahead to hold the buses so that riders don't have to worry about making connections. Take a look outside your windows, requests a third. I'm making the very best time I can, but you can see for yourselves how this road is all tore up. Complain to your elected officials, not to me.

On one memorable occasion, a driver who talked tough to the cops after he received a speeding citation got a standing ovation from his passengers. Thank you for your patience, he intoned solemnly into the microphone. For those of you who don't believe that the bus ever gets ticketed, he continued, waving the bright orange scrap of paper in the air, here's your proof! If we weren't expected to make up time when we're running late, these things wouldn't have to happen. Then he eased the bus back into the stream of cars, knowing full well that the infraction would be written up in his employee file. Schoolteacher, drill sergeant, comedian, disciplinarian . . . add "folk hero" to the list. Commander and commandeered, united in a moment of populist sentiment.

Next to the "Safe–Reliable–Courteous" placard above the windshield on my Chicago-bound bus is a decal that displays the logo of the ATU, the same union that will guide the New York transit workers to an unprecedented victory when they strike in 2005. Inside the circle a greyhound stretches out at top speed beneath U.S. and Canadian flags. Although the contract hammered out between Greyhound management and the ATU is not due to expire for several years, Local 1700, the national bargaining unit for Greyhound workers, is already making plans. Its website hosts a new rallying cry: "Reversing Decades of Decline on the Highways and in Labor." Repeated demands for salary concessions, cutbacks in positions and pensions, lower employer contributions to health care, two-tier packages that offered inferior compensation to new employees, declines in union membership, overworked employees, massive amounts of corporate money poured into union-busting campaigns: these were developments that most unions had had to confront. At Greyhound the national trends took on a peculiar poignancy, because the company had participated in some of the early downsizing initiatives during the 1980s.

After Ronald Reagan assumed the presidency, deregulation became the watchword, particularly in sectors of the economy such as transportation. Brand-new low-budget airlines gave trains and buses a run for their money. Increased competition impacted passenger numbers and damaged profit margins to such an extent that the bus companies began to lay off workers, discontinue routes, and close stations. Many small towns where bus service had offered the only quasi-public form of transportation now had no service at all.

The Great Greyhound Strikes of 1983 and 1990–1993 shook the transportation industry in the United States to its core. Both strikes took place in the long shadow of the 1981 walkout by air traffic controllers, a pivotal labor action in which government took measures to break the strike and the majority of workers faced termination. At Greyhound the circumstances that brought workers and management to an impasse were rather different. In contrast to the air traffic controllers, who had walked out in pursuit of better wages and improved working conditions, the ATU found itself fighting a rearguard action. Greyhound had demanded significant concessions, including a 9.5 percent wage cut. In 1983 the company argued for concessions based on falling profits. In 1990, when profits were up and employees expected a raise, the company argued that it needed to trim labor expenses in order to pay off debt, including the loans that had underwritten the buyout of its major competitor, Trailways.

The long-running strike from 1990 through 1993 was especially acrimonious. Greyhound continued to put buses on the road by recruiting strikebreakers (euphemistically called "new hires") and sending executives into the field to oversee operations. Fistfights broke out on the picket lines. Bomb threats were phoned in. A new hire killed a striking worker in Redding by running him over with a bus. In a move some described as a tactic calculated to break the union, Greyhound filed for bankruptcy in 1990. The ATU countered by filing charges of unfair labor practices with the National Labor Relations Board (NLRB). Both parties got tied up in court.

What began as a labor action turned into a war of attrition. Drivers who hadn't worked in three years began to cross the picket line. The ATU called its members back to work without reaching a satisfactory agreement, although it did manage to defend a few key union principles such as seniority. The NLRB eventually ruled in favor of the union on most counts, awarding strikers $22 million in back pay, but the bankruptcy filing protected the company from paying out anything close to this amount. While the union may have lost the war, labor historians have argued that the Great Greyhound Strikes represented a defeat for the company as well. What emerged from the strike was a company of diminished geographical reach, diminished carrying capacity, and embattled management.

Knowing this history, when a driver outside Reno mentions how glad he is to have enough seniority to pick his routes so that he can spend evenings with his family, it's not surprising that I hear a union struggle talking. When a driver outside Elkhart, Indiana, worries about how to get the care he needs for his epileptic six-year-old, I hear the losing side of that struggle. When a driver outside a city that shall remain nameless complains about his night vision and the difficulties of financing his retirement under the new pension plan, I hear a disaster waiting to happen. I worry about him. What place is left in a neoconservative world for a bus driver with failing eyesight?

And there's a more personal problem: None of these gentler ghosts of drivers future, drivers past, are available to talk sense to the irascible commander of the coach I'm riding tonight. The driver who just reprimanded me like a child for taking up two seats is busy glowering at a new set of passengers. Good. Good for me, I mean, but what about them? There he goes, jumping up to play the petty despot. I clutch the cake box—gently, gently!—and await the return of the aunt, knowing his time will come. From here to Milwaukee, the miles are littered with scheduled driver changes.

I Just Hate to Travel Like This

No sooner does Diana's aunt return to claim the cake box than she hurries to change buses and disappears into someone else's day. A shuffle of new passengers wafts a sixty-year-old white lady named Evie into the seat beside me. Everything about her says "sensible." With her cropped hair, lace-up shoes, and dark-colored pants (the better to conceal stains), she's the very picture of Middle America. If your picture of Middle America comes from the evening news.

Earlier, when we stopped in Worcester, the middle-class passengers melted away with the light. The ones joining us in Albany are, for the most part, riding for the longer haul, and this woman is no exception. Before the luggage doors under the bus slam shut, I already know three things about her: she's on her way home from Europe, she can't afford to take a plane the rest of the way, and she imagines she's better than the rest of us.

Ever had the chance to leave the driving, period, by taking to the skies? No idle question even in a wealthy country, where significant numbers of people have never had the credit or the funds to step inside a plane. Thirty-five thousand feet up, you'll find airline magazines cluttered with advertisements from financial services companies trying to sell elites on the virtues of long-term planning. Trusts, insurance policies, tax dodges, gifting strategies, liquidity needs, retirement accounts, incapacity preparation: every future anticipated, every contingency provided for, every stage of life mapped out. For a price. If, as theorist Geeta Patel points out, the companies don't fold.[3] Those ads push the message that you can master your fate by getting your years and funds lined up, like ducks, in a row. People on the bus know different. The years don't waddle along in stages, hoping for sensible provisions. Life passes unexpectedly, in vignettes.

I just *hate* to travel like this, Evie mutters the minute she drops into her seat. It's *so* low class! Her hazel eyes roll sideways to see if I agree. When I shrug my shoulders, she tries again: Don't you think? When I don't reply, Evie turns her attention to the aisle, where people are banging one another with oversize gym bags ("Sorry!" "Excuse me!" "Was that your foot?") in a desperate search for places to stash luggage that they won't trust to the bottom of the coach. One woman in particular garners Evie's disapproval. She's pretty, African American, and what my grandmother would have called "heavyset." Since all this woman is doing is trying to work her way toward a free seat, I get the feeling it's more than her old-school Jerri Curls that have attracted Evie's attention.

In the mouths of white Americans, even white Americans who are themselves living poor, "poor" and "low-class" often serve as code words for black or brown. It doesn't seem to matter how many statistical studies are published emphasizing that the majority of people living below the poverty line in North America identify as white. In the face of entrenched beliefs, numbers can easily be discounted. So can a person's own experiences.

Take Evie. She tells me she works on and off as a school monitor in the classrooms of upstate New York. The year we share seats on the bus she has earned a grand total of twelve hundred dollars for the entire fall semester. It's not much, she admits, but it's something. The anthem of the working poor. Just try to put the best face on things and keep going.

Evie is here because she felt determined to attend the wedding of her best friend's son. One glitch: the son was stationed on a U.S. military base in Germany, where the wedding would take place. The only way for someone of Evie's means to realize this dream would be to engage in a little creative financial planning of a sort that doesn't appear in airline magazines. First she took the bus to New York City, where she had secured an airfare at a reduced rate. That "cheap" airfare required her to draw down the little savings she had left from her married days. Well worth it, Evie said, for friendship. By the time she reached Iceland, where she was supposed to change planes, the weather had taken a turn for the worse. By the time the storm cleared, she had missed the wedding.

A wealthier woman with time on her hands could have turned what Evie called a "wasted trip" into a vacation. With no friends in Iceland or money for a hotel, Evie had to turn around. Exhausted and understandably grumpy, she found herself back on the bus. Not voluntarily, to save a buck, but because they told her when she landed at LaGuardia that a plane ticket to the small city she calls home would cost four hundred dollars she doesn't have.

A person might call Evie "in denial" about her current class position and she wouldn't be wrong. Evie herself said her financial situation took a dive after her husband passed away, although she did come into a small fixed income through Social Security. Divorce and the death of a spouse represent two of the most common routes to poverty for middle-class women. In Evie's case, however, her husband's death did not precipitate a fall from some sheltered middle-class existence. Her husband had held a steady job in a factory until the Rust Belt began to creep eastward during the 1980s; then he was laid off. After that, they were struggling. When he got sick, friends passed the hat to send the two of them off for a last-wish vacation to Aruba. What a time they had! White sand beaches, jazz every night in the hotel lounge, buffets like you've never seen in your life. Believe it or not, Evie tells me in the conspiratorial tone she favors, I even tried the goat stew. It's better than it sounds! On the return trip, after the plane landed and they completed their journey by Greyhound, she remembers how they emptied their pockets and counted out forty-five cents between them. Evie might hate to travel like this, but she is no stranger to the bus.

Evie also knows well enough that she has something in common with the people occupying the rest of the seats. The problem is, she hates it. She doesn't *want* to be like them, or whatever she imagines they are. She can't stand the feeling of diminished possibilities—who could?—and she doesn't think she should have to reconcile herself to it.

Just when I start to think I've got Evie figured out, she interrupts the story of her husband's passing to come to the defense of a boarding passenger. He is slightly built, with hands the color of mahogany jutting out from a nylon windbreaker with too-short sleeves and a broken zipper. The man clearly doesn't understand which part of his ticket the driver is demanding. Rather than detach the part of the ticket the bus company keeps for its records, the driver feels compelled to berate the man: Speak English? ENGLISH? E-N-G-L-I-S-H? English, yes! the man replies, holding out everything in his hands.

That's awful! Evie shouts, rising up out of her seat to tell the driver just what she thinks of his approach to customer relations. There's no reason to treat him that way! And Evie has to shout, because the driver subscribes to the common belief that language skills can be taught by turning up the volume. Only when the driver backs off does Evie sit back down. Some people, I tell you, she says, staring off into the night. As the recently intimidated guardian of a cake box, I admire what it took for her to do that.

After copious tongue clucking and head shaking all 'round, we settle back into our seats and return to our conversations. It's been ten years since he died, says Evie. You know, my husband. And I'll tell you, the Social Security payments do not keep up with the cost of living. (Officially Social Security payments are indexed to the cost of living, which is supposed to allow them to keep pace with inflation through periodic adjustments.) You can say that again! declares an elderly woman across the aisle, who apologizes for listening in. I do everything to stretch my check, but there's no way to make ends meet. Just go to the supermarket, says Evie, turning around. The prices go up and up, so you know things must be different than they tell you.

I jump in. Did you know that some people claim Social Security payments would be 40 or 50 percent higher if the government hadn't changed the way it measures inflation?

What do you mean? they ask. Well, the people who measure such things decided to leave certain things out, like the price of heat and gasoline. What craziness is that? the woman behind us asks. This is upstate New York! A person's got to heat their home. Wait, I say, it gets better. Did you know there's no inflation to speak of, so long as you can buy tuna fish for the price you used to pay for lobster? What!?! they exclaim in unison. They think I'm joking. No, seriously, I reply, that's the way the government counts now. Economists even have a name for it. It's called "the substitution effect."

John Williams, an economist and the author of the online newsletter *Shadow Government Statistics,* would have plenty to say about playing the numbers:

> In 1996—the middle of the Clinton economic miracle—the Kaiser Foundation conducted a survey of the American public that purported to show how out of touch the electorate was with economic reality. Most Americans thought inflation and unemployment were much higher, and economic growth was much weaker, than reported by the government. The *Washington Post* bemoaned the economic ignorance of the public. The same results would be found today. Neither the Kaiser Foundation nor the *Post* understood that there was and still is good reason for the gap between common perceptions and government reporting... Inflation and unemployment reports are understated, while employment and other economic data are overstated deliberately.[4]

Four years before Williams posted a summary of his work on his website, the grassroots critique of government reporting to which he refers was being refined in the civic arena called the bus.

Can I ask you a personal question? says the eavesdropping

woman. Sure, I say. Are you some kind of teacher? Sometimes, I say. Sometimes. I've been called worse.

So you mean, Evie persists, if I was rich and I used to be
able to afford one of those plush Icelandic sweaters (which I
couldn't, but let's suppose I could) and now I can only afford
to shiver in this little sweater here, we pretend like nothing
has changed? I nod. Just because I've still got a sweater? I
nod. The three of us stare reverently at the maroon pills that
cover her thin acrylic vest. It's hard to think of what to say
after that.

Y'all Shouldn't Have Ate That Chicken

Forty miles later, when the tickling sensation starts working
its way up the back of my throat, there's not much to take my
mind off it. This chapter should have been the interlude between action-filled adventures. (You know: the one where the
vehicle's tires hum on the road.) Evie has drifted fitfully off
to sleep. The altercations in the aisles fizzled out hours ago.
My head pillows into a blue-black picture window that reflects more of the dimly lit interior of the bus than the lakes
and fields that must lie spread out on either side of us in the
dark. And that's how my not-so-excellent adventure begins.

I may be en route to Milwaukee, but my intestinal tract
has taken off on a journey of its own. The process starts in-
nocently enough, with a bubble of gas. That tiny bubble
multiplies, expands, multiplies again, jamming my diaphragm
against my liver, guts into spleen, churning, churning, until
finally the queasiness roots in my stomach.

This is not good.

I reach into my pocket for a scribbled copy of the schedule. Next stop, Utica, 2:05 a.m. Rummage around for Pepto-

Bismol chewable tablets to quell the nausea. Congratulate myself ever so briefly for riding prepared. I *have* learned a thing or two from my experience in Salt Lake. But self-satisfaction quickly gives way to a curse when my body won't respond to the drug. Come on, think: What else can you do? Meditate, follow your breath. In, out, in, out, in, ouwww... The world beats in syncopation with my stomach. Time slows. 1:21. Close your eyes, try not to check your watch. 1:23. I can barely hold myself together.

At first I don't know what to make of my suddenly desperate circumstances. Could this be some allergic reaction to the harsh cleaning chemicals that permeate the bus? Every time I breathe, the synthetic citrus scent cuts my lungs. Yet I've ridden dozens of buses without ever reacting to the chemicals. No, it's more likely that feeling nauseous has heightened my sensitivity to smell. What, then? A fierce case of motion sickness? No, I tell myself, that doesn't make sense, either. I don't usually get motion sickness, especially when I'm riding so far forward. And who ever heard of motion sickness accompanied by rumbling intestines with fever and diarrhea? Maybe it's the flu.

I'm considering a run for the restroom when a calm voice whispers through the crack that separates the seats: Y'all shouldn't have ate that chicken. I turn around, cradling my belly. Huh? You heard me. Y'all shouldn't have ate that chicken. That stuff was probably laying out there all day. My food critic turns out to be an elderly man, stoop shouldered, with lopsided stubble on his chin that I find oddly comforting. I remember seeing him back at the food court in Boston. He watched me plow through a dinner of grilled chicken, green beans, and rice, hurriedly shoveled into Styrofoam just before closing time.

That's when I realize that any dreams I might have entertained about waking up in the Midwest are about to take a radical detour through the underside of the country's deregulating food supply chain. How could I have been so stupid? If I were traveling in Mexico or India, this version of "rumble tummy" would have been immediately recognizable for what it was. Only because I'm looking through the illusion of the rich world, the allegedly safer world, do I try to explain away my symptoms as allergy, car sickness, motion sickness, the flu. But the wealthier side of the world has its own divisions—isn't that why I'm riding the bus?—and I am about to land badly on the down side of one of them.

Ten minutes ago my temperature was so elevated and my teeth ached so badly I could feel my incisors wobble. When I jiggled my bottom front tooth between my fingers to check, I could swear it moved in my jaw. Maybe I should see a dentist when I get back, I remember telling myself through the haze. Then: Where will I get the money for a dentist? It will be another day before I understand that I am riding the edge of hallucination.

While I could still think, I had asked myself if maybe I had come down with influenza. Isn't that what most people in the United States say when the fluids riot in their bellies: It must be the flu? There's just one problem with that ready diagnosis. Diarrhea and vomiting don't accompany influenza. They are, however, classic symptoms of food poisoning.

Not again! That would make this my second case of food poisoning in as many trips! Later, trying to understand my bad luck, I will come across a little book by Nicols Fox called *It Was Probably Something You Ate.* According to Fox, Americans have been too quick to blame fate or the flu for their upset stomachs and even their near-death experiences. Cases of food poisoning are on the rise in the United States. When I was a child growing up in Chicago in the 1960s, the government worked rather diligently to keep noxious bacteria out of the food supply. My mother put raw eggs into our milkshakes for the protein, when we could afford them, and never thought twice about it. Schoolchildren took to heart the lessons of *The Jungle,* Upton Sinclair's famous exposé of the nefarious practices of the meatpacking industry earlier in the century. Inspectors would show up at restaurants or packing plants and shut them down if the food contamination was too severe. Well, usually.

By the time I started riding the buses in earnest, food was traveling farther and sitting on the shelf longer than ever before. Lax regulation, budget cuts in inspection services, overuse of antibiotics, sweetheart deals between government and industry, and the global reorganization of agricultural production had given bacteria a leg up on the consumer. Spot testing in the United States uncovered salmonella rates upwards of 90 percent in poultry and eggs. When similar results became public in Sweden, shoppers revolted. They stopped buying chicken, which put the necessary pressure on producers to clean up their game.[5] In North America, it was a different story. Instead of cleaning up the food supply, public health authorities warned consumers to cook the hell out of their food.

Only nobody cooks on the bus. With a private car, at least there are options: traveling with a propane stove, reviving the lost art of radiator cooking, stopping to visit friends along the way. (What's that? You've never had the pleasure of being introduced to radiator cooking? It's a simple technique you can adapt to whatever ingredients you have on hand. Thin-sliced zucchini, say, with carrots, potatoes, cilantro, a little lamb if you so desire, double-wrapped tightly in aluminum foil and secured to the hot block of a running engine. Depression Era cooking with a cosmopolitan twist.) When you travel, it's hard to take the government pronouncements seriously, because they depend on having control over food preparation. When you're traveling on little or no money, it's even harder. Thirty hours into a cross-country bus ride, those burritos you brought from home will be long gone. Then what? If you're passing through Omaha City, how in the world are you going to "take responsibility" for what you eat?

The problem goes beyond people getting sick from bad food. In every area of life, the corporate reorganization of production has downloaded responsibility onto individuals for matters beyond individual control. Buy a filter for your tap (again, if you can afford it) rather than organize to stop the leaching of hazardous waste into the groundwater. Cut your chances of developing lung cancer by throwing away your cigarettes, but leave the muddied skies to "Clean Air" legislation that raises the levels of pollutants permitted by law. After the brand-new wrench you bought breaks in a week, spend an hour fruitlessly trying to activate its ten-year warranty by working your way through a robotic phone tree. Or spend your hard-earned cash on what you hope will be a wholesome meal. Then find out what you've really bought: a five-day pass to clearing toxins from your body with every rapid-ejection device known to human physiology.

Like the man said, it could have been the chicken. For that matter, it could have been the rice, reheated and reheated until *B. cereus* got the better of it. Who knows? And that's the point: as individuals, we can't know. But we can pay. Oh yes, we can pay.

It's no secret to anyone who rides the bus that any long-haul ticket includes a whirlwind tour through the fast-food nation. Gone are the days when truck stops stocked with chicken stew and homemade barley soup dotted the highways. With a few very welcome exceptions, the meal breaks take place at franchises: Burger King and Taco Bell in the north, Popeye's chicken in the south. Riders don't need to read Eric Schlosser's send-up of the fast-food industry[6] or watch Morgan Spurlock's struggle to survive on a McDonald's-only meal plan in the documentary *Supersize Me* to understand that this kind of steady diet doesn't count as nutrition. I can still hear the rallying cry of "Real food!" that went up in White River Junction, Vermont, the minute a bus full of tired passengers realized that the station shared a building with a family-owned Chinese restaurant.

By laying my bets on that chicken back in Boston, I was hoping to postpone the inevitable, at least for my first day on the road. Little did I know I would soon be in the business of swearing off food, period. Here I ride, belly cramping, as laid out as a person can be while seated in an upright position. Go away, little girl. Don't you even think of coming near me with that bag of chips.

What I want is for the bus to stop rolling so the fire in my stomach can die down. I want the bus to stop rolling. Wait. Stop? I never want this bus to stop. I never want this bus to stop because then I will have to move. Can't move. Too dangerous to move. Open my eyes and the world spins onto its side. Oh. Please. Stop.

Too-Tired Meets His Maker

Stop we must, eventually, but not yet. Not yet. Now is the time for reverie. Now is the time for murmured confessions between riders whose fears won't let them rest. Now is the midnight hour of mislaid plans and unredeemed intentions. Now is the moment for a recruitment party laid on by the gods.

Behind me two men trade silences, and words. Do you

believe in the Almighty, son? whispers the elderly man who advised me about the chicken. (No answer.) You awake, son? he persists. (Mmm.) I asked you if you believe in the Almighty. I got to sleep, the younger man replies. You can sleep when you get where you're going, son, the old man insists. This is the most important conversation you'll ever have in your life.

Tell that to my sergeant, says Too-Tired, rolling over to face the window. Sergeant? You in the service, son? Yessir, Too-Tired mumbles over his shoulder, 10th Mountain Division out of Fort Drum. Infantry, that's infantry, right? (A pause.) Light Infantry, mm-hmm. (Silence.)

The Recruiter clears his throat. Render unto Caesar, eh? Of course, that's right, he says, smoothing the stubble on his chin. You do what you have to do. But what about the other part? The Good Book says you got to render unto God the things that are God's. Listen to me, now. We're talking about your immortal soul here. "Do not love sleep," the Bible says, "or you will grow poor; stay awake and you will have food to spare." That's the Book of Proverbs, son.

But I *got* to sleep, protests Too-Tired, pulling a gray sweatshirt over his head. I know, I know you do, son, says The Recruiter. This won't take but a minute.

You haven't been saved, have you? I can tell. But it's never too late. Never too late, unless of course you was to get yourself shipped out somewhere, mixed up, blown up, without accepting the Lord as your personal Savior. But he doesn't want that to happen. No sir. He's giving you the chance here tonight, right here on this bus, to make things right.

Look how he's watched over you so far. You got yourself a good job. You can travel. One day you'll get to study. The army pays for all that. No, says Too-Tired, stirring in his seat, not all of it. Most of it. Some of it, he corrects himself, remembering the way that "incidentals" add up while traveling.

Tell you the truth, Too-Tired explains, the army doesn't pay all that much. And just like that, The Recruiter has his attention.

The roads are filled with itinerant preachers and spiritual practitioners of all sorts, but not many have the chance to work the captive audience that the bus so readily supplies. In the post-9/11 years, devout Muslim riders tended to improvise as best they could when it was time for prayer, worried about calling attention to themselves in a land where media commentators fomented anti-Islamic hysteria. Far from proselytizing, they were more likely to shield their translations of the Quran (not to mention any texts written in Arabic) from the eyes of fellow travelers. The occasional Buddhist rider was in a better position to welcome debate. Outside Fayetteville, Arkansas, I sat next to an engineering student from Malaysia who delved into the concept of "real Buddhism" with the same passion other passengers devoted to the topic of "real food." Did I think that all those new forms of Buddhism coming out of Japan should count as "real Buddhism"? I wouldn't know, I said; what do you think? Definitely not, he replied. Why not? Because, he explained, relishing the contradiction, they believe they're the only true Buddhists and that's not so Buddhist.

Ride long enough and you might come across the Hindu Sanatan Temple in Quincy, Florida, whose multicolored "Om" mural borders a thrift store, or Muhammad Farms near Albany, Georgia, a sustainable agriculture project sponsored by the Nation of Islam. You might even notice how the lines at Port Authority thin out on the Jewish High Holy Days. When it comes to spreading the word on North American bus routes, however, it's not Buddhism or Judaism, Zoroastrianism or Hinduism or Islam, but Christianity that holds sway.

While my stomach roils on our way to Utica, Too-Tired and The Recruiter talk into the wee hours, with the old man insistently working the conversation back to religion. He's as genial as he is determined. What does the size of a paycheck matter? he asks, picking up the thread about low compensation in the army. "If I give all I possess to the poor and surrender my body to the flames but have not love, I gain nothing" (First Corinthians 13:3).

This time Too-Tired rises to the bait: How can you say it doesn't matter? It would matter to you if your family had to live on *my* check! True, says the old man, true. (More silence.) Then, as a last resort, The Recruiter decides to challenge the kid's manhood. What's the problem, he says, you afraid to talk about God? No! shouts Too-Tired, causing the girl across the aisle to abandon her dreams. Well, says the old man, why won't you talk about Him, then? You're afraid! I'm not afraid, Too-Tired repeats, lowering his voice. I just don't want to talk about it. I've got to get some sleep. (Another long silence.) Sure you do, sighs the old man. Get some rest, he says. He relinquishes his quarry. And the young recruit closes his eyes to make good his escape.

In 2003 troops from the 10th Mountain Division—"the most deployed unit in the U.S. army"—shipped out of Fort Drum, headed for Afghanistan and Iraq.

Ladies and Children First

You know, a woman told me once on my way to the Boston bus station, I've never heard a guy tell another guy he's scared. Guys don't do that. They might be scared, but they don't do that.

I'm thinking to myself that I don't do that either. Not on

a bus full of strangers. But by the time we reach the outskirts of Syracuse, I am sick enough to be scared. Very. And I'm ready to take advice.

Evie, awake now and apprised of my predicament, dispenses prescriptions: Try Pepto-Bismol. Oh, you had some and it didn't work? Poor thing. Let's see, what else could you do? Okay, I've got it: Find a place where they make tea when the bus stops, then get a lemon and suck on it. A lemon should do it. It'll settle your stomach. You know, it's not good to put chemicals in your body.

Excellent idea, I think to myself, however unappealing at the moment. I'm comforted by Dr. Evie's impulse to help, even as I acknowledge to myself the impossibility of following her orders. Where in the world would I find a lemon in Syracuse at three in the morning? Slowly, almost imperceptibly, fresh lemons have disappeared from the condiments offered at coffee stops and snack bars, replaced by carefully measured doses of reconstituted lemon juice preserved in little plastic packets. With chemicals, of course.

What I do find waiting in Syracuse is a pay phone. Coin-operated phones are disappearing too in the era of mobile devices, but bus stations still tend to provide them. A concession, of sorts, to the limited income of the average passenger. The vanishing pay phone has made everything from job hunting to funeral arrangements harder for people who live poor, not only while they are traveling, but also when they can't afford a landline, when the company disconnects their home phones for lack of payment, or when they find themselves living on the street. On the bus the dulcet tones of the theme from *Ghostbusters* or Daddy Yankee's *Gasolina* do ring out more often than they used to, but it's nothing like the plane, where passengers whip out their mobiles like six-shooters at high noon as soon as the aircraft touches down.

So when I step down off the coach in Syracuse, the shining bank of telephones that greets me is a godsend. Although it's the middle of the night, I use the brief stopover to call directory assistance. In the name of competition and free markets, I have to place my call on equipment that belongs to a private carrier: $1.75 it costs for a number that used to be free, just another in a long line of regressive charges that ask poorer people to pay more for the services they access. Theoretically, of course, anyone can put the canary-yellow receiver to her ear, but who is more likely to be traveling without a mobile in her pocket?

There's only one person I know in upstate New York, an old school friend who lived in Buffalo the last time I checked. That was ten years ago. It's clear to me from the state of my innards that I will be lucky to make it that far, so I figure looking her up is worth a shot. I score: she's listed. Then I make a run for the women's room, do what I have to do, and climb back aboard with her number in my pocket.

Our driver, the first woman driver I have encountered in many months of riding, has presented herself as tough as nails from the get-go. It's easier to play Master and Commander if you're a hulking six-foot-two ball of masculinity on a day run, so now she's overcompensating in order to establish an authority that's already in question. All you women traveling with small children, listen up! she says into the microphone. This bus is full. You will have to hold your kids on your laps so other people have a place to sit!

A frustrated *Puertoriqueña* holding a two-year-old by the hand blocks the aisle and refuses to sit down. I paid for my son's ticket, she insists, so he gets a seat. Sit down and put him on your lap! the driver orders. No, says this incarnation of Justicia, not until my son gets a seat! Can't you see we're late? shouts the driver. I can see we're late, replies Justicia. Can't you see my son has a ticket?

Why is *she* driving? mumbles a young man behind me
who's seventeen if he's a day, the whiteness he shares with the
driver no bond at all. The driver ignores him. She's too busy
attempting to force Justicia and her son into the two re-
maining unoccupied places, which are aisle seats separated
by four rows. My son is two! He can't sit up there alone!
his mother protests. She stamps her foot for emphasis. The
purple-flowered diaper bag slides off her arm.

Unfazed, the driver keeps yelling at Justicia: Shut up! Sit
down! Evie and I can't take it. After a hurried consultation,
we agree to give up our seats so that mother and son can sit
together. I end up next to a skinny white girl who pulls her
howling eight-month-old onto her lap because, she apologizes, she doesn't have enough money to get the baby her
own ticket. It costs sixty-nine dollars to get from New York
to Denver if you pay ahead, she explains, and that's a lot right
there. She adjusts the fuzzy elastic holding back her ponytail
with a hand that tapers off into impeccably manicured nails.

Once she gets to Colorado, the girl says, her cousin will
watch the baby while she looks for work. At least she's heard
there's work. What do I think? she asks, balancing the baby
with one hand while she fiddles with the buttons on her
peach cardigan. Have I ever been out there? What are her
chances of finding a decent job?

I have no idea, I tell her, though in fact I do. I just don't
want to discourage her. In this service-oriented economy, the
growing occupations likely to be open to a young woman
with a high school diploma include home health aide, food
preparation, waitress, amusement and recreation attendant,
janitor, and hazardous materials removal worker. According
to the 2006/2007 edition of the Bureau of Labor Statistics
Occupational Outlook Handbook, with some postsecondary
training my companion could reasonably aspire to join the

swelling but notoriously low-paying ranks of preschool teachers, aerobics instructors, or customer service representatives.
Rule in gendered wage differentials and rule out the jobs like
truck driver that are tough for a single mother to hold down,
and you end up with a poverty rate for single female heads of
household well above the national average. There's a reason
Diana Pearce coined the term "feminization of poverty" back
in the 1970s.

Some things have changed since the 1970s, of course. On
average, women working year round in the United States in
2004 made seventy-six cents on the dollar made annually by
the average man. That's a real improvement from the fifty-
eight-cent figure for 1975. Or is it? These numbers look better in part because men's wages, especially white men's wages,
have declined, not because women's wages have risen to meet
men's in real terms. According to the Institute for Women's
Policy Research, "Women's apparent progress masks worsen-
ing economic conditions for all workers."[7] These numbers
are also based on comparisons between full-time workers.
Young mothers are more likely to work part time, whether
voluntarily, because they cannot afford child care, or because
they cannot find full-time work. Part-time jobs tend to pay
poorly, bringing down the numbers even further for female
breadwinners overall. Whether a woman finds herself raising
a child on her own as the result of unanticipated circumstances, choice, or divorce, single parenthood "increases the
probability of experiencing hardships."[8]

If the gender wage gap doesn't sound like much to you,
consider the calculations offered by the Economic Policy Institute on the cumulative effects of this difference over time.
Because the gap grows larger as people age, college-educated
women who worked from 1984 through 2004 accumulated a
loss of $440,743 compared to their male counterparts.[9] That's

almost half a million dollars, more than enough to give the Howling One the university education her mother could never afford.

The majority of those living poor worldwide in 2006 were children. In this, despite its wealth, the United States has followed the trend. According to a 2000 UNICEF study on children in rich nations, this country weighed in with an astronomical 22.4 percent child poverty rate. That figure ranks worst among "developed" countries and puts the world's most powerful nation-state in the same league as many "emerging" economies. But it doesn't have to be this way. On an annual basis, Belgium reduced its child poverty rate from a 17.8 percent figure (based on pretax income) to 4.4 percent through a program of transfers and taxes. Government policies that favored more equitable income redistribution made all the difference. Nor can America's problems be laid on the doorstep of shifting family composition. If all countries had 10 percent of their children living in single-parent families, Belgium would still come out ahead, with the United States near the bottom of the list, behind Turkey, Poland, and France.[10]

You might think that, growing up in the fabled Land of Opportunity, a babe in arms would at least have a chance to make her own way, regardless of the resources her family can offer. Yet the Howling One's birth had coincided with the conservative push for economic and political restructuring called neoliberalism, with its punitive cuts in antipoverty programs and hollowing out of the middle class. If middle-class families in the early twenty-first century find themselves operating "the Bank of Mom and Dad" to subsidize their grown children, what resources can the child of a financially struggling parent expect to lay her hands on while she pursues higher education or looks for a job?[11] If she ends up with younger siblings, she's liable to have spent a good portion of her childhood helping her mother raise them.[12] Down the road, that cousin out in Denver will probably have to go to work herself rather than carry on as babysitter.

For a single woman, the Howling One's mother does have certain advantages. For one, she is riding toward "free" (family-provided) child care. For another, she's white. If you start breaking out wage statistics by race as well as gender, the picture for working women changes drastically. White women might have made seventy-six cents for every dollar earned by white men in 2003, based on median annual income, but African American women earned only sixty-eight cents. According to the U.S. Census Bureau, "Hispanic" women averaged closer to fifty-six cents on the dollar, worse than white women were making back in the 1970s when analysts started focusing on the gender wage gap in the first place.

My teenage companion remains hopeful. The future holds nothing but possibilities. Isn't that what futures are for? There's something about the journey to a new home in a country with a deep history of colonization that makes it easy to mistake relocation for a brand-new life. All the evidence suggests that you're more likely to end up with your old life in a brand-new place. But why disillusion her? Hope is the only tangible asset she has.

After an hour of jiggling, cooing, and cajoling, the baby finally stops fussing when she falls asleep across both our laps. I don't have the heart to move her. Maybe it's just self-interest. I can't help thinking that if I shift, those blood-curdling yodels might start up again.

At this point the driver comes back on the intercom, reiterating her list of "don'ts" for anyone who could possibly have missed them the first time: There will be no smoking, no drinking, no foul language on my bus. As the prohibitions mount, she improbably adds, in the same censorious, deadpan tone: The bus company now asks that you turn and take a moment to introduce yourself to the person sitting next to you, because the company does not approve of people who haven't met sleeping together. This gets a rise out of the Howling One's mother. We are unlikely bed partners at that.

Our bus *is* getting hot, but not for the reasons implied by the snickers now rippling down the aisle. The heater is malfunctioning. I soon discover that elevated temperatures don't do a thing for nausea. Meanwhile, there's half a baby splayed over my thighs. I wrap my fingers around a heel, the infant's mother cradles a head, as if the two of us are sitting here waiting for Solomon to decide where this steaming little slice of humanity should go.

If it's too cold, you can cover up, complains a jaggedy-edged woman in tights, loud enough for the driver to hear. If it's too hot, though, she continues, not a damn thing you can do about it! Go on, says a man at the front, you tell her! Mm-hmm. Mm-hmm. Turn that thing down! The driver gets back on the intercom to admonish us. With regard to the heat, she explains, it needs repairs. I've got the air-conditioning on full blast. It's either this or a two-hour wait by the side of the road while somebody comes out here to fix it.

Everything about the driver's tone screams, "Get off my case!" Listen, says the jaggedy-edged woman to the driver, you was the one that asked us to tell you if it was too hot or too cold. You didn't tell us it was *smoking*! Somebody whistles. The Howling One's mother applauds. For the second time that night, I give up on sleep.

Somewhere between Syracuse and Rochester, we pull unexpectedly into a deserted rest area. Stay in the coach, the driver orders. This time everyone obeys. She hops out, rummages around behind the sheet metal that screens the motor from view, then gets us quickly back on the road. In her best microphone voice, she announces that she has "successfully disabled" the heater. But if it gets too cold in here, she continues, you tell me. I don't want to pull into Buffalo with a load of popsicles. Ooh-ee! the man in the front calls out, turning around to look at us while he runs his fingers through his salt-and-pepper hair. Leave her alone now, you hear me? That girl knows her engines!

Anybody Asks You for the Time, You Don't Have It

As our refrigerated compartment creeps toward its next scheduled stop, we get a glimpse of the landmark elegance of the Kodak Tower, a 1914 homage to what would become one of America's leading companies. Down the street the boxy modernist outlines of the Xerox Tower rise from the pavement, with a red *X* to mark the spot of another declining corporate power. Economic succession is layered into the landscape here: The Broad Street Bridge uses the old Erie Canal Aqueduct for its foundation. Ghosts of the nation's first trackless trolleys ply the streets. Rows of nineteenth-century button, box, and saw factories with red brick friezes have either gone derelict or resurrected themselves as condominiums and office space. The art deco Times Square Building, with its quirky Wings of Progress on the roof, could serve as a symbol of the straits the city finds itself in today. Commissioned during the exuberance of the 1920s, the building was completed in 1930, just as the Great Depression blanketed the country. Those four twelve-thousand-pound aluminum wings still reach skyward without a hint of irony. Welcome to Rochester, New York, a forward-looking city that has once again fallen on hard times.

Rochester, Evie explains from across the aisle, used to be the middle-class town, as opposed to Buffalo, which was supposed to be the working-class city. But now Rochester, too, is "going down," and taking the middle class with it. Well, what do you expect? she asks rhetorically. Kodak can't carry the economy all by itself. Now they've got digital cameras to contend with. A lot of people here have been losing their jobs.

Indeed. Rochester could serve as a poster child for the harsh effects of the layoffs that swept the country after downsizing gained acceptance as a tool for producing corporate profitability. In *The Disposable American,* Louis Uchitelle documents the irrationalities and the hardships created by this managerial sea change. For most of the years following World War II, layoffs were relatively rare. When a company had to shrink its workforce to grapple with changing business conditions, it tended to hire employees back in as orderly a fashion as possible. Both middle-class and working-class employees considered a job with a major corporation a good job, in the sense that the work was steady and promised a remunerated future. Beginning in the 1980s, though, these same companies began to shed workers by the thousands or even tens of thousands, without ever hiring them back. "Do more with less" had become a corporate mantra.

Many of the laid-off aircraft mechanics, bank loan officers, and assembly line workers followed by Uchitelle tried to upgrade their skills, with minimal or no government assistance. They dug into their pockets to go back to school and accepted jobs for which everyone admitted they were overqualified. Very few—including the ones with enhanced skills—ever again attained the income levels that they had enjoyed before being laid off. "In the competition for the jobs that do exist, the educated and trained have an edge," Uchitelle affirmed. "But you cannot earn an engineer's or an accountant's typical pay if companies are not hiring engineers and accountants, or are hiring relatively few and can dictate the wage, chipping away at it."[13] The temporary furlough had become a one-way ticket to the nether regions of an economy restructured on the backs of its workers.

These leaner, meaner corporate policies were understood as such by those they affected most intimately, yet Uchitelle also found that laid-off employees kept blaming themselves. They couldn't get over the thought that some mistake they had made accounted for the sudden turn their lives had taken, or that a different boss might have saved them. If only I had... If only they had... Their emotional damage was extensive enough, Uchitelle concluded, to warrant a comparison with trauma survivors. It's about what you'd expect in a land "inundated with self-help books that urge individuals to create, from within themselves, their own job security."[14]

To see these changes played out in Rochester was particularly poignant. Eastman Kodak, one of the city's major employers, had also been one of the first corporations to introduce the concept of job security. A century ago, Kodak had joined DuPont, Sears Roebuck, Procter & Gamble, and other elite companies in a drive to boost profits by curbing employee turnover. Welfare capitalism, they called it back in the day. The large corporations offered generous pensions, wage increases, health insurance provisions, and profit-sharing plans. These perks also supplied one of the less tangible staples of a middle-class life: the ability to plan. In return, the companies discouraged union activity and demanded loyalty from their employees.

Fast-forward to the twenty-first century, when the same corporations pursued market share by canning workers rather than cultivating them. These were business decisions, yes, but arguable ones. In the long run, studies had shown that a steady diet of layoffs could have negative effects on a company's bottom line. Not to mention household budgets.

This little detour through labor history helps explain why, at our 5:00 a.m. rest stop, our driver warns us not to leave the coach unless absolutely necessary. Rochester, she explains, has become one of the most dangerous stations on the route. If you do choose to get out here, she continues, let me give you some advice: Anybody asks you for the time, you don't have it. Anybody asks you for a cigarette, you don't have any. Anybody asks you for money, you don't got that, either. Anybody tries to talk to you, just keep on walking. Those of you who want to step outside, you must do so now. For your own safety, I will lock the rest of you in the coach while I complete my paperwork.

Thank you! shouts the jaggedy-edged woman on her way to use the bathroom at the back of the bus.

Sick as a Downsized Dog

At seven in the morning, Buffalo never looked so good. A light drizzle has the streets shining like obsidian. I wait for the Howling One's mother to join the other passengers in search of a coffee shop, then gingerly rise to my feet, grasping the back of the seat for support. Evie offers to carry my things. With her stooped shoulders, she shouldn't be carrying much of anything, but I have little choice but to agree. Knees quavering, stomach lurching as though we were still on the road, I make my way across the freshly cleaned terminal to another pay phone and bid goodbye to one of the more loyal companions that circumstance could have provided.

In the 198 miles since Utica, I haven't been able to come up with any better recovery strategy than to try to roust my old friend from bed. A little layover here in Buffalo and I can be on my way, I think to myself, somewhat unrealistically. Not exactly an airtight plan. I have no idea if my friend will be home. Even if she is, how well will she remember this raggedy acquaintance ringing her up from out of the blue? It really has been years. For that matter, will she remember me at all?

She does. Not wanting to put her out, I ask her to recommend a cheap hotel that's not too far from the bus station, secretly hoping she'll say, "Don't be ridiculous. Come over to my place until you feel better." She does. Invite me to stay with her, that is, with a ride from the bus terminal to boot. It's the kind of magnanimity that leaves you feeling like you owe someone your life.

When my friend pulls up at the curb with her golden retriever, Rosie, in tow, it's a wonder she can recognize me, bedraggled and ailing as I am. My hair is standing up every which way and one shoelace has come undone. But, again, she does. The next hours blur, yielding only the vaguest memories of dragging myself from bathroom to bedroom to bathroom, too queasy even to watch TV. (All that unbearable light, movement, intensity on the screen! Why didn't I ever notice it before?) For some reason, despite the evident cause of my distress, I haven't gone off poultry. The only thing I want to see in a bowl is Campbell's chicken rice soup with crackers.

This is the first time in quite some time that I've had to ask a favor when something truly terrible would have happened to me if my benefactor refused. Favors as luxuries rather than necessities: that's a hallmark of the privileged life I've been leading as a professor during the times when I've found work that utilizes my training. Favors as necessities rather than luxuries: the unforgettable lesson from years of living without money. *A su servicio:* a little something for you, your comadre, or your neighbor. Hey, it could have been me. Don't mention it. *De nada.*

Rosie the Rescue Dog stands guard at my bedside for two, three, four days that melt into five. If had been traveling to a job, I would have lost it by now. I don't want to cut my trip short, but it's looking like that's what I'll have to do. I don't have health insurance at the moment and I'm too weak to go on.

Luckily or unluckily for me, at this point in the project I'm, well, not exactly unemployed, since the research for the book employs most of my time. Let's call it "unwaged." My cash flow is nil, but I have something stashed away for emergencies that many riders don't. It's a double-edged weapon called a credit card. The same one I had to pull out when I got stuck in Salt Lake City.

Like many people who have moved in and out of resolutely middle-class jobs, I have leveraged my position by securing credit during the periods when I could qualify. No matter that if I filled out a Visa application right now, jobless, the fiduciary powers that be would turn me down flat. No matter that I have no idea how I'll pay off the $436 added to the balance when I book a last-minute plane flight back to Boston. The important thing (or so it seems at the moment) is that my card is not maxed out. If I had had to resort to paying inflated fees at check-cashing outlets for my "banking" because my credit was bad, the hardships of this trip would have compounded. One thin slice of laminated PVC makes the difference between not wanting to impose and not having to impose on the kindness of a friend.

Then again, the very idea of imposing only makes sense if you imagine we should be living separate lives. Viewed another way—say, through Rosie the Rescue Dog's eyes—a friend is someone who opens her home to the needful, no advance reservations required. If you ever want to know who your real friends are, try showing up after years and years with nothing in hand but the likelihood of puking your way across their newly tiled kitchen floor. You'll know.

Scooby-Doo, Where Are You?

This time I've really learned my lesson. Determined to try again for Milwaukee, I set out months later from Boston with an entire knapsack filled with "inside" food: the kind you take from home and carry wherever you go. Peanut butter sandwiches nestle next to apples, nuts, and other vegetarian fare that should survive a long trip without refrigeration. On this twenty-one-hour jigsaw of connecting routes to Chicago via New York, I'm not taking any chances.

From Newark to Scranton, a smooth-faced Puerto Rican kid in a do-rag paces up and down the aisle with his prepaid mobile, trying to get a better signal. "Roaming charges" never looked so literal. In the closed container called the bus, cell phone conversations bounce off the sheet metal and pass quickly into the public domain. I told you, he promises the receiver, I ain't gonna do no more of that stuff! I know. I know. It'll be different this time. I'm going straight. Maritza, she what? She gotta pee? She peed all over? That's messed up! All right. All right. I'll be there. I said I'll be there. Next stop. Don't go nowhere, now!

He throws himself into a seat next to two young African American men in quilted leather jackets who say they're riding to Binghamton. A picture of a toddler, hair neatly braided into pigtails, peers out from beneath one of the jackets on a customized T-shirt above the legend "I'm Daddy's girl." These two are deep into a friendly argument about the romantic and sexual virtues of black women (not necessarily in that order) that started while we were waiting in line back at Port Authority. The smooth-faced kid listens for a minute, shrugs, then looks away.

Outside the action never quits. An old man shuffles a path to the highway to retrieve his recycling container. There's a crowd at the Wet, White, and Blue carwash. In the parking lot of a local dog-training academy, impatient mutts vie with equally impatient owners to discover the virtues of obedience. Big-box stores share the fields with vineyards near the Pennsylvania border. Shoppers in, shoppers out, like a vast circulatory system with a cash register at its heart.

Along the back roads of upstate New York, many of the buildings look rundown yet cared for, in a scruffy sort of way. Ancient wooden barns bloom under coats of lemon-yellow paint. Improvised railings, pieced together by hand from iron pipe, guide visitors up porch steps. In Binghamton our route skirts the restored Lackawanna train station, its name spelled out in the optimism of raised brick, as though its day must last forever. We start and stop and start again, passing towns with names like Ovid that date to the neoclassical revival, rivers with names like Chenango and Genesee that watered the land before the Iroquois Confederacy.

At this time of day, the Willard Correctional Facility near Romulus, New York, is a flag stop. If no one flags down the coach or tells the driver he wants to get off, the wheels just keep rolling. Where the turnoff to the prison meets the road, there is no razor wire, no guard tower, no closed-circuit camera, just a sign claiming jurisdiction for the Department of Justice. All signs of life sequestered.

On a day with visiting hours, this route could be a prison run, packed with wives, girlfriends, homies, cousins, mothers and uncles, daughters and sons. Most of New York State's prisoners come from New York City, yet most of the prison cells are located in rural parts of the state. This out-of-sight-out-of-mind policy has imposed serious hardships on relatives and friends of the accused, who can't keep the ones they love out of *their* minds, yet now often lack the means to visit them.

It's well known that the criminal justice system in the United States disproportionately imprisons people from poorer communities, especially communities of color. Many writers, including Angela Davis, Tara Herivel, Paul Wright, and Tiny a.k.a. Lisa Gray-Garcia, have called attention to the subtle ways in which laws work to criminalize the poor. When I was a child, for example, it was perfectly legal to sleep on many coastal beaches. Today the public beaches "close" after a certain hour, rendering people subject to ticketing or arrest for surrendering to one of life's most basic needs, even if they have nowhere else to go.

So say you're hard up for cash and your best friend has just been arrested on one charge or another. It's one thing to ride the subway between jobs to visit him in prison. It's quite another to come up with long-distance bus fare plus a day off work to do the same, especially if you also have to pay for children. That's assuming the prison in question is even served by a bus.

By the time we reach the college town of Ithaca, everyone is ready for a jailbreak. Two middle-aged ladies stuff Chinese movie magazines into their handbags before they hop off. A nurse with an indifferent haircut jumps out to chain-smoke, her free arm curled around the largest teddy bear I have ever seen outside of a toy shop. Better than a pillow, she explains

with a wink. The driver, trying to get the attention of someone or other, for some reason or other, keeps yelling, Hey!
Young man! Eventually he brings his hands together with a
crack, the way you call a dog, in front of the face of a white
guy who has fallen asleep on a bench. Young man! Oh, says
the guy through a haze, me? You, says the driver, time to
board!

And we're off. Past the "Honor Our Treaties" sign near the
Big Indian Smoke Shop outside Fredonia. Past the Through-
way Holiday Motel, where we make a hurried rest stop. In
Cleveland, a new driver finishes counting heads. This bus
should be gone, she informs a passenger holding his ticket at
the foot of the stairs. He seems to have more Russian than
English. Why are you so late? she asks. When she doesn't get
an answer, she repeats herself three times until he apologizes,
though whether he is supposed to beg forgiveness for his tar-
diness or his language skills isn't clear. Let's go! someone
shouts. Finally she lets him on. The coach backs out of the
terminal, horn blaring.

Many cities in the Great Lakes region still have working
waterfronts. The United States might have embraced a service economy, but that economy includes some old-fashioned
services, too, like shipping. In this part of the country, rail
bridges and roads are engineered to let boats through. Ma-
chinery plants flank storage silos at the water's edge. The silos
are old but the slogan painted on their sides is new: "Port of
Toledo, Your Link to World Markets."

Our driver's modus operandi becomes clearer, like so
many things in life, farther down the road. Drive fast in the
passing lane, make up time, then stretch out the breaks. At
each station she announces the official time allotted for a rest
stop. We all take her seriously, of course, since to do otherwise is to risk being left behind. By virtue of the madcap driv-

ing, our "on time" becomes her "early," which means we all end up sitting in the bus, waiting.

Three Amish girls in white caps and plain dress pass the time by reading a teacher training booklet to prepare them to teach in Amish schools. "The teacher who has rules and stands by them and gives an occasional surprise or hot lunch does not have such demanding children," the booklet explains. "They are happier and more respectful than children with lots of surprises and planned fun." Perhaps the driver's been reading over their shoulders.

At the next stop, mustard and ketchup live in huge push dispensers on an open counter out in the eating area. Mayonnaise, on the other hand, has a higher value. Mayonnaise shelters in little packets with serrated edges, held close in a bowl where the cashier's fingers rest, lest anybody take too many. And how many is too many? When you're living without, when does helping yourself shade into rudeness? Into stealing? When the wrong person looks at you sideways across a class or color line?

By the time we finally make it to Chicago in the dark, we're greeted by a Korean woman who hands out leaflets to the passengers straggling off the buses. "Heaven or Hell: Which for You?" reads the first one she gives me. "This Could Be Your Last 5 Minutes Alive!" warns the other, its bold red type set against a backdrop of clock faces. True, true. But the lake-freshened air on our cheeks feels so good after God knows how many hours hugging our knees. The world is suddenly here for us, now, not five minutes later.

Though Chicago is my hometown, my relatives here have moved on. At the Raphael Hotel on Chicago's Gold Coast I've booked a room for a night at a rate that's cheaper than any of the downtown dives. But while I may have secured the room at last-minute, bargain basement rates, my lodgings come with pretensions. In the lobby doughnuts have been elevated to "pastries," $6.75 with coffee. I pass. I could definitely do better back at the depot.

When I walk over to Lake Michigan to practice *qigong*, a kind of moving meditation related to tai chi, I join a couple of other people on the edge, to whit: one man with a happy-face muscle shirt and a huge yellow hoop earring who is jogging on the beach in flip-flops, and one man who has spent the night on a bench making a list of reasons why a person should never, ever trust the cops. After showing them a move or two, I take a Harlem El train to the past. Well, my past, anyway.

California Avenue, where my great-grandparents made a home when they first arrived in the United States, remains scarred with a patchwork of vacant lots. In the poorer neighborhoods, decades of urban renewal, housing project demolition, and knock-'em-down city planning have created urban prairies where kids shoot imaginary hoops and a few families try to farm. At Kedzie four uniformed men with leashed German shepherds wait for a train going in the opposite direction. I step off in Oak Park, where I was born, to take a self-guided (i.e., free) walking tour of Prairie School houses designed by Frank Lloyd Wright.

Dinner, as usual, is on me. For old times' sake, I drop by the Cozy Corner, where my godmother used to take me sometimes when she had an errand to run up on Lake Street. She never married, so it seemed she always had pocket change. I have a taste for fajitas, which I can get down the street, but I eat here because it strikes me that after thirty-five years in operation the restaurant just might not be here if I come this way again. A woman who looks old as Methuselah occupies the picture window. Sit wherever you want, she tells me, with the regular's sense of ownership. Then she returns to her conversation with the new waitress.

I was in the service industry, too, she confesses. You know, you don't make much in that business. But I'd rather have my own money than depend on someone. The waitress nods. Me too, she says. Methuselah's sister hasn't finished yet. If you have money, you have power, she says. If you don't have money, you have no power. It's that simple. You're a pawn.

It's then that I remember my second-grade teacher announcing to the class that we must learn to stop calling the janitors janitors and start calling them custodians. The nuances of power escaped most of us, although the teacher carefully explained that "custodian" was more respectful. What the janitors—I mean, custodians—didn't realize was that they were the ones with the keys, the ones with the power to open any door and so, to our childlike eyes, the rulers. Even the teacher faced by an emergency or a stubborn lock sent one of us running for the custodian. What's more, they were the keepers of the eraser-cleaning machine, a vibrating contraption that earned our respect by its furious efforts to turn yellow chalk dust into clouds whose effects on young lungs must have been second only to asbestos. None of us had one of those at home. And so the pawns turned into kings, for those who still believed in magic.

The next morning I'm up with the seagulls—literally—to catch an early bus to Milwaukee. Behind me in the line, a young man talks on the phone about trying to get out of the game. He's just finished house arrest. He has plans to go back to school. A free man, he says. Freedom is sweet. No, he doesn't want to come back through town. No, he doesn't want to do that one more thing.

A loudspeaker suddenly proclaims that the lines for the Twin Cities and Milwaukee buses will be combined. Anybody who does not make it onto this coach will have to wait for the next scheduled Milwaukee-bound bus two hours later. After the predictable scramble sorts itself out, the free man and I get the last seats. I find myself next to a woman in her early twenties, white, good-humored, exhausted, with a ringlet through one eyebrow. She's slightly built, so you wouldn't describe her as tough, yet there's something street-wise about her.

Sonia has been riding since Delaware. Her boyfriend, who works construction, is stuck out there building houses while he waits for the long Minnesota winter to wind down. She showed up as a surprise. He didn't really believe she'd come. If only she'd had the money to take the train instead of spending days on the damn bus. Not that she's desperate or anything. She has a steady—well, pretty steady—job installing hardwood floors, plus construction when she can get it.

First time out, they had her doing gofer work. Carrying loads of gravel, sweeping up, whatever they needed. Besides her supervisor, she was the only other woman on the site. Having the supervisor there, it helped.

I ask Sonia if she's ever been to Chicago. Once, for a tat-too convention. Tattoos, she says, are a big part of her world. At the conventions, they invite all the top artists. Do I know that they have contests? First thing she did when she got to the convention, she entered her Scooby. Even though I didn't win anything, she says, I didn't mind. Scooby? I ask. Next thing I know, this child is pulling down her shirt to show me: a rainbow-colored cartoon of Scooby-Doo adorns her right breast, while Shaggy, another member of Scooby's gang, graces the other. I admire without staring. It's a fine line to walk.

Sonia says she's not sure if things with her boyfriend will last, because he's older than her, he's got kids, and he doesn't like to talk when things bother him. For example? For ex-ample, he didn't tell her when his ex moved and took his kids, even though it was weighing on his mind. Do I have kids? she asks. Nope. A boyfriend? No, a girlfriend, actually. Sonia wants to know how long. I tell her I've been with my partner for thirteen years. In the long pause that follows, I hope she's not going to freak out. With the limited understanding most people have of gay relationships, I wouldn't be surprised if she thought better of her impulse to take Scooby out for a walk. Okay, she says finally, that works. Yeah, I reply, it does.

About the time Sonia found Scooby-Doo, she lost her brother. Their mother, you see, has a "thing" with drugs. She can act pretty erratic, Sonia says. One year, when her mother decided to take off with a new boyfriend, Sonia offered to take her brother in. That way he could finish school. Sonia even went so far as to begin the paperwork necessary to get official custody so that she would have the legal authority to make decisions that affected him. Although Sonia had their mother's approval, when her brother's school sent home forms that a parent had to sign, she had to forge the signature. What if he had ended up in the hospital? Half the time they didn't even know where their mother was.

The arrangement worked for a while, but eventually her brother started missing his mother. When they found out she was living in a small town in Arizona, Sonia saved up for bus fare so that her brother could go to live with her. After all, she said, it's his mom. It wasn't my place to stand between them. I mean, I could have, but I couldn't.

Sonia didn't call Arizona a lot after her brother left, because calling was expensive. Then one day her mother's boyfriend picked up the phone. I have no idea where they are, he said. I woke up and they were gone. Sonia tells me that she shouldn't have been surprised: Our mother does these things.

For the last three years, she has been trying to track down

her brother using directory assistance. Every weekend she gets out her map of Arizona and dials up more cities and towns to request information on someone with her brother's last name. But it's not working. So Sonia and I spend the time from Waukegan to Kenosha generating some new possibilities. What about his school records? Maybe Minneapolis has phone books at the public library and computers where she can search the Internet for free. Yeah, I heard something about that, she says. I should check it out.

Someday, Sonia knows, they will all find each other. She can feel it. Then everything will be perfect. Or maybe that's just a fantasy. The only way to make it perfect, she explains, is to accept her mother and her brother the way they are.

When we say our goodbyes on the platform in Milwaukee, things have a way of circling back to food. There's no lunch break because the bus has pulled in late. Sonia confesses that she's run out of things to eat. But don't worry, I'll be okay, she insists, the tough girl after all. Before I leave, I bequeath to her my last bag of spicy cashew nuts. In exchange, she has gifted me with stories. When I ask her permission to include them in this book, she says sure, maybe my brother will read it. There's something wistful in the smile the tough girl flashes then.

III.

Going Coastal:

Five Hundred Years of the Poverty Draft, New York to St. Augustine

Port Question Authority

Now he's lost. On every side a bewildering array of folding gates hedges him in, rolled out for the night on little wheels. He peers through the diamonds that the steel bars create, hoping for what? Something to differentiate among the rows of greyhound-studded buses? A compatriot from whatever country he started in? A sign? What he gets instead is a gym-enhanced security guard shouting for him to get back. Don't touch those goddamn bars!

Oh, he knows where he is, all right. Everyone knows Port Authority, the biggest bus terminal New York City has to offer. There's a more insidious reason why Rafael has wandered the cavernous building for an hour with a blue nylon jacket clinging to his back and work-chapped hands stuffed into his pockets. He can't find his way because he travels in a land where few make the effort to cross over into another language so long as English is the first tongue they speak. If this had been New Delhi, say, or Mumbai, where hundreds of languages converge, where people consider trial and error part of communication, Rafael would already be at his gate. Instead, he's facing arrest in the surveillance society that North America has become.

Why don't you help him find his bus instead of hassling him? I ask the guard, who shrugs me off and reaches for his walkie-talkie. Look, I persist, the man's got a ticket. (Show him your ticket. Ticket, umm, *papel,* no, that's not it. *Boleto, sí, boleto! Dónde está su boleto, como*—I reach into my pocket for my own ticket—*como* this?) See, I continue, he has a ticket. He's not causing any trouble. He has as much right to be here as you.

This man disobeyed my direct order, says the guard. He had his chance. I told him twice! This man doesn't *understand* your order, I tell the guard as he shifts from foot to foot. What I really want to say is: Who died and made you king? What I really want to say is: When did touching a barricade become a chargeable offense? But the satisfaction isn't worth sending a man to jail. Okay, I counter, how about this: I take this guy off your hands and escort him right to his gate. Less work for you.

And that is how I come to know Rafael as Rafael. We walk over to the ticket counter together, putting as much distance between ourselves and the guard as possible. I am shaking. In the neighborhoods where I came of age, contrary to what they teach schoolchildren, the policeman might be your uncle but he is not necessarily your friend.

You look sleepy, I say to the woman behind the desk, angling for a more human response. She smiles, though she does not look like the smiling kind. Don't think I didn't see what happened, she says, tugging on one earring. It's a shame how they treat people. Tell him he can ask me a question.

I follow her gaze to the far end of the counter, where Rafael in his battered Yankees cap now stares intently at the departures listed on the monitor. Would you believe, the woman says, that before you came, he spent twenty minutes looking at the screen? Tell him he can ask me a question.

I try. *No comprende,* says Rafael. I try again: *¿A dónde?* Spring Valley, he says. *Trabajo.* With this revelation, the woman behind the counter explains that he wants a different bus company altogether, not Greyhound but something called Red & Tan. She writes the name on an envelope for

Rafael, who looks like he might not be able to read but seems happy to have something to show people. I tell him in seriously broken Spanish that he must search for another bus company, but to get there he has to go outside. The interior pathway will remain blocked until the guards roll the anti-homeless folding metal scissors gates away at 6 a.m. "Anti-homeless folding metal scissors gates" exceeds any Spanish I will ever know, but he seems to get the idea from *"ahora es cerrado"* (now it's closed). The barricades themselves do most of the talking.

In the end I can't escort him, because I have to get in line for my own bus. So I gesture in the same direction as the woman at the counter, hoping that will be sufficient to get him where he needs to go, because I am out of words. It looks to be enough.

Language is not the prison house that keeps us from one another. The bars arrive with suspicions that border on the farcical but pass for common sense. Why is that shabbily dressed fellow loitering inexplicably in front of the monitor? Why would he refuse to obey security staff unless he's up to no good? Yet people have to be inculcated with fear to have such worrisome questions occur "naturally," in place of the much more mundane (and also more likely) suppositions that the man is bored, preoccupied, needs help, or operates in another idiom entirely. What are bus stations, if not places where people wait?

In the post-9/11 debate framed as security versus freedom, discussion tends to skirt the sorts of questions that have intimate bearing on the lives of the poor: Whose lives do particular measures make more secure? If you go through a nasty divorce and end up without a roof over your head, are you better off because you can't get into Port Authority to use the bathroom? Does one type of security require giving up another? How much power and money do you have to have to qualify for "protection"?

Aren't you afraid? a friend asked me before I left. She meant to ride the bus. It's a question I often get, though the nightmare scenarios conjured by middle-class and working-class friends tend to differ. Wealthier folk draw upon nineteenth-century associations of violence with poor people themselves. The dangerous classes, as it were. Poorer people worry about repetitions of violence that they themselves have seen or experienced, a violence more often directed at the less powerful. Living poor is not a romance, but neither is it a crime. Sometimes I *am* afraid, but mainly if there's a need. Not generically. A corporation that eats your pension fund can shorten your life as easily as some aspiring hood.

The business of closing big-city stations at midnight to all but ticketed passengers is a relatively new practice, advertised as an anticrime and antiterror measure but rooted in an earlier push to keep out people who live on the street. When authorities decided to "clean up" Times Square, for instance, major hotels relocated their lobbies to upper floors so that nonpaying visitors would have to run a gauntlet of staff. Like most security measures that depend on lock, guard, and key, both the lobby relocation and the overnight partition of bus terminals have the ironic effect of penning in the paying clients. One of the most practical and effective measures of personal security, having friends and relatives meet you or see you off at the gate, has become impossible at America's transportation hubs.

In the case of the scissors-gate fences, farce is certainly on display. Any enterprising body who lives on the streets can get through the perimeter by ducking into the station a few minutes before the cordon takes effect. When I stop by the toilets, I meet a woman with nappy red hair putting towel and soap back into a shopping cart that is filled to the brim with sleeping bag, aluminum cans collected for cash redemption, and whatever else she needs to get through the week. In hushed tones she confesses, I like to use Dove when I can get it. Feel! she says, pulling my hand up to her cheek. It leaves your skin so soft.

Suppose she had not figured out a way to use the place to freshen up? Besides forgoing the pleasures of smooth skin, she would have laid herself open to the circuitous logic of what used to be called blaming the victim, but what actually amounts to blaming the excluded. Decline to erect public facilities, bar people from availing themselves of quasi-private locations such as bus depots, then condemn "the poor" for traveling the world in an unsanitary condition. What's that they say? Point a finger, and there are three fingers pointing back at you.

Not all lines of exclusion are so obvious. Some are embedded in the way facilities are set up. On the other side of the cordon, my last task before joining my queue should be a simple one: I need to phone home. An electronic security measure, you might call it. Knowing how difficult it can be to trace people who get lost in the bus system, I've promised my partner that I'll call when I reach New York. But the pay phones near my gate don't register as touch-tone, so I can't use the cheap prepaid calling card I've purchased with the rest of my change. The effect is to force passengers into the much more expensive route of calling collect or doing without. Just like the phones in prison.

I have to pass by the guard who almost arrested Rafael on my way to catch the bus for Washington, D.C., but luckily he's distracted. Maybe it's Vivaldi's *Four Seasons* playing over the loudspeakers, over and over again. (They will add up to at least eleven seasons by the time the bus to D.C. actually pulls out.) More likely it's the sound of two grown men arguing in the underground waiting room to the strains of a particularly delicate violin passage. "Fuck you." "Fuck you back." "Fuck you." "Fuck you back." "Fuck you." "Fuck you first." "Fuck your mama." Oooh. The insulted man moves away with his coffee cup, and it's a good thing he does, because his antagonist is about to swing. Then the instigator sees the security guard and thinks better of it. Seasoned travelers look up only long enough to see whether the two men are in earnest, whether they might need to dodge or duck. No one seems to know what it's all about, or care, particularly. The night is young.

The Amazing Debt-Defying Disappearing Bus

Already the line for the D.C. bus winds twice around the little passageway allotted to our gate, with some places marked by left luggage. The time was short for getting in line but not for leaving. I try to sleep, sitting on the cold concrete floor with my head balanced on my pack, which topples over every time I begin to drift off. It may be one in the morning and I may be dead tired, but the geometry just doesn't work.

At a bend in the line, a woman from the islands looks up from her Bible. Too many soldiers, she says, watching a boy who could be her grandson adjust his gear. Life is not meant for this.

With the mobilization of troops to fight in Afghanistan and Iraq, young people in uniform have become an everyday presence. More so as you travel further south into poorer communities where the military offers the only steady employment.

In my country, observes a man from another part of the Caribbean, people rather party than fight. We got sugar cane rum. My country, too, the lady with the Bible says. Is it 150 proof? he wants to know. How much is that? she asks. I don't know exactly, he says. Whiskey is about 80. In my country, she says, people party eight days a week. Someone's going: Let's have a party. Someone's coming: Let's have a party. Breakfast? Here, have a drink.

The two start comparing notes in earnest. In my country, he claims, women can do more than they used to. It's not like before. They're educated now. They stay in the school. They can work. In my country, she says, even if women don't have education, if they have to feed their children, they will find a way. They will work. Because, she says, catching my eye, we are stronger. The man, if things are not right, he just feel sorry for himself. He sit there and drink.

When two African American girls run up, dragging gym bags and completely out of breath, the Bible lady's interlocutor looks grateful. I can't believe we missed it! one exclaims, bemoaning their bad luck. Missed what? The D.C. bus scheduled to depart at 1:30 a.m. You didn't miss anything, the woman at the head of the line insists. I've been here since 11:00 p.m. If you missed the 10:00 bus to D.C., you have to wait until 3:45 in the morning.

But she told us we just missed the bus, they protest. Who told you? inquires the middle-aged Puerto Rican man who is second in line. The woman at the window! She said it just left! She's lying, he says. I ride this bus every ten days. Very seldom does that 1:30 bus go. They list it to get people in, get the money, get you in line. If there's enough people, they send a bus, but it almost never goes.

My heart sinks. I had been hoping that the 1:30 was simply late. I should have known better, because the phenomenon of the phantom bus is one with which I've become well acquainted.

Many's the time I've stood in line for hours, only to see my departure time come and go without an engine ever firing. In Boston's renovated station, where electronic boards above the gates lent departures an air of substance, the red letters that spelled "NEW YORK CITY 11:30 a.m." would flicker out to be replaced by "NEW YORK CITY 12:01 p.m.," with no signs of life from the darkened interior of the bus parked at the dock. Once things finally did start to move, a driver might appear to announce, "Passengers for Framingham, step aside. This bus will be making no stops. Your coach will leave from Gate 5 in ten minutes." Ten minutes could mean anything.

At Port Authority I have no way to evaluate the analysis offered by the cynic at the head of the line—he admits he's just speculating—but regardless of intent, the practice of creating phantom buses does save the company money. Certainly there's a need. Laidlaw Inc., Greyhound's parent corporation, best known for its fleets of yellow school buses, filed for bankruptcy in 2001. Like many companies caught up in the wave of mergers and acquisitions during the 1990s, this one had acquired mountains of debt along with its subsidiaries. In the second quarter of 2000, Laidlaw reported a loss of $1.46 billion after writing off a bad investment in an ambulance service and losing money when the company expanded into hazardous waste management. On top of these deficits, the corporation agreed to a $55.4 million settlement in a lawsuit over priority payment of debt after it failed to pay interest on nearly $2 billion in bonds. Although Greyhound was not named in the bankruptcy papers, Laidlaw had cut off its credit funding two years earlier, forcing the largest intercity bus company in the United States to seek alternative financing. By 2007 ownership of Greyhound, along with its debt, had passed to FirstGroup, Britain's largest bus company.

With the rise of loose credit early in the new century, bankruptcy became a strategy with which government, corporations, and individuals all had to engage. Workers in legacy sectors (a corporate euphemism for heavily unionized industries) found themselves playing a cat-and-mouse game in which employers used bankruptcy to undercut union power. Local governments reduced services to lift their bond ratings and keep insolvency at bay. Passage of a bankruptcy reform bill would soon make clearing personal debts more difficult, even as corporate bankruptcy moved closer to standard practice. War debts, well, almost nobody talked about them in terms of payments owing.

On the way into New York, our bus almost scraped its roof negotiating an underpass in Central Park, where workers were busy patching a bit of what reporters call "America's crumbling infrastructure." Wire mesh provided a cheap fix to keep the old bricks from falling onto the windshields of cars below. As we headed south from Harlem, we passed botanicas, skyscrapers, lawyers' offices, schools, bodegas. Cleaners drifted home from their night jobs. Bakers reported early to work. Now *this,* my seatmate proclaimed, is a city. Where you live—Boston—is just a village. With neon rising and bricks falling all around me, it was hard to deny.

Todos Que Hermanos

By the time we leave Port Authority, the city that never sleeps is beginning to nod off. It's January 18, 2003. By the time we wake up in Washington, people from all parts of the country will have gathered to protest the impending bombing of Iraq. Not all the passengers are going to the antiwar rally, of course, only a few. But they will join a distinguished history of riders who have traveled on overnight buses to march on the nation's capital.

At the D.C. bus station, a young black woman calls across

the room to a man who looks like her younger brother. Get me a doughnut! Glazed. If it's some two-dollar doughnut, you just leave that shit lay there. Her brother returns empty-handed.

I have an hour to kill and it's too cold to wait outside, so I try to buy grapefruit juice from the only vendor who isn't standing behind a counter. A single bottle retails for twice what it costs in the store. Less expensive than medicine if I end up getting sick after two nights on the bus, I think to myself. I offer the vendor exact change, but she refuses my money. Crumpling the dollar bills into a ball, she throws them back at me. It's dirty, she says. My customers won't take that dirty money. So I head down the street to Union Station, where grapefruit juice can be had for $1.65 and everybody's dollars, apparently, are green.

The price difference between the bus and train stations is interesting, because people who commute to work by rail tend to command more money than bus travelers. Although the bus depot lies only a few blocks away, it operates as a micro-neighborhood where poorer people pay higher prices.

As I pass out into the street, a cab driver falls in with my stride. Are you here for the peace march? he asks. He had hoped to solicit a fare, but I tell him I plan to walk to save money. He wants to talk. No charge for that. I have an eighteen-year-old daughter, he explains, as we shiver in the midwinter air. Have you heard? Now they're talking about drafting everybody.

He's referring to a bill introduced into Congress by Representative Charles Rangel from New York's Fifteenth District, which includes parts of the Upper West Side and Harlem. Rangel, a senior Democrat, veteran, and founding member of the Congressional Black Caucus, promoted the bill as an antidote to the poverty draft. Both women and men between certain ages could be called upon to serve. The reasoning went like this: What better way to encourage peace than by making privileged Americans confront the costs of war? The effect would be to extend military ranks beyond the many "volunteer" troops from poor families who enlist because they can't find another way to make a living.[1]

Once that draft happens, the cab driver continues, they just snatch you up. They just snatch you up, doesn't matter who you are. Just like Vietnam. I served in Vietnam. That's why I'm worried for my daughter. These people in there now [in the Bush Administration], they never served. They've got the wrong idea.

Twenty minutes later, we're still talking. Julius formally introduces himself and asks me where I'm from. Chicago is my hometown, I explain, but now I live in Boston. Is it expensive there? he wants to know. About fourteen hundred dollars per month for a studio apartment, I tell him, maybe a one bedroom if you're lucky. So you know, he says. You know how it is. It's bad enough keeping a roof over your head, putting food on the table. We got enough trouble fighting the war in the streets without starting some war over there.

Julius promises to look for me when he drops by the rally later—a sweet idea, given that the event is expected to draw hundreds of thousands—and points me in the direction of the Mall.

So many peace marchers have congregated around the city's transportation hubs that security guards force their way through the crowds shouting, Pipe down! Pipe down, please! It's hopeless. I merge into the slipstream behind the Union de Trabajadores and a percussion troupe sponsored by a coalition of Filipino American and Korean American organizations. Somehow the drummers manage to keep their banner unfurled while laying down a beat and crossing traffic. Coming up on our right are the Raging Grannies, who infuse old standards with newly politicized lyrics in three-part harmony. "United Nations, we don't need it, international law, we don't heed it," they croon, a satire set to the tune of "Yes Sir, That's My Baby."

Placards are everywhere. They range from soon-to-become-clichéd slogans, such as "No Blood for Oil," to the heartfelt ("Iraqis Are People, Too"), idiosyncratic ("Just Stop It!"), and wise ("The Road to Peace Is Peace"). Some voice populist sentiments ("Good Fat Cat" scrawled under the picture of a calico). One features a picture of the president over the caption "Psychotherapy for a Peaceful Resolution." There are signs that seem more hopeful than historically accurate, like the one that reads "Starting War Is Not American." Martin Luther King, whose holiday arrives tomorrow, gets the last word on many of the posters. Among the more popular quotes attributed today to Dr. King: "War Is the Enemy of the Poor."

There are so many people milling about the rolling lawn that it could be mistaken at a cursory glance for Central Park on a Sunday morning. Caramel corn and bumper stickers are both on offer from hawkers working the crowd. I wander over toward the other side of the Mall, where the group Veterans Against the Iraq War has formed a circle. Don't be led to war by those who've never been there, a man intones into the portable microphone. Chickenhawks want war; we don't. His colleagues break out into an outrageous buck-bucking and cluck-clucking. Some are Gulf War veterans who say they believed in that conflict but not this one. Others hold signs with pictures of men who run the government but never served a day in the military.

Near the street, a jovial white guy hands out oversized currency with a cartoon of the president on the front. Why should the rich get all the money? he shouts. Let's print our own! Let's get the economy going again! It's worth as much as Enron stock, he adds, referring to the collapse of the energy trading corporation. Face it, your human worth is measured in how much you have. Isn't it time to increase your wealth? Get your Deception Dollars! Deception Dollars here!

Through it all, a man in a black ski mask stands listening silently, intently, to the speakers, who talk about how the government spends money on bombs while cutting subsidies for housing. The stage is so far away it shimmers. A homemade sign pinned to the man's chest proclaims, "U.S. Marine Corps Infantry Officer Against the Bush Oil War." He's taking quite a risk to be here. Although members of the armed forces on active duty may attend political meetings and rallies as spectators, taking a partisan stand is another matter. Department of Defense Directive 1344.10 specifically bans the use of "contemptuous words against the President." Words are notoriously open to interpretation and never more so than in the matter of war.

Despite the bright sun and my thermal socks, I've spent the last three hours freezing in increments from the ground up. As the rally winds down, I duck into the National Gallery of Art, hoping to rediscover what circulation feels like in my legs. Unlike the national parks, at the time of my visit in 2003 the national museums had managed to evade the worst excesses of "cost recovery" and privatization. Handbags and backpacks must be surrendered for inspection, but admission is still free. I float through the galleries in a sea of protesters. Sculptures by Degas and Rodin draw the usual crowds. A peace marcher in a watch cap explains trompe l'oeil rather unsuccessfully to a five-year-old who has clearly had a long day.

If I had a slogan to write on a placard at this point, it would be "My Imaginary Kingdom for a Shower." I've traveled eleven hours, spent another six hours at the rally, and still have 578 miles to go to reach Savannah, Georgia. There I'll stop to find myself a proper bed before continuing on to Florida. Luckily I've planned ahead. Before leaving, at my mother's suggestion, I logged onto the Internet at the public library to find a hotel near the Mall that allows anyone to use its gym facilities for a fee.

When I arrive at the hotel, however, no one has heard of this policy. They're not set up to deal with cash. After I tell my story to the attendant, who probably makes minimum wage, she lets me in for free. I have to promise not to tell anybody. In the uninhabited gym I pick a spot to practice *qigong*. The room dissolves into Eight Pieces of Brocade. Then I give myself over to indoor plumbing's answer to rain.

Back at the bus terminal, a discarded rally poster leans against the wall. It reads, *"Todos Que Hermanos."* Not *Todos Somos Hermanos,* we are all brothers, but *Todos Que Hermanos,* everyone united *like* brothers. To conjure one another as sisters, as brothers, there is a little work involved.

Some of the experiences on the road can lead a person to ask, What kind of *hermanos* are we? Imagine: The last seat on a crowded route—your seat—is soaked through because somebody didn't think about the next rider when she changed a diaper. You watch a station agent in a small town treat customers with such rudeness that four impeccably raised Mississippi teenagers step outside to call him "Peckerwood." Then one day your bus pulls out of D.C. with a little boy named Tony falling asleep against your shoulder. This is not the stuff of romance: The child is as mischievous as they come, repeatedly summoned by his full name, Antonio, when his grandmother gets serious about discipline. But she has trusted him to your care, *hermana*. And in that gesture lies a path.

Little Box of Terrors

Did you see that? He threw it! she exclaims, surveying her luggage in dismay. She's looking out the window and probably wishing she hadn't. Be nice with the bags! shouts her traveling companion to the handlers loading the bus. These two are perfectly put together, dressed to the nines like it's Sunday morning. That bag is on wheels, says the first lady, and he just threw the damn thing up there! He could have rolled it. I tell you, people don't want to work. She directs her last comment to the driver, who has just stepped onto the coach.

I don't got nothing to do with baggage, the driver protests. Those gentlemen are real independent and they got their own union. Be that as it may, the church ladies in the front still expect him to intercede. Look, he says, they don't want me cussing them out. If anything's broke, you can . . . If I get that bag and something's broke, interrupts the woman in the feather-trimmed hat, I'll get a good lawyer. He will sue them until they see dollar signs. And I'm your witness, says the other. Now both ladies are giving the driver the eye. Let me go so we can get out of here, he laughs, before we all go to jail!

The atmosphere on this bus out of D.C. filled with Latinas and middle-aged African American women couldn't be more different from the one on the bus I rode last evening through Hartford. On the earlier run, a crew of underaged white guys sprawled across the seats, blocking the aisles with their ripe stocking feet and shattering the stillness with music blasted through headsets. On our Savannah-bound bus, entertainment arrives the old-fashioned way: with banter.

After the driver hands in the last of his paperwork, he springs into his seat with a younger man's energy. Don't make things hard for me now, he requests, using his silkiest voice as he puts the coach into reverse. You don't need me to tell you we've been waiting up on this bus two and a half hours. Remember, I'm the one got you out of here. Aren't you glad?

I was glad until I saw them throw that bag, the church lady with the battered suitcase persists. Her traveling companion sees the humor in the situation. Take your time, honey, she says to the driver. God's the one who's going to help us get out of here, before we do anything un-Christianlike that we'll regret!

When the driver finally picks up the mike to say good evening, his greeting resembles the usual prologue to a dry list of rules and regulations, so at first he gets no response. Good *evening,* he repeats until he finds his chorus. Good evening! we shout in unison. With a rare personal touch, he tells us his name is Sterling. Are you married, Sterling? calls out one of the church ladies. This one merits a pause. The pressure builds as everyone starts clapping. Come on, Sterling, tell us: Are you married? No, Sterling finally confesses into the mike, I'm not married. Well, honey, says the proper woman in the feathered hat, tonight you could get three for the price of one!

Things go smoothly, flirtatiously, until I have to change buses in Richmond, Virginia, where I take my leave of Sterling and his ladies. Federal regulations, intones the captain of my new ship, say do not cross the yellow line. No matter what. If you must speak to me, do so at the next station stop. Little does this curmudgeon know that he'll be begging us to speak long before the bus gets to Florida.

The line to which he refers is painted on the floor at the head of the aisle. This simple stripe, which adorns every bus, began not as an "anti-terror" measure but as a sensible precaution to prevent riders from needlessly distracting the operator while the coach was moving through traffic. Like federal regulations on smoking, the yellow line is taken quite seriously. I have only seen it violated once, when an overflow of passengers who had waited in 116-degree heat for passage to a station stop on the other side of a river threatened to block the bus unless the driver took everyone across.

After 9/11 Greyhound introduced a rule of its own to prohibit passengers from sitting in the front row of seats unless they were disabled. It would be nice to think that this initiative had people with disabilities in mind, but that seemed unlikely. In a 1998 test of the company's compliance with the Americans with Disabilities Act (ADA), 25 percent of the testers reported being dropped or hurt as they boarded the bus. Despite pressure from advocacy groups, the company for years refused to install lifts on its vehicles. "People like you should not ride the bus," testers were told. No matter that people with disabilities, on average, constitute one of the poorest segments of the American population, which means they suffer disproportionately from lack of access to public transportation.

As late as 2005, when members of the activist group ADAPT attempted to ride the bus to demonstrate the seriousness of the problem, Greyhound refused to seat 32 percent of the test riders, even after selling most of them tickets. New coaches conform to ADA requirements, one driver told me, and most drivers can recite the ADA by heart. But then they don't bother to make the bus "kneel" for riders with canes.

The primary purpose of the empty seats in the front of the bus—and they generally remained empty—seemed to be to put distance between driver and passengers. Shortly after the destruction of the World Trade Center in 2001, Greyhound had to contend with a disturbing incident in which a rider knifed one of its operators. Six people died on Interstate 24 in Tennessee when Damir Igric, a Croatian war veteran, slashed a driver's throat while the coach was in motion. The driver, Garfield Sands, fought for control of the bus, but Igric overpowered him and flipped the coach into a ditch. Somehow Sands managed to crawl out a window to seek help.

In an unprecedented move Greyhound temporarily grounded its fleet, although an investigation by the Federal Bureau of Investigation later concluded that the incident was not "terrorist related." Two more attempts to commandeer a coach took place before the end of the year. The company issued emergency mobile phones to its drivers and started using handheld metal detectors at depots in larger cities. Violence on the bus became a headliner in the edgy political climate of the times. Ironically, buses remained the safest method of highway travel in the United States, according to the Centers for Disease Control and Prevention.

Two years later, our Florida-bound bus is retrofitted with a clear plastic gate that cordons off the driver. What that thin piece of plastic would do to deter a motivated attacker is beyond me, other than buying the driver an extra second or two to respond. Like many innovations associated with the "war on terror," this one seems less serviceable than symbolic.

If you're not making it economically, you get accustomed to having authorities herd you to one side or the other of a line, although you may never reconcile yourself to the crudity of such measures. Lines and counters are ubiquitous in the wait for health care, food stamps, soup kitchens, and cheap transportation. As far as the government is concerned, of course, the most prominent marker of your condition is the poverty line. The poverty line or poverty threshold is a concept developed in the early 1960s by Mollie Orshansky, an economist employed by the Social Security Administration. Although Orshansky emphasized that no one can put an absolute monetary figure on the struggle to get by, the use of a threshold to identify the needy gained popularity during the Johnson administration's War on Poverty.

Many economists now consider the poverty line outdated. As calculated in the United States, for example, it assumes that a household allocates a third of its budget to food. That assumption made more sense before the decline in food prices with the industrialization of agriculture and the real estate inflation that catapulted housing to the top of household expenditures. Nor does the poverty line provide much insight into the travails of relative poverty, which has more to do with how your standard of living compares to others' than how you have fared by any fixed measurement.

"Were poverty defined more reasonably—like, say, half the median income, a common metric among academic researchers—U.S. poverty rates would be half again to twice as high as they are," argues Doug Henwood, the author of *After the New Economy*.[2] Yet as we head south, it strikes me that the notion of poverty as a strict cutoff does lend itself to creative analogy. Unless you get behind the yellow line, your bus doesn't move. Unless scores of people step behind the poverty line, the economy doesn't move, either, at least not with its current dependency on low-wage, impoverishing jobs.

Our new driver, dubbed Hardline by my fellow passengers, takes the exclusionary process engendered by every line in earnest. Many of the passengers on our run have their tickets routed incorrectly, or at least inconveniently. This coach stops in Jacksonville, precisely where they want to go, but the computer has routed them via Fayetteville, North Carolina, which would require a layover and another change of buses. They insist that the ticket agent told them to ignore the computer-generated itinerary and remain on this bus. The driver insists that they have to follow what's printed on the paper. Heated negotiations ensue that eat up most of the hour gained by the previous driver.

Hardline is no humor, all rules. After I watch him for a while, I start to feel bad for him. He struggles a bit with the controls. Okay, more than a bit. The man goes forward when he means to back up. He switches on the overhead lights by mistake when he's searching for the map light to illuminate his schedule. Still, it feels rich when we start prowling the back streets of the next city on our route. After a few minutes going up and down, up and down, he reaches for the microphone. Anybody here know where the station is in Raleigh? he asks. Maybe it's his first day. Oh, the cynic behind me remarks, *now* the man wants us to speak! From the back someone shouts, We just passed it! We passed it? the driver says incredulously. Yeah, on the left! Hardline does a beautiful job of turning the coach around in the dark.

Dr. King on the Waterfront

By "early check-in," I don't suppose the budget motel I've booked has 5:00 a.m. in mind, so I hang out until 7:00 a.m. in the Savannah bus station. It's clean, comfortable, and desolate at this hour. Coming into a new town in the dark you have only a notional idea of where you are and no idea of how things play locally, so it's best to wait until dawn to set out walking in any case. After several false starts I find the motel, where a kind woman at the desk gets me into a room and offers me an extra, illicit continental breakfast. But you might just want to get some sleep, she says, taking in my state.

A few hours tucked into my dreams and I'm ready to explore. During the nineteenth century, Savannah served as a mercantile hub for the cotton industry. According to a commemorative plaque that no one stops to read, the city once laid claim to hosting the second-largest port in the world for cotton shipping. (I wonder to myself where the first would have been . . . Egypt? India?) In years since, the local economy has embraced a different sort of finance: tourist dollars. The hulking red grandeur of the Cotton Exchange, better known at the time as King Cotton's Palace, is now a historical landmark. A festival calendar published by the merchants' association ranges from the de rigueur—Fourth of July fireworks—to an annual Boat Parade of Lights. River Street, which fronts the water, has become a pilgrimage site for art galleries, boutiques, and upscale seafood restaurants. A cotton warehouse built in 1790 has reincarnated itself as a tavern.

Somehow, in the midst of all the hoopla, Savannah's waterway has managed to preserve its character as a working river. Tugboats guide barges to docks where they can offload against a backdrop of street artists, jugglers, and strolling couples. Even the city's sidewalks come from the sea. Specks of oyster shell give the concrete luster, set off by the sandy earth and hanging moss.

Upriver near Augusta, at the Savannah River nuclear materials processing center, things must look less evocative of the Old South. The Savannah River National Laboratory, which advertises its "safe, secure, and cost-effective management of the nation's nuclear weapons stockpile," has its hands full cleaning up the site. Over at the Savannah River Ecology

Laboratory, a watchdog organization run by the University of Georgia, environmental impact monitoring of nuclear facilities is the order of the day. Both answer to the Department of Energy.

Savannah's historic district, for all its proximity to the bus station, remains racially divided. People share space, all right: folks of color, mostly African American, staff the service jobs; white people, with a few exceptions, patronize the shops. The civil rights movement put paid to overt, Jim Crow–style segregation, of course. Now real estate prices and the ties that make for comfort appear to do the sorting, along with the occasional hard stare.

A few short blocks from the waterfront lies the Owens-Thomas House. With its English Regency architecture and sumptuously furnished interior, it boasts all the qualities expected of a residence turned museum. From the copper fountain in the manicured garden to the filigreed brass banister, the place radiates ease and stature. In the main house, a carpet runner echoes the Greek key pattern that graces the dining room window. Transoms give the benefits of air cooling with none of the electrical expense. A water-harvesting system, installed when the house was built in 1819, would put many contemporary "green" houses to shame.

If you take the Owens-Thomas house tour, you might be greeted, as I was, by an extremely knowledgeable white guide who unconsciously frames every detail from the point of view of the white families who lived there. Imagine, she says, you lose your fortune in the depression of 1820, like the Richardsons who built this fine house. Imagine, she goes on, how it would feel to watch your dream home converted into lodgings for travelers. Imagine that you are Margaret Thomas, an Owens by birth, who has to decide whether to bequeath the property to the Telfair Academy of Arts and Sciences. Such financial struggles and dilemmas of estate planning are judged worthy of narration. But the Richardsons, Owenses, and Thomases are not the only ones who frequented these hallways.

Across the garden in the carriage house where the tour starts, you'll find what the brochure describes as the "earliest intact urban slave quarters in the South." On the tour these "urban slaves" go unnamed, but not because their names have gone unrecorded. Displays on the walls of the quarters confirm that historians have used tax records to uncover information about individual slaves who worked in the house. Exhibits on African American history frequently open here. What today's tour conveys about the lives of the people who lived here under duress, however, reduces them to labor and superstition. The "haint blue" color was painted on the ceiling in an effort to ward off ghosts, our guide explains, nodding sagely. When we get to the dimly lit basement, she has a quick word for the dangers of working in a laundry with lye and heavy irons all 'round.[3]

Even the name of the white family that commissioned the house, Richardson, gets short shrift. After all, they are the ones whose financial reversals allowed the Bank of the United States to repossess the property. A lesson, perhaps, for our even more highly leveraged times.

On my way back to the motel I go window-shopping, trying to stay awake long enough to get back on a daytime schedule. In an antique mall by the river that has the cozy air of a thrift store, I come across a stereoscope card dated 1900. The caption reads, "Sheikh el Rachid and his Escorts, most famous Bedouins of Palestine." Next to Sheikh el Rachid in the foreground of the photograph stands a European woman, perhaps the affluent adventurer Gertrude Bell, who visited Jerusalem about that time. Behind the cash register an otherwise bored employee scrutinizes the print before handing it back to me. Sheek, she remarks in a tone of wonder. Is that how you pronounce it? Shake? I guess, she says, that was before they became suicide bombers.

For all the talk about how insulated Americans are from their country's military incursions in the Middle East, the war is everywhere, emerging in palpable fear and unfounded comments like these. On a holiday dedicated to Dr. Martin Luther King Jr., it's discouraging. It's also complicated. People seem determined to find small ways to care for one another across lines that still divide, though to my mind the lines of care more often run toward privilege. An hour later, while I'm sitting in the motel lobby, the white manager sticks his balding head out of the back office to complain, Hey, it's cold in here! Cold? What you mean, cold? Feels fine to me! responds the African American cleaning man, who has worked up a sweat polishing the plate-glass windows. Feels fine to me, too, says the big guy running numbers on an adding machine behind the front desk. Y'all need to eat some greens. Your blood is too thin! My wife makes a mean pot of greens. She cooks some, I'll bring them in.

The next morning when I shoulder my pack and head back to the bus depot, the streets in the historic district have completely changed color. What's happening? I ask a girl in pigtails who peers out from behind an armful of T-shirts. Parade! she grins shyly, then scoots down the block in search of sales. I chase after her to get a better look at her wares. A pensive Martin Luther King adorns the front of the shirts, reproduced in little squares ten times over. Dr. King is seldom separated from his words and this T-shirt is no exception. Gold-edged letters affirm that "Unarmed truth and unconditional love will have the final word." On the back the designers have added a sentiment of their own: SOONER OR

LATER ALL THE PEOPLE OF THE WORLD WILL HAVE TO DIS-
COVER A WAY TO LIVE TOGETHER IN PEACE. At ten dollars,
the shirts push the limits of affordability for many people
in the crowd, but they are half the price of similar ones sold
at the D.C. rally.

Much of what Dr. King had to say about unity apparently
has yet to sink in, because although we are celebrating a hard-
won national holiday, the parade is far from a multiracial
gathering. Except for a few politicians smiling their way
down the street and a mixed group of drag racers on tricked-
out motorbikes, white Savannah is scarcely in evidence. The
high school bands, with their stutter steps and bell-bottom
uniforms, haven't changed much after years of court-ordered
school desegregation. Then again, maybe today Dr. King is
in the house. When I drop my pack on the curb and settle
my light-skinned self back to watch, nobody pays me any
mind.

The parade takes almost an hour to pass by, yet it feels
small in the intimacy it creates. Tissue-paper flowers lend a
homemade quality to the floats. Afrika in Savannah, Haram-
bee House, and Citizens for Environmental Justice have
decked out a truck in prideful shades of red, black, and green.
FM radio station vans play the latest hip-hop. The Rough
Riders ATV club pulls off wheelie after wheelie without
mishap. MLK Skaters for Freedom live a bit more danger-
ously, scattering spectators as they barrel down the pavement
on roller skates. Dignitaries safely ensconced in convertibles
call out to friends, neighbors, and pastors they recognize on
the curbs. Mr. Ross! Mr. Ross! Bobby Johnson! You doing all
right?

Every block or so, a megaphone broadcasts one of Dr.
King's speeches, with a heavy emphasis on love. "One people,
one freedom!" chants the congregation of a Baptist church.

From the African Episcopal float comes a more critical view: "War abroad is war at home. Peace abroad is peace at home. No war! No war!" That's right! shouts a man in a fedora from the curb.

When a bus rumbles down the street representing the Savannah local of the Amalgamated Transit Union, I figure it's time to be on my way. One people, forty kinds of freedom.

Ready to Die but Never Will

When my father considered me old enough to understand, he called me to the basement to teach me about war. On a table lay an open cigar box that once held White Owl Invincibles but now housed his treasures. Do you know who this is? he asked, pointing to a black-and-white glossy photograph. I scrutinized the picture. A debonair man with a pencil mustache crooked a cigarette between two fingers, celebrity style. Very 1940s. Without waiting for an answer, my father explained, It's your great-uncle Willard. Uncle Willard, I replied, why haven't I heard of him?

That's when the Silver Star came out of the box. The government sent the medal to us after he got shot, said my father. And you know how he died? He ran out in front of the guns. They said he was a hero. They said he ran out to save someone's life. Later we heard from one of his buddies. You know why he really ran out? The guns, the mud, the trenches . . . I guess you could say he went crazy. Battle fatigue. He couldn't take it. He might have saved somebody, but he ran out to end his life.

Heroism in our family was never a simple subject. My grandpa Ervin, Willard's brother, spent World War II in a ball bearing factory, exempted from the draft because the government considered his work essential to the war effort. Ball bearings made tanks and jeeps run. If you are Roma, you don't have to live your life through the life of the nation. Why defend a border you live to cross? Not every Roma feels this way, of course, but that was the thinking in my father's family, where people were bound to serve, but seldom in the military way.

Perhaps that's why, when the man in the hooded Marine Corps sweatshirt boards the bus out of Savannah, I am dumbfounded by the gold lettering on his back.

> Devil Dogs
> Born to Fight
> Trained to Kill
> Ready to Die
> But Never Will

Is death something a person can survive or—worse—hand off to another by asserting it cannot happen? Never is a longer time than most of us will ever know.

What Did You Do with My Aunt?

Pine trees and palmettos. Trailer parks, broken-down apartments with kitchen chairs set beside the door, an old man whose gaze fills the potholes in the road. A U-Haul center that turns into a Greyhound depot at 4:10 p.m., then goes back to renting trucks to people who can't afford to hire movers.

I'm on the damn bus! a white woman complains into a cell phone, her bejeweled fingers giving "ringtones" another meaning entirely. No, I couldn't get anything else; it was all booked up. Last time I had a seat on Delta, it took me two hours to get there. Now it's going to take me twenty... What, him? The company's going to keep him there another five months. They're paying him good money, so... Of course I wish he was supporting me. Oh well, at least I'm not supporting him!

There's a baby screaming its head off. Are you bored out of your mind, buddy? my latest seatmate asks rhetorically. Join the club! Want to come up here? Look, birdies! She takes the child from his mother and the screams subside. With my good hand, I pull out a set of keys for him to grab. Try these, little man. When he starts to fuss, some girls across the aisle toss him a package of sandwich cookies.

My bad hand was a good hand until ten minutes ago when I put my weight on it to shift in my seat. Now it throbs where the tip of a ballpoint pen hidden between the foam cushions has carved an ugly bloody furrow into my wrist. The consummate traveler, I have Band-Aids in my pack, but I'll have to think long and hard about the last time I had a tetanus shot. Notice, dear reader, the dawning of relative affluence: sometime, somewhere, I *might* have had a tetanus shot.

My next thought is a strange one, or not, depending on where you stand: It occurs to me with relief that finding the pen this way saved my pants. Otherwise they would be marked with indelible ink stains. I experience the kind of relief in a moment of duress that arises from a history of doing without. Freak accidents and blood poisoning be damned. A person can grow new skin, but money doesn't grow on trees, so she can't grow a new outfit. These reveries are the product of a mind long schooled to think poor, regardless of changes in income. To see a dish or a piece of clothing is to say to yourself, "Irreplaceable." If you break it or ruin it, there might not be another. For a very long time, if ever.

In Jacksonville we pull in and pull out but only get as far as the parking lot, where our driver comes to a halt with a screeching of brakes that rivals the sound of the baby. Apparently the windows need spraying. A scant 45 minutes later—no time at all in the bus universe—we arrive at St. Augustine, Florida, my next stopover. Inside the tiny depot, the game show *Jeopardy* poses indecipherable questions from a television set with the volume turned down so only the station master can hear. Before I have time to ask directions, a man and a woman with Pepsodent smiles and bad teeth fling the door open. What did you do with my aunt? the woman demands. She's not smiling now. Answer me! she says. My aunt should have been on that bus!

Calm down, now, the station master says. He peers at his computer screen and types with an air of authority, checking connections. The niece's mouth continues to move silently with worry. You're right, he says, she should have been on that bus. It's the last bus of the day. Then he proceeds to intone a list of scheduled stops longer than the Catalogue of Ships in Homer's *Iliad,* as though this would bring her closer.

Aunt Matilda called us before she set out, the husband says. Nothing since then. (Matilda? I think to myself. Who has an Aunt Matilda in real life?) I volunteer descriptions of the passengers who reboarded in Jacksonville. There weren't so many, after all. Let's see. Me, of course; the mother and baby, both African American; a young white guy with a beard more hope than promise; two Asian American kids toting a skateboard; and an elderly white woman. They perk up at the mention of the older woman. How old was she, exactly? Hard to tell, I say. Seventies. Sixties, maybe.

That's her! the woman exclaims. She's sixty-seven! What

color was her hair? Snow white, I reply. That can't be her, then, the husband interrupts. Aunt Matilda's hair is auburn.

I suggest that their image of dear old Aunt Matilda might be out of date. What if she stopped dying her hair? That could be it, the wife says. Maybe it *was* her and she forgot to get off. Her memory's not what it used to be. We could trace her!

The station master tries to break it to them gently. Without a reservation system, he explains, there's no way to trace people on the bus. People get on and off. If they use a credit card to pay for their tickets, their names go into the computer, but no one can say for sure who actually rides. If you're trying to disappear, now, that can be an advantage. There are those who don't want to be found. There are those who are so lost they haven't the slightest idea where they are. You work here a while, you'll see.

For some reason, Aunt Matilda's niece is not interested in hearing his prescriptions for invisibility. Tell us what to do, she begs. My aunt shouldn't be out there on her own. If it was me, he yawns, I'd go home to see if she calls. Got to show up sometime.

I remember Diana's aunt, balancing that homemade birthday cake on her lap on our way out of Boston so many months ago. Good god. Maybe she's still riding.

After the couple leaves, I ask the station master which way is north. It's early, only 7:15 p.m., but the streets of "America's oldest city" are dark. He takes a long look and points me in the direction of the local homeless shelter. Sited, appropriately enough, on a road called St. Francis, patron saint of the poor.

If I had any doubts about how disheveled I would look after a week on the bus, that settles it. The station master has gifted me with a new anxiety. As I trudge through the cobblestone streets, my bags getting heavier, heavier, I wonder if they will let me into the inn where I've booked a room, light skin and MasterCard notwithstanding. After having just had my dollar bills thrown back at me in D.C., it seems not an unreasonable fear. While I was raised to be white, a Romani kind of white, I am also the granddaughter of a man who drove in the dark "to make better time" whenever he took his family out of the city. It's what people of color historically have done to lessen their chances of being stopped on the roads. We never grew up with the sense that the world waited for us with open arms.

Luckily it turns out to be a slow season at the inn; they look happy to see my plastic. So I buy my way into privacy, which consists of a high brass bed, a brocaded chair that's too uncomfortable to sit in, and something even more unsettling. I can't quite put my finger on it. Then I realize what it is: silence.

The Castillo Economy

People come to St. Augustine for the historical ambience and to visit the Castillo de San Marcos, a four-bastioned stone fort that dates to 1672, complete with ramparts, sally port, and drawbridge. This onetime Spanish colonial city is old in the way that only a marketing campaign can make it. Adobe buildings, wooden houses that list to this side or that, high-priced margaritas, historic plaza, the pedestrian mall where anything can be had so long as it isn't a necessity. Wooden *santos* line the shop windows, but few of the shopkeepers know which saints they represent. It's contrived and utterly charming.

St. Augustine is not really the oldest continuous settlement in the United States, of course. That honor would more likely go to Sky City, the pueblo on top of the mesa at Acoma in what is now New Mexico, where people were plastering walls and husking corn long before Spanish galleons anchored off *La Florida*. What's distinctive about St. Augustine is its thrice-colonized, multiply militarized history, which extends the poverty draft back into the sixteenth century and foreshadows the armed economy of our times.

Before the Americans, there were the British. Before the British, there were the Spanish. Before the Spanish, there were the French. Before the French, there were the Timucuans. Each wave of colonists arrived with soldiers and fantasies of prosperity backed by guns. In 1565 when Pedro Menéndez de Avilés, a member of the landed gentry who moved in and out of royal favor, claimed the place for Spain, he led his impoverished, dreaming troops to stage what may have been North America's first lynching. At nearby Fort Caroline, an outpost of France, he ordered every inhabitant put to death, hanging the bodies from trees with the apologia "not as Frenchmen, but as heretics." That cleared the way for rice and citrus cultivation, based on techniques acquired from others they considered "heretics," Moors and African slaves.

To visit the Castillo is to step into the complexities of seemingly endless military ventures. The coquina walls, often attacked but never breached, were built with slave and convict labor. On one side as you walk into the Castillo's courtyard, you will come across a storage room used in the 1830s to imprison Seminole, who came together as a people in the fight against enslavement and colonization. It's a small cell, practically airless, and the vaulted ceiling does nothing to keep out the damp. In 1702 those same walls sheltered Indians and blacks who took refuge when the then-Spanish garrison came under attack by the British.

After the fort passed into American hands, it became a place where black Buffalo Soldiers served a white government and Native people who fought to keep their lands served time. In the late nineteenth century, the United States government transported seventy Plains Indians to the Castillo—Arapaho, Kiowa, Cheyenne, Lakota, Comanche. They were forced to cut their hair and engage in military drills in the uniform of the troops that had massacred their villages. When Geronimo's band of Mescalero Apaches finally surrendered in 1886, they, too, were housed here, after a fashion. Few survived.

The mostly white tourists who explore the bastions with me are in awe, but not of this history. What they're after is the view from the battlements overlooking the harbor, where they adopt the conqueror's point of view. Ponce de Leon stood where we're standing now, a woman in track pants murmurs to her husband. Isn't that just amazing? You always read about it in books, but to actually be here!

Of course it's unlikely that Ponce de Leon ever stood on this spot, since he reached Florida in 1513, when the Castillo was yet to be built. His name leads because he is the "explorer" associated with Florida in grade school textbooks. And who could forget his legendary quest for the fountain of youth, still the grail of many a biotech company? Much easier to forget that de Leon died of wounds inflicted by Calusa warriors when he tried to seize their lands. Now Osceola, there's one whose memory should inhabit these stones. U.S. Army officers took the widely respected Seminole leader into captivity in 1837 when he arrived to negotiate a truce. The Castillo was the site of his betrayal.

A Castillo economy works like this: Militarize in a way that profits the few and yokes the rest to nationalist dreams. Institute policies that impoverish. Coerce people quietly into choices. Take and call it giving. Talk truce all the way to prison. Draft without calling anyone up. Then move the pieces around the board so quickly that it's hard to tell who's doing what to whom, though a body might have her suspicions.

In the early nineteenth century, Thomas Jefferson pursued a deliberate strategy of getting indigenous people into debt to pressure them to give up their lands "willingly." In the mid-twentieth century, African American sharecroppers were free to join the army to work their way out of debt, though not to share rank with those who set up the inequities of the sharecropping system in the first place. In the late twentieth century, well-to-do commentators blamed low-income people for their profligate ways while companies peddled zero-money-down deals on easy credit. In the century that cradles us now, a government at war has increased recruitment quotas for its all-volunteer military while cutting entitlements and even burial benefits for active-duty soldiers. When the armed forces instituted mandatory reenlistment after soldiers' contracts expired, some reconciled themselves to the country's need for them to continue to serve. Others called the arrangement a new form of slavery.

By the time I hop the bus back to Jacksonville, a different kind of game is going on. Or is it? There's a man in the back of the bus with a velvet-covered board balanced across his knees and all eyes are on him. Call him The Taker. He's got four twenty-dollar bills and a couple of ones creased between the fingers of his left hand. The other hand's in constant motion. I'm not asking you to play, he says. His braids swing down past his eyes like little pendulums, keeping time as he moves the bottle caps around the board.

Just watch. I'm not asking you to play, The Taker repeats. He needs that line, because most of his customers know the game, even if they don't quite understand how it's rigged.

The bottle caps swirl in figure eights, up, left, right, down. Every so often the Taker pauses to reveal a little red ball beneath one of the caps. Remember, he says, I only want you to watch.

The Taker's latest mark scratches his elbow nervously and shifts his baseball cap back on his head, but he watches. Come on now, says The Taker, pay attention. Where's it at? Where's it at? He transposes the caps with a dexterity born of practice. You don't have to put no money up. I just want to know where you think it's at.

The Taker has a confederate who plays and wins, plays and wins. After a while, The Taker pitches again to the mark, who has switched seats to get away from him or perhaps away from temptation. Try it, says The Taker, I'll let you play once for free. C'mon, it's free! I won't even charge you.

Now the mark is in. Thirty dollars later, he's emptied his pockets. I know you switched it, the mark says, abashed at his own naivete, or was it hubris to believe he could win? I *know* you switched that ball.

Naw, I didn't switch it, insists The Taker as he folds up the board. Why would you think that? You can see every move I make.

IV.

The Fine Arts of Moving in Circles:
El Monte to Bishop and Back

What class are we, Mom? The year is 1967, I'm tall for my age at four foot ten, and I have just learned a new word from television. I tug at my mother's new Sears Roebuck jeans, purchased with the grace of our aunt's employee discount card. Mom, what class are we?

My mother looks distracted, but then she often looks distracted, her mind in Tasmania while her right hand stirs the pot. I am the insistence in the corner of her eye that convinces her to pause long enough to say, If you're not doing anything, set the table.

But Mommmm . . . don't you *know* what class we are? Understanding the pride my mother takes in her reading and her knowledge, I figure that ought to get a response. I don't yet understand that she believes life should have treated her better.

Well, honey, she finally replies, I guess you could say we'd be lower middle class. I head for the silverware drawer, satisfied to be answered, dissatisfied with that part about "lower." Lower sounds like less. Lower than the other kids in my class? Lower than the president? Lower than what?

Tonight we're having gravy bread. I circle the table with the brown-and-white Melmac plates that familiarity has taught me to love. My younger sister gets a bowl with a picture of Mary Poppins at the bottom that she can uncover as a reward for finishing her food. Six places. One day, after financial aid sends me to college, it will dawn on me that

gravy bread is not necessarily a special treat, as my belea-
guered parents have pretended in an effort to protect us, but
a supper of last resort when the money runs out at the end
of each month.

My sisters and I look forward to this meal above all. It's
easy to prepare. Mix up brown gravy from a package (no
meat, of course, for drippings), season with an onion if you
have it, then pour over spongy white Tip-Top bread from the
day-old bakery outlet store. My mother usually manages to
set aside a bit of money so she can purchase the loaves by the
baker's dozen and defrost as needed. Call it our little hedge
fund.

President Johnson's War on Poverty is all over the airwaves,
but it doesn't occur to me that the policy has anything to do
with us. Not when an elderly lady in Chicago was discovered
last week eating cat food out of a can. Not when the parents
at my school have banded together to collect old clothes for
Desiree, a girl in my class, so she can have more than one
outfit to wear. We were the collectors, after all, never yet the
collectees. But then, we have my mother's aunts and my
grandmother to help.

The headlines finish at the top of the hour and Petula
Clark comes on the radio crooning *Downtown*. "The lights
are much brighter there, you can forget all your troubles, forget all your cares..." It's my mother's favorite song. Me, I
never think of going to downtown Chicago and having the
money to shop in the Loop. I just listen to the trains at night
rattling through the yards a block away from our house.
Trains, not buses, carry dreams of escape for children who
fly kites along the tracks. I fall asleep riding to places those
commuter trains could never have taken me.

What do you want to be when you grow up, little girl?
Moving.

*   *   *

Since my childhood, the lines of class have become both sharper and more obscure. Across the world, advertisements urge you to better yourself, in a market-directed way, of course. Across the world, as the tiny fraction that commands wealth systematically insulates itself from the systemically impoverished, more and more people go without. If you're one of those outside the gates, admitted only, perhaps, to wash the castle floors, how do you understand your position? As the way things are and will be? As the injustices of the few visited upon the many? As a staging ground for flight? As something to nurture your art? As a plight that should elicit the sympathies of royalty?

In the Philippines, says Marcelina, who climbs aboard the Greyhound with me in Los Angeles, people *love* Princess Diana. I love her, too! Because she did a lot for the poor. Her husband, no, we don't like him. But Princess Di! Not like the politicians. Estrada, he should have stayed an actor. Cory Aquino, she too was corrupt. The new prime minister, she might be good. Wait and see. Imelda Marcos, she did one good thing, buying all those shoes: now everybody has heard of the Philippines. But Princess Di, she was different. How terrible, Marcelina says, the way she died.

Ever since the day Marcelina's husband gave her a coin with Diana's picture on it, she has collected everything she can find relating to the princess's life. See for yourself! she says. She pulls a scrapbook from her mustard-colored bag to show me the object of her devotion. There's Princess Diana attending an AIDS benefit with the caption "Queen of Humanity." There she is again in a smart white suit, walking hand in hand with Mother Teresa. Farther along she reappears in jeans, her hands cupping the face of a grandmotherly woman from the Landmine Survivors Network. You see,

Marcelina says, Princess Di was just like us. So much love for the people!

As Marcelina turns the pages, the rhinestones embedded in her nails catch the light that sifts through the grimy bus window. Near the end of the book comes a young Diana with a tiara perched uncertainly upon her head, looking new to the life of a princess.

This business of collecting things, Marcelina explains, is new to me, from when I came to America. My husband, he sells old things. What do you call them? Antiques. Coins, old papers. People pay a lot of money. Rich people. Sometimes they buy a lot, sometimes not so much. Lately not too much.

My husband, she continues, he started his business because after he got out of the army, he couldn't stand a boss. He doesn't want somebody telling him things. The money isn't reliable, though. Sales go up, sales go down. We live together in one room in San Francisco. What do you call it? A loft. Only one room! In the morning you can see the sun on the water, like in the Philippines. But it's so expensive! One thousand five hundred, six hundred dollars a month, for that!

Sometimes I think I want to get a job, Marcelina confesses, but my husband doesn't want me to. Hers is the classic story of marriage as a path to upward mobility, of a sort. The couple met years ago at a bar in the Philippines. When Marcelina and her girlfriend came back to their table after a dance, her future husband stuck his foot out and she almost tripped. Later he admitted that he did it on purpose to talk to her. One thing led to another and he took her to America.

We fight a lot, Marcelina admits. A lot over money. I tell him someday we might get divorced. Then what will you do? But he doesn't care. Maybe because he live without a woman so many years. Sometimes I think, he is so selfish! Not always to me, but to everyone else. I tell him, "Don't be so mean," but he doesn't listen.

When I pass the poor people, she adds by way of illustration, I want to give them something. He says, "No! Don't give them nothing. It makes them lazy. They're young. They can get a job. They should work." I think it's okay to give them something. I feel sorry for them. But he says no. Me, him, we are different people.

Through marriage Marcelina has found a way up, if not out. Out would mean that past struggles no longer touched her. But Marcelina's experience is also the exception. Get a job, get two, work hard, flirt hard. If you are born into a family with little money at a time when economies funnel wealth toward people who already have it, your story is likely to turn out rather differently. For you, life will loop back like the route we're now riding: El Monte to Los Angeles, San Francisco, Reno, Bishop, Los Angeles, El Monte. With a little luck, you finish where you started.

All Snakes, No Ladders

We've already passed through Little Tokyo, where Latinos Pizza advertises asparagus topping and vacant lots jostle strip malls. Marcelina asks if I mind if she sits up front for the rest of the trip. That old lady up there, she explains, she's from the Philippines, too. She wants somebody to talk to. So I am left to contemplate the sign coming up on the left for the Japanese American National Museum, with exhibits on history, sculpture, and the incarceration of Japanese Americans in concentration camps during World War II. During the war authorities seized people's property and Little Tokyo changed into a short-lived African American enclave called Bronzeville. After the camps shut down, former residents returned to reclaim their homes and businesses, but not all were successful. All those lots not empty, then. Haunted.

This being Los Angeles, it's not long before we find a freeway. No sooner do we pick up speed on Interstate 5, however, than the cars slow to a crawl. So much for all those Hollywood movies where teenagers race around the city in convertibles. In L.A. terms, there are traffic jams and there are traffic jams. We're caught in something that exceeds the usual 24/7 rush hour.

Stop-and-go traffic on the steep grade leading up to Coalinga has left scores of vehicles marooned at the side of the road, radiators steaming. Must be an accident, passengers murmur. "Gaper's block" is the diagnosis an elderly white lady offers. I'll never understand it, she says, shaking her head. Why does everybody have to slow down to look at somebody else's misfortune?

We inch along, inch along, inch along for miles. Door's open! our driver calls out to stranded motorists. This is the Greyhound. Hop aboard! There's pride in the way he says "Greyhound" but defiance as well, because all the seats are occupied and this magnanimous gesture violates much-touted federal law.

When we finally come upon the burnt-black shell of a Ford Galaxie, we stare at the fire crews still dousing the carcass with foam. We stare at the drivers, a young white couple dressed in muscle shirts and cutoffs. Their eyes brim with disbelief. Jailhouse tattoos on the man's arm curve protectively around his partner's shoulder. How incongruous it must seem to them when a cheer goes up from the bus. At last we're rolling.

Near Coalinga we pull into a Burger King for a rest stop. The smell that shrouds the little building comes not from sizzling burgers, but from the pre-burgers corralled into stockyards over the hill. There's a McDonald's barely visible in the distance. One girl risks losing her possessions, along with her place on the bus, to substitute a Big Mac for a Whopper. I like choice! she calls over her shoulder, as she takes off for McDonald's at a run.

When it comes to stretching our legs, the choices here are few. I take a quick jaunt around the building and call it exercise, though in truth most of the workout comes from dodging the cars that whip around the drive-through lane. Greasy smoke from the exhaust fan wafts up to seed the clouds. Many of the fruits, nuts, and vegetables grown in the United States come from fields in this onetime desert.

You might think we are in the middle of nowhere, some nonplace invented to bleed money from the highway, unless you notice the graffiti. "Norte" glows orange in the dusk, stylized letters on charcoal pavement. El Norte, the North. When tensions between Mexican Americans and Mexican nationals crystallized in the 1990s—over money, work, style, immigration, identity—"Norte" became a strike for the U.S.-born side in the graffiti wars. Even the burger kingdom apparently is one worth fighting for.

Soon everyone piles into the coach. I settle back to nap, can't sleep, open my eyes, and...wait a minute. This looks familiar. Isn't that the Burger King sign? A Latino kid in a Lakers jersey is yelling—A tall white girl! A tall white girl!—at the top of his lungs. While attempting to pinpoint the source of this commotion at the back of the bus, the driver has steered our San Francisco–bound coach in a perfect circle through the parking lot. We're back where we began and it's no metaphor.

Someone's missing and, as usual, the riders have to figure this out. It's not the McDonald's girl; she made it back in plenty of time with an extra order of French fries to share. Our driver stops and sends the kid in the jersey to trawl the restaurant for absent-minded passengers. He returns with two sheepish-looking girls in tow. Before they sit down, one of them sticks her hand in the overhead rack, feeling for her violin case. Judging by the instrument, their clothing, and their incomprehension at the idea of being left behind, I'd peg them for middle class. Maybe they're in school. Maybe they're out for an adventure. Maybe they're short of money. Whatever it is, they're definitely not used to riding the bus. The ratio of privilege to vigilance is completely off.

Is that a bite? the woman across from me wants to know when the bus finally gets under way. She wrinkles her nose like a rabbit and points to an impressive welt on my arm. No, I explain, it's a bad reaction to a shot. Oh, she says, I had to get one of those too, when I went overseas. You know, with the military. Would you believe I made sergeant? (Her little boy nods behind her back: he believes it.) Of course, she says, that was before I had the kids.

Her eldest passes the time by reciting the names of the states backwards and forwards in alphabetical order. Someday, the little girl tells me, she wants to be a poet. Or a lawyer. Maybe a cashier. Her mother says she should be a lawyer, but her aunt thinks a cashier is just fine. She sighs. It's so hard to decide. But it doesn't really matter, she concludes, cheering up. When I get big, I'll work really hard. Then, she whispers in my ear, we'll have enough money for toys.

Rising, sinking, circling, sticking: the imagery of class mobility. Rising, that's the sort of mobility mothers wish for their children. Sinking is the one no one wants to talk about, the kind that's all too prevalent. Circling can be harder to discern because loose credit allows people to get ahead on their possessions by falling behind on their bills. Sticking is a new term, coined to describe how people in constant motion end up staying put. Think of it as the flypaper principle. Rich stuck to rich, poor stuck to poor, the middle torn away.

When the British magazine *The Economist* reported on declining social mobility in the United States, it chose "All Snakes, No Ladders" as its headline. Citing a study by Thomas Hertz of American University, the report concluded that "a person born into the top fifth is over five times as likely to end up at the top as a person born into the bottom fifth."[1] Whether or not it has become harder to get ahead in the United States, increasing inequality in the way that income is distributed has certainly not fostered greater mobility.

Like the player in the classic children's board game Snakes and Ladders, a person who lives poor in this wealthy country is supposed to advance by landing alternately on squares with ladders that bypass rows of obstacles and snakes that send him slithering back from whence he came. But what happens when punitive social policies and a corporate economy rig the game? With ladders removed, a player theoretically can advance square by square, but sooner or later he'll land on a snake—a job that disappears, a health problem, a car that breaks down—which will negate his best efforts.

Ladders make a better recruiting story than snakes, however, even on the bus. Suppose you're riding through Raleigh, like one of the passengers on my last journey. You toy with the idea of picking up the woman sitting next to you, who swears she's eighteen. I don't mind to talk about my past, you tell her. I came from nothing; now I *am* something.

Six years ago, you explain, I was a crackhead. Ended up living on the street. I got attacked. There was two of them. I fixed one but couldn't deal with the other. I spent eighteen months inside for that. Got out of prison. Started up with the crack again. Three years later, I didn't recognize myself. Cranking, at first it was fun, but then it got to where I wanted myself back. It wasn't fun no more.

I had people who cared for me. I don't know why. The way I was, I couldn't care for them. They helped me get a job in sanitation. I went from $6.30 to $10.30 an hour in a year. (Well, exclaims the young woman you're trying to impress, that was worth it!) Most definitely it was worth it. My boss told me, he said, When you started you were worthless. Now you do the job of three men.

The two of you disembark at the next stop and say your goodbyes on the platform. I keep riding, keep thinking about your conversation. "Now you do the job of three men." Ah, but were you paid the salary of three men? That is a question seldom posed when people are recruited back into the market. By middle-class standards, by the cost of what it takes to live in expensive American cities, $10.30 in 2003 was not a pittance, but neither was it a living wage. And for every redemption song like yours, there are ten, twenty, about going around and around and around.

I've tried everything, the taxi drivers, security guards, saxophone players, and unemployed carpet cleaners tell me. Nothing seems to work.

So there you are, riding in circles when you know things could be better. You open your eyes and . . . you're stuck. How do you handle it? These questions, too, circle round. You can place all your hopes on the magic square with a ladder that will anoint you as the lucky one. You can say to hell with it. Or somewhere along the way where there is no way, the lights come on and you become a different sort of player.

Swagger

In an age of public relations, everybody knows that spin has become something of an art. If you're living poor, you, too, have a chance to spin your story. When you meet strangers on a bus, the promise of a job without benefits at a meat-packing plant becomes a promising future in the food-processing industry. Part-time work as a telephone solicitor gains glamour when presented as a job in advertising. "We have relatives with Re/Max" might mean that your nephews work as cleaners for the big real estate company. These are more than euphemisms, more than attempts to put a re-spectable face on difficult circumstances. Spin keeps other people's hands off your dignity.

If spin is an art, swagger often represents its epitome, es-pecially for men of color. "For that marvelously mocking, salty authority with which black men walked," James Bald-win observed, "was dictated by the tacit and shared realiza-tion of the price each had paid to be able to walk at all."[2] Not everybody has it. Not everybody understands it. And even once you master it, swagger can be hard to sustain.

When we get to Oakland, an African American couple in their seventies tries to board. Tries and fails, because the cane carried by the striking woman in pearls doesn't provide enough leverage to get her into the coach. Somehow the two have wedged themselves into the little stairway leading up to the aisle. Errant passengers have to pull them to safety.

The whole bus knows that the name of the woman in pearls is Edith, because every time she levels a charge against her husband, he responds in a plaintive voice, But Edith! Edith's leverage comes from cataloguing her husband's imaginary offenses. He looks dapper in his driving cap, but frail, too. Edith comes across as someone long accustomed to having the upper hand in marriage.

Now that Edith's memory has begun to tremble in syncopation with her legs, her husband has trouble managing. It takes him ten full minutes to convince her to release her grip on her shopping bag so that they can sit down and stop blocking the aisle. Come on, Edith, he pleads, give me the bag! I've always made my way, she objects. (Edith, give me the bag!) What business is it of yours? (Edith, give me the bag!) You know I've always handled my own bag. (Edith, give me the bag!) The lady's convictions certainly have not gone the way of memory. Edith, she's got swagger.

So does Dartanian, who joins us the next day in San Francisco. What are you listening to? he asks the girl across the aisle the minute he sits down. She pretends to ignore him and then, when he keeps after her, points out the obvious: a tape. Yesterday's technology, but not by the standards of her budget.

Needless to say, a man with swagger cannot be deterred by such paltry delaying tactics. Not with miles to go until he reaches Seattle. Not the way Dartanian rolls. What tape? he wants to know. She shows him, looks away. He follows up with a commonplace, the perfect riposte: Where you going? Weed, she says. What? Weed, she repeats. Weed, he says, looking confused, what's that? It's a place, she says. Where that? Weed, Oregon, she says, I *know* you never heard of it. That where you stay? he asks. She nods, headphones still on. I stay in East Oakland, Dartanian volunteers. Going up to Seattle to shake the town.

He takes a swig from his Coke bottle, in the manner that

"swig" would suggest, while the driver runs through the usual list of prohibitions. No smoking, no music without earphones, no alcohol. Mm-hmm. Anybody three seats in any direction who can breathe knows that this child has laced his Coke with rum. But that's all fine, because the point is to show respect—and ingenuity—by making a flourish of following the rules. Thus the plastic soda container. It's 12:30 in the afternoon.

We edge past a corner where workers, all Latino, have gathered to try to sell their strength. Casual labor, economists call it. As the sun peaks, the chances of finding work diminish. There's nothing casual about the way they hold out their arms, waving hopefully, desperately, even at a passing bus.

I bet you and me is on the same route, Dartanian tells the girl. What if I want to see this place, Weed? Anything happen there? Bet there's no black stuff there.

No, she agrees, it's boring. You like it? he asks. She nods. Don't you miss town? Uh-uh. She won't tell him her name. He manages to find out her age, though, which turns out to be seventeen, clearly a bit of a surprise. Dartanian shrugs. A youngster, huh? Then he starts to explain why Seattle is worth the daylong trip. You can get a zipper-bomb up there for two hundred something. In Oakland the same thing would cost you four hundred.

He has misjudged his quarry—for some strange reason she's not interested in the price of an ounce of marijuana, much less a woman for hire—so the conversation, such as it is, turns back to the other kind of weed. Hot up there in Weed? he asks. She nods. Real hot? She nods. For all Dartanian's street-smooth, I'm-running-this-game demeanor, this girl is making him work. Not like town, huh, he says. These long sleeves and beanie cap, I'd have to get up off of these.

He bums a couple batteries for his machine, then complains that her batteries are old. Bums two more and complains about those, too. Takes another swig. Insists on lending her some of his tapes. Pulls down his gym bag from the overhead rack, rustles through a plastic bag filled with CDs and tapes, passes her one by P. Diddy. Takes another look at hers and exclaims, That's old shit! Girl, you been up in Weed too long!

Now why would you want to cultivate this prickly, prideful, sweet-talking style, designed to bring the world close when you want it and otherwise keep it at bay? Three hundred years of history aside, the answer lies back in Los Angeles behind Door 16. That's the number of the gate at the bus depot where the ticket taker for this route, white as the day is long, had trouble distinguishing humor from humiliation. Nice print, she commented to the carefully made up Mexican woman in front of me, mocking her green floral sundress. Sure you're not Hawaiian? The woman grew attentive, a question in her voice: Ha...why? Although it was clear that this rider knew very, very little English, the ticket taker decided to force a conversation. You better change to something else, she persisted, or you're gonna freeze up there in San Francisco. When she still got no response, she raised her voice to an insulting level and began to scream: CHANGE! SAN FRANCISCO!

At this point the woman's husband tried to defuse the situation by picking up on words he recognized. *Qué bonito,* San Francisco! he offered respectfully. While the ticket taker stared at him, he repeated slowly, as if for the language impaired: San-Fran-cis-co, *qué bo-ni-to.* Then, taking advantage of her distraction, he reclaimed the boarding passes from the ticket taker's frozen hand and helped his wife drag their battered suitcase through the door.

Now it was my turn. The ticket taker met the demand in

my gaze with a shake of her gray curls. Looking down at the floor she muttered, I never could get that *español* in school. Flunked it my first year. As though that would be explanation enough for a woman who returns tickets to black passengers with the words: Step aboard. You're bought and paid for.

So when Dartanian makes his way to the back of our bus with that assertively crafted bounce and glide in his step, it's a joy to watch. Into the tiny bathroom he vanishes for a solid twenty minutes or more. A succession of passengers who need to use the facilities rap on the door to no effect. Nothing is going to roust Dartanian out until he's ready. Riders begin to comment on his disappearance in low tones. Something's going on in there, says the old lady who's been passing around pictures of her family's Doberman. The old lady's lips purse like she knows. A middle-aged African American guy in khakis takes the occasion to explain to the driver why he moved to Sacramento from Oakland. If I was back there in Oakland, he says, I'd be messing with the same ones from the neighborhood. Sacramento gave me back my life.

When we pull into the terminal on L Street in Sacramento, Dartanian is still in there. The rest of us file off the coach, never to see him again unless we, too, are headed for Seattle.

Which we're not. Although some of us will continue on this bus to Reno, we still have to haul every last piece of baggage around with us on our lunch break. It's time for the bus to be cleaned, which usually involves only the interior, but this time the cleaners leave the luggage bays wide open. The driver has duly announced that the company will not be responsible if everything we own is gone when we get back.

The last time I arrived in Sacramento on a bus, I was nineteen, working as a courier who shepherded documents to state government buildings in the days before overnight delivery services created a global market. Things look different now.

A taxi grinds to a halt just outside the bus bay. The minute its driver raises the hood, fellow cabbies rally to help. A flurry of back pounding, chin nods, and handshakes ensues, but in the end it all amounts to a clutch of Latino, South Asian, and Native American men staring at the engine block. Passengers waiting to transfer either watch this little drama unfold or shoehorn themselves into plastic chairs that are bolted to the floor and fitted with black-and-white pay televisions. At a time when airports, with far wealthier clientele, provide free TV, most bus stations charge for electronic means to while away the wait.

A young mother who keeps drifting off to sleep calls to her son, Trey, keep close! Don't go running off! The minute her eyes close, running off is exactly what he does. To an eight-year-old, the strip of video games along the back wall is a siren song, even if he doesn't have quarters to play.

Over in the restaurant the crowd thins out. Most likely it's the prices. On second thought, maybe it's the food. Sandwiches come prepackaged; grilled cheese is made to order. I settle for Cup O Noodles Chicken Flavor Noodle Soup. With all that MSG, what's the worst the cook can do to it? All she has to do is add water. I hadn't considered that the hot water poured into the little Styrofoam cup wouldn't be boiling. Crunchiest noodles in the West.

Between crunches a page for a missing passenger on the bus headed south comes over the loudspeaker. I nudge the shoulder of an infinitely elderly white lady who has fallen asleep over the debris of her lunch. Could it be her? She's disoriented. It's hard to wake her. Plus she's entirely too well brought up. She can't bring herself to leave the restaurant without cleaning off her table first.

Hurry! You're going to miss your bus! I exclaim over and over again, hoping for some hypnotic effect. I go on ahead to try to hold the coach, since it's obvious that with her arthritis she can't move fast enough. When I get there the southbound lane is empty. They left as soon as they made the announcement, offers a skinny guy in the neighboring line to assuage my disbelief.

My bus is leaving too, so I can't even go back to tell her. In the toilet at the back of my coach Dartanian has been replaced by a Chicana in her fifties who cries out in alarm, No light! No light! A veteran rider realizes that this isn't a job for the repair crew. You got to lock the door! he yells. Or else fiddle around until you find a hole. If that don't work, I don't know what to tell ya!

Before the bus starts to move I decide I might as well use the toilet too, especially now that it's been cleaned. Only it hasn't. On the little shelf where a sink used to be lies Dartanian's stack of brand-new CDs. Or rather, a bag filled with jewel cases stripped of their discs. It seems the purse-lipped grandmother was right. Something *was* going on in there. Not to mention wherever that music came from.

Three rows up sits a guy who just got out of prison. He keeps talking about how bad he is. Bad as can be. And how, then again, when you really get to know him, he ain't.

The Philosopher-King Does Sacramento

If you've ever been to a Barnum and Bailey circus, you've seen them: the clowns with their ostentatiously patched trousers and worn-out shoes flapping at the toe. There are other sorts of clowns, of course: the fools in European circuses who poke fun at politicians, the Zuñi *heyoka* who tease people when they misbehave. Patches the Clown takes a swipe at a rather specific target: the hoboes and tramps who dotted the American landscape during the Great Depression. Without even realizing it, audiences are being schooled to laugh at a caricature of poverty.

A real tramp like Arthur could set them straight, if he thought it worth his bother. He's one of the few passengers on the Sacramento–Reno bus who isn't traveling on a casino package. The others have booked discounted rooms at the Sands Regency. Once they arrive at the hotel, they will show their bus tickets to receive food coupons and free plays at the roulette wheel. It makes for a cheap vacation, if they can avoid reaching into their pockets for that extra bit of change to feed the slot machines. The hotels are betting they can't resist.

In the row for disabled passengers, a balding man with emphysema and a lucky feeling is heading for the Sands with his oxygen supply. His seatmate spins a cautionary tale about somebody who lost all his money at craps, overstayed the five-day limit printed on his casino bus ticket, and couldn't get back home again. No one wants to hear a story like that when he's feeling lucky, so the exchange peters out. I take advantage of the lull to immerse myself in *High Country News,* a newspaper with a focus on environmental issues in the West.

That's when Arthur decides to strike up a conversation. You reading about wolves? he asks, gesturing toward the illustrations that accompany an article on wolf reintroduction in the desert Southwest. Arthur's white mustache grazes the top of the headrest as he turns around. He's wearing a soft yellow tatter of a shirt that ripples because it's been washed so often. This man either loves that shirt or he hasn't got much of a wardrobe. Wolves, uh-huh, I mumble. My distracted nod becomes the entrée for some first-rate philosophizing about the dangers that wolves don't pose and never have posed to ranchers.

Take your average coyote, Arthur says, pronouncing it "cay-oat," the way westerners tend to do. Coyotes don't deserve their bad reputation. I worked on a ranch outside Elko one time. The coyotes would come and make a meal of the dead carcasses, but never the live cattle. That helped the ranchers out, because they didn't have to dispose of the dead stock. Saved us ranch hands the trouble of hauling them in, too. People that badmouth these animals haven't lived around them, or haven't really looked. Same thing for wolves. It wouldn't be any different for wolves.

The Philosopher-King's face is as sun-darkened as his arms. He poses a rhetorical question. When you look at me, Arthur asks, would you know I'm a tramp? Not a bum, mind you. A tramp.

Do you know the difference between a tramp and a bum? Arthur asks. I shake my head slowly, feeling like I should. A bum, he says, is a guy who's down and out. A guy who doesn't take care of himself. A guy who's not responsible to anybody. A bum has no philosophy. Where's his pride?

It occurs to me that Arthur's definition of a bum has something in common with the propaganda about tramps put out by farmers' associations during the hard times of the 1930s. According to Carey McWilliams, a chronicler of migratory farm labor, the so-called blanket men were said to be "shiftless fellows who actually *preferred* 'the open road' . . . chaps who adored lice and filth and vermin."[3] This pernicious slide from love of the open road to the love of lice created a rationale for low pay and substandard conditions in the early days of industrialized agriculture. Like the "happy slaves" of an earlier era, tramps were supposed to be satisfied with their lot. Masters, farmers, and governments need take no responsibility for their wretched condition, except insofar as they claimed to have improved it.

Arthur says that the new generation of tramps still has to contend with slanders leveled during the Great Depression. A tramp, he continues, is also not to be confused with travelers on the work-to-ride plan. By way of explaining the distinction, the Philosopher-King poses a hypothetical: Suppose a man scrapes together the money for a one-way ticket to spend Thanksgiving with his ninety-two-year-old mother because he hasn't seen her in years. He knows he has no way to get home. They have a great reunion, celebrate the holidays. He makes his mother happy. When the money runs out, he finds a job, says to himself, Guess I'll have to shave, and works until he earns enough money to buy a ticket back to wherever he came from. That's a great thing to do, but that's not me, Arthur insists. A tramp is part of something.

When our bus pulls into one of the small towns that dot the roads heading up into the Sierra Nevada mountains, Arthur points out a nondescript bar that backs onto the railroad tracks. There's a whole society of tramps, he explains. This is one of the ways we find each other. You see that sign? (I look. The sign reads, "Ma Barker's.") There are places like this where we meet all over the country. We even have a convention. People get to know one another, travel together, separate, meet up again.

The Philosopher-King rides the rails, moves from job to no job, travels from city to countryside to town. Once in a while, if he has the cash and he has to get somewhere quickly, he takes the bus. The way I live, he says, I guess it's what you'd call voluntary poverty. So far at least. Another few years and I'll be too old for anybody to want to hire me. Then I'll be living this way whether I want to or not! But right now, I live this way because I want to.

A person who lives to get a new car, a new television, a new lawnmower, can you really call that living? he asks. The way I've spent the last decade of my life, *that's* living! You see so much. You learn so much. Bet you didn't know the Mormon Church owns the Union Pacific!

Whatever the Church of Jesus Christ of Latter-day Saints does or doesn't own, what interests me is the interest the Philosopher-King takes in the political economy of his favorite mode of transportation. He knows that Brigham Young and other church leaders recruited work crews to lay track for the first transcontinental railroad back in the 1860s. He knows all about the history of the so-called Mormon Roads, the railroad spurs created to link early LDS communities. He knows all about the railroads' dismal safety record at present. He knows that the Union Pacific remains one of the largest landholders in the country.

Maybe ownership interests Arthur so much because he barely practices it. I've got a brother in Atlanta, he explains, with the expensive home, the fancy office job, the boat. My brother keeps asking, "Why do you choose this life? Why would you live on the road? Why do it to yourself? You used to have a good job. You could have it again." But my brother, he's miserable. He can't get any real pleasure out of that big, big boat. Somewhere deep down inside, he knows it.

Well, sighs the Philosopher-King, to each their own. He is torn between relativism and visions of a society ruled by the way of the tramp. If everybody left the rat race and took to the road, Arthur is convinced they would be better off, but he also tells me he tries not to judge. He knows a tramp's life isn't for everyone. It can be hard. You get thrown off the trains. You get cold. But, he adds, you get to do things and see things that other people never will see. Riding boxcars through river canyons where no road goes. Can you imagine it out there? The old, old trees. The eyes of a cougar staring back at you. Red rocks covered in snow. That lonesome whistle in the dark when you hit a tunnel.

The Philosopher-King cups his work-chapped hands together and blows.

To See What There Is to See

Of course, you don't have to become a tramp to take to the road for the pleasures of it. On the bus, you don't even have to have much money. There's no need for hotels. You can ride all night, night after night, if you book the right kind of ticket.

In Detroit, Jorge was trying to figure out how to get to Cooperstown, New York, to visit the Baseball Hall of Fame, with one day left on a two-day bus pass. In Portsmouth, New Hampshire, Eric was working his way across the country to get to a Rainbow Gathering on the Clark Fork River in Montana. In St. Louis, Yvonne was determined to see the Grand Canyon once before she died. A skilled nurse's aide with little compensation to show for it, she was quite proud of having figured out a way to put the trip together. In hundreds of college towns across the country, students without the money for cars were taking the bus on the weekends to get a taste of life in the nearest big city.

While most people ride for a limited purpose—work, school, a political protest, a wedding—some are out to reclaim tourism for low-income people. The bus companies have recognized this constituency with some of their advertising campaigns, including Greyhound's "See America" pitch, which dates at least to the 1940s. And what is it these riders end up seeing?

Classic tourist destinations are on the list, no doubt. En

route to Flagstaff, a backpacker from the United Kingdom with long, curly hair and an American flag embroidered on his fishing hat was on his way to Sunset Crater Volcano. If you want to see a big hole in the ground, The Trucker advised, you got to go to Carlsbad Caverns. Where's that? the backpacker wanted to know. New Mexico, The Trucker replied, down by the border. It takes you half a day to walk down, then they make you take the elevator back up. There's a cave, bats, everything. You can even eat lunch underground, I offered, caught up ever so briefly in the romance of travel. Why would you *want* to walk up if you spent the whole day walking down? this budget tourist from the UK wondered. If a backpacker can't answer that question, I remember thinking to myself, I'm surely not going to try.

Others were headed for attractions visible only to the mind's eye. On the Jacksonville bus, a heavily muscled sanitation worker described what happened after a friend gave him an old camera. That camera, he explained, made the whole world look different. The birds, the cardinals, they're the ones that got me started. Had to get me a zoom lens. See, they're skittish. You can't get a picture of them close up. Now I got one in my traveling bag—a zoom lens, not a cardinal. This trip I'll maybe be able to get a picture of a gator. Down by where my father lives. I'll be able to get the eyes of the gator, shooting from here to where that truck is parked. You don't know what that feels like.

Indeed I didn't, and given the quarry, I wasn't sure I wanted to try. But even without a camera or an eye for the peaceable kingdom, sightseeing by bus entails another kind of art. There are no showers, no flat beds, no towels on this road, not even a hint of home cooking. Yet these very privations can promote less consumerist forms of travel. Lots of people travel only to arrive. They're bored out of their minds and can't wait to "get there." A few riders cultivate another approach entirely.

On the bus, if you sight-look rather than sight-see, you can glimpse angels as well as devils in the details. Turcotte's Shoe Repair testifies to the survival of an artisan in a country that encourages people to buy new goods when things break, even if it means going into debt. The exquisite play of shadows to the north speaks of an early winter. Shops near the depots with names like "Slightly Injured Furniture" and "Park & Pawn" remind you, as though you could forget, how class and race segregated urban space remains in the United States. The bumper sticker on the back of a passing patrol car that reads, "Next Stop, the Twilight Zone" suggests something of the post-9/11 erosion of the constitutional right to appear before a judge. The latest parking lot, just like the last parking lot, offers a mute commentary on homogenization. This place could be a bunch of places, a teenager mutters, turning up the volume.

If the Fleet Bank that was there on your way down has turned into a Bank of America by the time you head back, you have a clue to the reach of the mergers sweeping the global banking industry. Those three-inch cockroaches that scuttle across the floor of the depot in El Paso supply you with ammunition to shoot down boasts about the superior size of the roaches in Chicago tenements. The tedium of endless miles is just another person's awe at the vastness of the country. Children who dart across six-lane roads in sprawling western cities variously represent a hazard to motorists, a danger to themselves, or a refusal to bow to the reign of the automobile. When the bus sidles up to an overflowing convenience store dumpster at a stop in the Florida Panhandle, a songbird with amethyst stripes in the overhanging branches roots beauty in squalor.

Look, there's something there! That's the cry that set heads swiveling on the freeway outside El Monte. A woman with a filigreed gold cross hanging from her neck gestured toward a building in the distance. Must be police, she concluded, noting the helicopters on the roof. In a gated community or a different part of the country, other possibilities would have come to mind: a newsroom, perhaps, or a hospital. But in Los Angeles, anyone who has come up through the barrios has intimate knowledge of the military-style surveillance conducted from the air since the 1990s. Helicopter-mounted searchlights sweep through residents' homes; ultraviolet binoculars lead to the arrest of suspects under pursuit as well as the occasional resident bold enough to venture out into her own backyard in the dark. Police station, television station, trauma center? There's always more to see than what the view from the window reveals.

"The Biggest Little City in the World," otherwise known as Reno, poses no exception. The first place our bus halts in Reno is the Sands Regency, of casino package fame, which commands its own bus stop. The second is the Hilton. Third comes the bus depot itself. Although the depot is located a scant two blocks from the Sands, passengers who aren't here to play blackjack have to wait an extra half hour while the bus loops back around. That's the political economy of the New West in a nutshell. Tourism displaces ranching and mining, while the closest thing to public intercity transport is private.

Behind the Sands I enter a horizontal landscape of liquor ads, doughnut shops, and no-frills weddings. At the Candlelight Chapel, just down the street from Dunlop Tires, there are plenty of spots reserved for "Marriage Parking." Instant marriage facilities hark back to the days when people flocked to Nevada because the state permitted the fastest divorces and even faster weddings. The proprietor of the Candlelight says business is slow.

A row of little neon-clad motels left over from the 1950s advertise themselves as clean and affordable, with weekly rates. "Weekly rates" are the tip-off: A good portion of the working poor in the United States live in facilities like these, paying as they go, paying more than if they had the ready cash to go elsewhere. Where will they move when this strip succumbs to gentrification? The retro-1950s coffee shop at the Sands, which serves designer burgers and recycled Frankie Avalon songs, is thronged, while the motels look rather desolate. Not an auspicious sign.

Near the riverfront, it's now easy to find an organic coffee shop frequented by white women wearing jeans so tight they prefer standing up. The coffee arrives in a turquoise mug and tastes better than anything I've had on the road. It's also three times the cost of a cup on the other side of the hotel. Along the Truckee River pathway that the city has installed in an attempt to upscale its charms, mountain bikers, drinkers, and gamblers out for a stroll strike uneasy compromises as they share the space. The ducks, however, seem quite satisfied.

I decide it's long past time to get my hair cut. The definition of serendipity is this: In an effort to escape the twentieth repetition of "Send in the Clowns" while I wait outside a Chinese restaurant for my order of hakka noodles to come up, I cross the street to discover a cut-rate hair salon right next to Goodfellas Bail Bonds. *And* there is no one waiting. The young African American stylist who trims my hair claims that locals never see the inside of a casino if they can help it. Even so, she says, gambling makes for a rough town. Times are difficult right now, for her and for the hotels. Haven't I noticed it's all vacancies? Her plan is to save her tips until she has enough to move with her baby girl to Vegas. That's where the money is. That's where she's got people to watch her back. How long will that take? I ask. Three years, she expects. Maybe two, if things pick up.

Afterward I drop by the bus station to check tomorrow's schedule. Behind the plate glass near the ticket counter, a police substation advertises the services of a liaison for the homeless. Apparently it's a town of instant weddings and instant homelessness as well. People get so caught up in the gambling, the liaison tells me, they lose everything. Then they're stranded here. It might seem a little strange to provide social services in a bus station, but believe me, we do a good business. This is where people come, trying to find a way back.

Whenever I reach my limit, four dollars in nickels, I quit, even when I'm ahead. Having doubled my money playing the slots, I figure it's time to head back to Los Angeles. The 7:45 a.m. bus turns out to be the only one that can deliver this high roller to Hollywood at a time when my *hermana* Lisa can pick me up. I make sure to get to the station by 6:30 a.m. in case there's a line, only to find that there is no line and no food, either. The coffee out of the machine is so bad that for a moment I consider chucking it all and going back to school to become an accountant so that I, too, can dress in tight jeans and drink organic coffee out of turquoise cups for the rest of my natural-born days. If you knew me better you'd understand just how bad that coffee was.

Books Mobile and the Secret Stash

Sometimes what there is to see lies between the covers. On sleeper coaches, no doubt, except that Nite Coaches with their Pullman-style berths have gone the way of observation platforms, deluxe buffet service, and the Purple Swan Line.

On a twenty-first-century bus ride from Reno down to Bishop, the covers in question are more likely to shelter a book. But how can that be? It's widely reputed that, when it comes to reading, poor people won't touch the stuff.

To all casual appearances, most bus riders don't. You'll see the occasional passenger pull out the occasional guidebook with USA emblazoned on the spine in red-white-and-blue block letters. But you can go for miles without encountering a single page written by Nobel Laureate Toni Morrison or, for that matter, bestselling romance novelist Danielle Steel.

Appearances don't always deceive. A 2004 study by the National Endowment for the Arts reported that reading literature in the United States is on the decline across classes, auguring what the chair of the NEA called "a general collapse in advanced literacy." The study piggybacked upon a sharp but ineffective flurry of media attention given to children in inner-city neighborhoods who felt pressured to leave their books at school in order to look good.

But the United States is also a nation where people held in bondage once risked their lives to learn the alphabet. Slave owners feared the power of the word. The people they tried to hold understood that power and the power of the fear as well. By moonlight and lamplight, they studied.

In the current electronics-saturated climate, bookworms have turned the art of reading back into something of a covert operation. There's plenty of compulsive reading going on as we edge out of Reno onto Route 686, but that's directed at the billboards that advertise hot springs, advise motorists to report smoking vehicles, and promote the Capitol City Cremation and Burial Society. More challenging subjects have to wait until I pull out a work of historical fiction by Michelle Cliff called *Free Enterprise*.

With the kind of timing that happens only in life, never

in quality paperbacks, my eyes graze the passage in which Annie Christmas reflects on her elusive journey to freedom from plantation-era Jamaica: "It was her fantasy, and she knew it, that there was a solution to the placelessness that had always been hers." Suddenly, as though he's received some kind of literary high sign, the amiable gentleman sitting next to me removes his fedora, reaches inside his jacket, and pulls out a well-worn copy of *Macbeth*. The thane's tragic ambitions are quickly buried under Louis L'Amour's *The Rider of Lost Creek*, A. S. Byatt's *Possession,* and *The Good War* by Studs Terkel.

Hi, I'm Rick, he says, offering his hand. He's particularly attached to the L'Amour, with its sepia-tinted cowboys on the cover. I found that one for twenty-five cents at the secondhand store, he explains. It's in pretty good shape. Ought to last me till Chicago. Macbeth, somebody left him at the laundromat. Now what would the old guy think of that? Rick chuckles. The rest I picked up here and there. Can't help it, I just love to read. Always have. You got anything you're finished with?

Like many people who continue their education as it falls into their hands, Rick reads with an avid eclecticism. He has compatriots everywhere the buses run. The titles, too, run the gamut: everything from *Identity Theft,* perused collectively by a Latino couple in their twenties, to fat Victorian novels, to memoirs about growing up on the mean streets of this town or that. Bibles are not uncommon, used as much for divination as inspiration. ("My girlfriend kicked me out. What should I do?") Once, but only once, I came across a man reading the Quran in Arabic. A brave soul, given the politics of the day. He garnered curiosity but neither hostility nor suspicion. I couldn't imagine that happening on a plane.

Unlike train stations and airports, bus depots seldom feature bookstalls. It's been a long time—almost a century—since working people in the United States pooled their meager wages to hire people to read to them in factories, until the owners put a stop to it in the name of efficiency. Nor is there the kind of reading culture that makes it profitable for hawkers to sell books on the street corners of a city like New Delhi. So it's all the more remarkable when someone like Rick shows up, willing to follow the trail of whatever books pass into his life through circumstance, without the luxury of buying individual volumes that interest him. Or perhaps not so much remarkable as encouraging, especially to this child of a father who came home from walking his mail route to immerse himself in *The Great Books of the Western World,* sold to him by a door-to-door salesman and paid for on the installment plan.

Somewhere along the Mojave Freeway I'm due to meet another closet reader, a white guy named Kevin. Kevin will carry a novel and a self-help book that promises to transform him into a vegetarian. In low tones he will divulge that he's trying to leave the party scene and make a change, since none of us are getting any younger.

I'm a shy person, he'll confess. Generally I don't say much. I didn't really think I'd be doing all this talking, but after riding for twenty-four hours, you just end up talking to people. Everybody's got a story.

I see you like to read too, Kevin will say, glancing down at my inexpensive edition of James Baldwin's *No Name in the Street.* Hey, he'll add, maybe *you* should write a book. You could call it *Stories I Heard on the Bus.* No, really, you could! Funny you should mention that, I'll tell him.

This Place Is a Dump

The skein of roadways stitched onto the back of the Sierra Mountains transforms green into an understatement. This is not the woods of my midwestern childhood, which sheltered in my imagination assorted and fearful goblins, most notably the Creature of the Black Lagoon. (Only well into my teens did I discover that many of the "woods" that lined midwestern highways were thin strips of foliage designed to hide cultivated fields and logging clear-cuts. The smallest sparrow, with its bird's-eye view, would never have been fooled by this impression of a forest.) No, the Sierras in the early twenty-first century still offered an ecosystem sufficiently intact to support bobcats, quail, black bear, and the occasional cougar.

But all is not well in the jungle. The rural areas of the scenic West are littered with incineration sites for outdated military ordinance, leaking tailings ponds, and dumps of increasing toxicity. Climate change has begun to drive species from the foothills to the mountains, while mountain species have nowhere higher to go. Proposals to renew uranium mining in order to lessen dependence on oil have been greeted with ambivalence, especially by Native communities still suffering the effects of radiation poisoning from the Cold War era.

Much of the road I'm traveling today lies downwind of the Nevada Test Site. On the California side of the mountains in the San Joaquin Valley, where a hefty portion of the nation's crops grows, the miracle of the irrigated desert is salting up. Land subsidence has become a problem, too, from too much groundwater pumping. And that's just a start on what ails the environment.

On our way out of Reno, we pass a bank of protesters, Indian and Anglo, with signs that oppose a new mining project. Old West meet New West: This time the miners intend to dig not for gold or copper, but for kitty litter. Projected environmental impacts on the Reno-Sparks Indian Colony include exposure to released carcinogens such as arsenic, lead, and mercury, as well as pollution of the waters in the underground aquifer. Culture is at stake, too. "Preserve our ancestral clay pits!" is the cry one protester hoists aloft.

There was a time, and not so long ago, when environmentalism in the United States was perceived as a luxury issue taken up by the white and the well-to-do. Even if they wanted to, people who had to worry about putting food on the table every week allegedly would not make jaguars or aspen trees a priority. That was before the environmental justice movement began to articulate a critique of environmental racism and classism in waste disposal, land use, public health, and transportation. The First National People of Color Environmental Leadership Summit in 1991 was a landmark event that brought together people from cities, towns, and reservations to strategize about how to protect the land, honor its sacredness, and confront inequalities in the way that environmental impacts are distributed.

Included on the list of problems that needed addressing were bus stations. In the United States, an advertisement that reads, "Immaculately maintained two-story home, conveniently located next to bus terminal," probably won't help sell a house. Why? Part of the explanation might be elitist prejudices against the clientele. But prospective buyers would also be deterred by the poor air quality, the health hazards, and the noise pollution.

In Atlanta in 2001 the Disability Law and Policy Center of

Georgia took the local transportation authority to court on charges of dumping its oldest, most polluting diesel buses in African American communities. In New York the non-governmental organization West Harlem Environmental Action pointed out that five out of seven of Manhattan's bus depots were located in the borough's northern communities of color. Small particulates in northern Manhattan's air exceeded government standards by 200 percent. Asthma rates had climbed right along with the particulates.

An Associated Press analysis of data contained in a 2005 Environmental Protection Agency report affirmed what activists had already established: On a national basis, the poorest communities scored highest on pollution indexes. Black Americans, to take just one group, were 79 percent more likely than white Americans to live in neighborhoods exposed to significant health dangers from industrial contamination.[4] Concern for the environment that fails to take class and race relations into account sometimes exacerbates these problems. The Basel Convention on the Transboundary Movements of Hazardous Wastes and Their Disposal, for example, prohibits exporting waste to countries that don't wish to import it. When wealthier countries can't ship their detritus to poorer nations, they have to reduce their waste or find a place for it at home. But whose home? Not surprisingly, the waste tends to end up in poorer, less powerful localities within the richer nations.

In Brunswick, Georgia, a bus I was riding got stuck in a line of logging trucks while the old drawbridge let a ship pass. Despite the advent of black liquor recovery furnaces and wastewater recycling, there's no mistaking a paper mill town. I went to school here, a middle-aged woman confided while we waited. First grade through high school. Still smells like it always did.

International treaties, paper mills, and the smoke swirling

over the bus depots of Atlanta seem a world away on our drive from Reno down to Bishop. The ponderosa pine trees here look healthy and the driver says the fishing up by the dam in Bridgeport can't be beat. There's just one thing. The driver also says the rural areas on this run are changing. In a sense, he says, they're trying to screw themselves. They want growth, but with a small-town atmosphere. Jobs. It doesn't have to be the smokestacks and pollution. Some towns have turned into bedroom communities. But now people can't pay the taxes. You pay a heavy price for all that privacy and your non-urban lifestyle.

Plus, the driver says, what if you get what you wish for? That thing they call growth? Even Sacramento was a cow town once. Nancy Reagan would go there to get away from it all and get her hair done. Not anymore. Now look at it!

Anybody been to Yreka, up near Oregon? he asks as we pass a billboard for Deadwood Fence Posts. All the riders within earshot shake their heads. Those folks in Yreka, he says, they want their own government. Put up a big sign: "Welcome to the State of Jefferson." They feel that San Francisco and Los Angeles can't relate to their needs. They don't want the cities sending their junk up there. And I don't blame them.

The most significant health hazard in these parts comes from Mammoth Mountain, where magma from the Long Valley Caldera releases carbon dioxide in concentrations large enough to kill trees and take campers right along with them. (Earthquakes, diseases, floods . . . the Bible predicted it all! declares a blond woman in the front of the coach.) Inyo County, where we're headed, had one of the best environmental scores in the United States in 2002. But even a "clean" county in a rampantly consuming country has to have its dumps.

On the outskirts of Bishop, not quite visible from the main road, sits the Bishop-Sunland landfill. Bishop-Sunland might bring a smile to the faces of environmental justice advocates, located as it is closer to the Bishop Country Club than the Bishop Indian Reservation. But the smile wouldn't last. For a two-dollar entry fee, residents can dispose of unwanted items, up to a collective maximum of 120 tons per day. The site offers free recycling for electronic equipment and has plans to install groundwater monitoring wells. Yet the very professionalization that has turned garbage dumps like Bishop-Sunland into "waste management facilities" has also had an impact on people who live poor.

Trash picking—combing the dumps for salvageable items —is a time-honored occupation across the world for people who need to supplement their incomes. As the composition of the trash has gotten more hazardous, so has the occupation. It used to be that black bears rooting for cast-off sandwiches posed the biggest threat at North American landfills. Now, in the name of toxicity and safety, people are often barred from working the dumps, while waste management companies reserve the right to any profits from recycling.

All this has come as a blow to people accustomed to recycling long before recycling was cool. Old tires turned into scallop-edged planters might not appeal to middle-class aesthetics, but they supplied one answer to the question of what to do with all that balding rubber. Soda cans and a pair of tin snips were all that was required to turn scrap metal into aluminum art. Ancient sofas given a second life as porch furniture could have counted as recycling if creative reuse was all that mattered. Yet they came under fire from zoning laws framed by middle-class planners who couldn't distinguish some people from "trash."

Just before our lunch break, a passenger asks the driver to

let him off. Rural routes in Buslandia feature the equivalent of whistle stops. Buses deposit passengers anywhere they desire along the road; aspiring riders flag down the bus by day and use a flashlight to get the driver's attention at night.

On his way up the aisle, the departing rider distributes announcements about a memorial service for a local couple. After he leaves, the God-fearing blonde asks the driver if he knows what the service is all about. Three years ago a couple got off this bus, the driver explains, on a day just like today. Next thing you know, somebody chased them down, ran them down, with a jeep. Here they were, just trying to enjoy nature. You know, it's strange. People tell you how to deal with bears, how to deal with mountain lions. They never mention what to do with the human beings.

In a couple of years, our driver says, this route down through Bishop might not even exist. There's a lot of local feeling but not much demand for service. It's a chicken-and-egg problem, he adds, because the fare is so expensive. You can ride all the way from Los Angeles to San Francisco for the price of a ticket from one little California town to another. Well, he sighs, surveying the gray-green of the mountain juniper bushes, the land will still be here, in some form or fashion.

In some form or fashion. Before the year was out, Inyo County would petition the federal government with concerns about its proximity to the proposed nuclear waste disposal site at Yucca Mountain.

Ride in Beauty

Across the world, more people than ever before are in a position to know a dream for a dream when they see one. Flat-screen TVs light up billboards, not the corners of poorer people's houses. The good life rides into town on long work hours and environmental "accidents." The impossible terms of the mortgages peddled to "high-risk" clients are matched only by the stink when they find themselves out on the pavement.

Even when mobility fails, not all nocturnal journeys send the dreamer climbing endlessly, branch after branch, or plummeting uncontrollably to earth. Some dreams are simpler. Some dreams follow the circle.

On the outskirts of Bishop, the God-fearing woman points toward a speck of clapboard on the horizon. How'd you like to live in that house there, she asks, way out in the middle of nowhere? It's another rhetorical question, but not an unanswerable one. Every unexplored space shelters possibility.

Possibility is just that, not to be mistaken for fantasies of escape. Anyone with any sense dreams of getting out of poverty if their best energies merely go to getting by. But the way out, if there is a way out, can acquire many meanings in the getting of it. To one, it means never looking back. To another, it means returning to give back. Nor is getting out, strictly speaking, a matter of money. The world of fast cars and easy credit can trap your heart under a stone.

My daughter, the God-fearing woman explains, she's what you'd call slow. She makes these rugs. Just look at the colors, the woman says, fishing a tumble of reds, oranges, and gold from her purse. Gorgeous! Isn't there something we could do with them? Something to bring in some money? I slide my palm across the yarn, so vibrant, so yielding.

As the bus passes a row of cow hides, scraped and strung across barbed wire to dry, we all pitch in with suggestions. Maybe her daughter could sell her art—for that is what it is, hey?—through a crafts cooperative. Have they tried auction boards? eBay? Oh, nobody they know has a computer. Let's see. The driver happens to know a consignment shop in the town where the woman is headed and gives her directions.

The bus station in Bishop abuts a trailer park, just down the road from the Pizza Factory. (We Toss 'Em, They're Awesome.) Everything in a town this size is just down the road. There will be no rest break here, just a crowd of people putting relatives on the coach.

In the parking lot, two men get out of a car with license plates issued by the Osage Nation. Outside town the reservations are mostly Paiute and Shoshone, not Osage, but people will travel. The men escort an auntie to the seat behind mine, arrange the smaller of her two traveling bags where she can reach it, and step off the coach. On the way back to the car, their braids reflect off the windows of a half-ton pickup with a decal that features two guys in sombreros pissing on *La Migra*.

It's a quiet ride down to the McDonald's at Mojave, where auntie is supposed to change buses. I only have a thirty-minute layover, but it will be a good four hours before her eastbound coach arrives. That's where we wait? she exclaims incredulously as the McDonald's comes into view. It's the first time she's spoken.

Yes indeed, I say, right inside on those uncomfortable-by-design seats. Is there anyone to help with our things? she asks, scanning the parking lot. When she finds out the answer is no, she wonders what they expect a person to do.

I offer to carry her luggage. There's no way she can manage otherwise and besides, she's an elder. This maneuver, however, requires that I leave my bags aboard while I ferry hers to the restaurant, which is not my usual practice. I can't lift everything at once and there's not enough time to make two trips, order us both French fries, and watch her things while she uses the restroom. I feel the tug of my unguarded

belongings and the worry that my bus will leave without me.
I feel the tug until I don't. That happens when Celia—a.k.a.
the auntie—shares her story.

It's been years since Celia has taken the bus. She's on her
way to supervise the cooking for a supper to honor veterans
at a powwow back on her reservation. Every year she goes.
Every year she supervises. Every year she thinks, how would
it ever come together if I wasn't here to supervise? Other years
she's gone by car, but no one else can get away to make the
trip this time. Either that, or their cars won't make it.

We're Sac and Fox, she offers. Mesquakie? I ask. She nods.
I tell her about the year I spent in Iowa living not far from
Mesquakie land at Tama. She tells me how her kids have been
invited to a United Nations conference for indigenous people, where her son wants to speak on the environment and
the state of fishing up in the mountains. I tell her about the
years I spent waking up at 4 a.m. to fish with my dad, back
when the rivers ran clear enough for walleye. We could both
have continued to sit together happily at the little plastic
table for hours, with or without the talking. It's hard to leave.
I wish I could stay to see her safely onto the next bus. With
the traveler's gesture of hope and longing, we scribble e-mail
addresses onto the back of each other's ticket envelopes.

Before you go, Celia says, I want to show you something.
From her bag emerge needles, thread, and an intricately designed pair of calfskin moccasins, half finished. I guess I can
use those four hours after all, she laughs. I got to finish these
for my niece before I get to Oklahoma! People know me for
my beadwork, she adds modestly. The interior of her hand
luggage glows azure, emerald, and crimson, a landscape con-
densed into tiny balls.

After Mojave I'm still thinking about Celia and her veterans as we head across the low desert, toward the kinds of vi-

sions only Hollywood engenders. I read an editorial once in *Indian Country Today* critical of "the socially pervasive European fable that eulogizes the pauper who would be prince." More important for "traditional" American Indians, the editors contended, is "leadership . . . valued on how their actions benefit those most in need, on how well they share."[5] What would they have said to the sign rising out of the dust on our right that urges travelers to *envio de dinero a Mexico*? You can send money, if you have it, but is that the same as sending dreams?

On the day before I started out from El Monte, I went with my *hermana* to an outdoor market in Long Beach. She pointed out how many produce vendors had gotten certified to accept food stamps. It's great, Lisa said, as she sorted through a stack of apricots. This way people can get their fresh fruit, their fresh vegetables. Some of Lisa's friends clipped coupons to redeem on double coupon days at area supermarkets. They saved a lot of money, but the food was all processed.

On the other side of the produce market, she treated me to fresh-squeezed lemonade from a stand where she knew the owner. It was the end of the day and all the stalls were shutting down. The lemonade lady gave us extra scoops from the bottom of her glass barrel. These people make it the way I like it, the way I grew up with it, my *hermana* said, sipping from her cup. Not too sweet.

V.

Living on Debts and Promises:

Montgomery after the Boycott, New Orleans before the Storm

Mickey's Hot Little Cousin

Two worlds. That's how elites have characterized the lives of rich and poor in the United States for ages. In the nineteenth century, writers such as Stephen Crane and Jacob Riis believed they had to journey cross-town to the slums to see how "the other half" lived. In the twentieth century, social scientists such as William Julius Wilson concluded that poor urban communities were becoming more isolated as public transportation disappeared, jobs shifted to the suburbs, and neighbors with the means to do so moved out. In the twenty-first century, some have even argued that America is fast becoming two nations, one privileged and gated, the other confined by hopelessness or necessity. If you make the trek from the bus depot to the airport in any major American city, you might be tempted to say the same. Yet this separation is built on a lie.

Take a city like Orlando, whose most famous resident, Mickey Mouse, lives a life so ethereal you can't even tell where he lives. On the outskirts of Orlando lie two suburbs, Kissimmee and Celebration. Kissimmee is where my sister drops me off to catch the bus. This economically mixed community has its share of gates and golf courses, but it also hosts tattoo parlors, vocational schools, and the Old Town amusement park, which offers Disney World lower-priced competition.

In this winter of 2005, Kissimmee's bus station is ringed by boarded-up buildings condemned after the last hurricane.

The terminal itself amounts to a single room with a sheet-rocked office, one snack machine (empty), one soda machine (dead), and a "Bathroom Closed" sign that does nothing to deter passengers from rattling the locked handle in desperation. A smiling attendant in cornrows works the phones, too cheerful by far for someone who has to listen to eight hours of the simulated squeal of tires emanating from the video racing game in the corner.

With a sudden urge to evade this electronic version of chalk on a blackboard, I set out in search of coffee. I find myself in the kind of neighborhood where grandmothers bring their utility bills to storefront offices to save a few cents on postage. Sidewalks overgrown with grass lead me past ramshackle bungalows and wrench-strewn garages, until I finally reach a lightly stocked mini-mart with the requisite brew. How's business? I ask the Gujarati man behind the counter. Quiet, he reports. Better to sell more, but my wife says, with all the shootings, people shouldn't wish for too much excitement. On my way back to the station the bicycle shop has no post-hurricane "Danger Do Not Enter" sign posted, but it is out of business nonetheless.

Life in downtown Celebration couldn't be more different. Kissimmee's younger cousin is a planned community founded in 1994 that cultivates nostalgia and trades on its connections with Disney. Its business center features a clutch of boutique shops and restaurants, priced accordingly. Some estimates gauge its cost of living as 98 percent higher than the U.S. average. If designer ice-cream flavors are your answer to the Florida heat and money is no object, Celebration is the place to go.

In the Celebration Company's realty office, expensively produced promotional materials take the form of a "Memory Book" crafted to look like a scrapbook. "This is it," the manila pages proclaim in a font that mimics handwriting, "the hometown you've been searching for, a place where kids still ride their bikes to school." Every front porch has its rocking chair, it seems, but on the day I visit, not a soul is rocking. The streets are manicured, sedate, hedged with neo-Victorian bric-a-brac and picket fences. At the heart of the town lies an engaging appeal to a kind of neighborliness more often found in stable working-class communities. It's sweet. Needless to say, the intercity bus doesn't stop there.

Now while you might not be able to get there (Celebration) from here (the Kissimmee bus station), especially if upward mobility is your aim, there is another sense in which the two are inseparable. Every Celebration sits atop the labors and exclusions shouldered by its poorer cousins. There are no barn raisings in Celebration, after all, no neighborly cooperation to hammer together the timbers of the next house. Nostalgia only extends so far. That labor comes from elsewhere. The staff in Celebration's restaurants come, primarily, from elsewhere. The capital that finances the town's growth derives from profits sweated out elsewhere. There can be no greater intimacy. If you insist on thinking of "poor" and "rich" as different worlds, it can only be as one holding up the other.

Nor is this to say that everyone traveling poor through life is eager to give themselves over to a Celebration-style hoorah. To begin with, most of the people stabbing sushi with chopsticks in downtown Celebration look nothing like them. What's more, many riders would find the atmosphere insipid. Why should they trust "nice"? Generosity, yes. Acts of kindness, sometimes. Sweetness edging over into saccharine—not a chance. As the anthropologist Sidney Mintz famously observed, ever since sugarcane growers who used slave labor convinced a thirsty public that beverages needed improvement, sweetness has steeped itself in power.

Cash-strapped passengers on buses in the South never

considered directing me to Disney World's astronomically priced attractions. Riders who knew Orlando advised me to check out the rides at Old Town in Kissimmee for some fun. Not simply because Old Town was affordable or because they wanted to reclaim the lower-priced knockoff. People down there know how to have a good time, they explained. Try bungee jumping off the high tower. You'll love it.

No worries, dear reader. You can unclench your fists, because we aren't jumping off anything taller than a supposition. Our final journey through Tallahassee, Montgomery, Mobile, and Biloxi will be strictly earthbound. Even so, you will have to make decisions about whether to soar. For we're riding in the time of glitter and debt, bubbles masquerading as promises, and pledges long, long overdue.

The Back Is Where It's At

When I was a child we used to play a game called I Spy on long trips. The leader would call out, I spy! The rest of us shouted in chorus, What do you spy? By way of response, the leader would offer various clues: I spy ... something shining ... something hairy ... something metal ... something blue. We very seldom managed to guess the answer. As the motorized world scrolled past the windows, there wasn't much time to catch the vision reflected in the leader's eye. My parents loved I Spy because it kept us occupied. The shouting they could have done without.

What a game it would have been on the road to Tallahassee. What clues we could have invented to describe the Christian day care crammed into a shack, suburban screen porches larger than houses, cattle in their winter coats grazing at the side of the road, two suited and booted motorcycle cops who stop to pick up litter before setting up their speed trap, Wal-Mart Supercenters redux, Floras de Mayo out of Santo Domingo, rusting silos near the tracks in Ocala, a neon-purple dump truck in the left lane tricked out in chrome, the girl at the next rest stop who will hold open the door with fingernails that perfectly match the truck's side panels.

For a while we ride neck and neck on I-75 with two flatbed rigs that have huge sections of a brick storefront strapped vertically to the bed. As we run alongside, the scene through the eyes of the storefront's picture windows constantly changes. Microwave towers, time share resales, concrete ramps, scraps of wetlands, Guns 'n' Gold Top Dollar Pawn (offering "Cash Loans on Anything of Value") all slide by, perfectly framed.

I spy Chambers Farm Powwows. I spy the Po'Folks restaurant chain. I spy pine tree plantations laid out with what used to be called military precision, before the much-vaunted precision of "smart bombs" got called into question. Near Silver Springs we pass roadside stands piled high with fresh citrus, knowing the bus will never stop there on a noncorporate whim. Now doesn't that look good! Like children gazing through the windows of the world's healthiest candy shop, we dissolve into craving.

What goes on inside the vehicle is also fair game. What else do you spy? I spy...A terminally confused sister in a white knit cap who has received three conflicting sets of instructions about where she needs to transfer. A divorcee from New Jersey who's riding to Texas because she's afraid to fly, although she can't understand why, because she was never afraid as a child when she took the plane to the U.S. from Puerto Rico. An aspiring lab tech who's late for work because the last bus was full and couldn't take any more passengers. A high school student who's behind in her classes because her school has been evacuated so often due to hurricanes. A University of Florida student who has her hands full juggling a suitcase, a sleeping bag, an open chemistry textbook, and the knowledge that she's the only one from her African American high school class to have made it to college. A young Cubano who swears into his cell phone as he tries to negotiate a better price for car repairs. The guy behind me, very hip, who throws his head back and breaks into snores to wake the dead, though not himself of course. The driver, who announces at rest stops, Don't go wandering off, I ain't gonna come looking for you. And means it.

Through it all, Kambui is sketching. What begins as a patch of cross-hatching on a sheet of bond paper slowly turns into the shadow under Brother Malcolm's chin. Kambui works with the assurance that pen strokes demand, coaxing eyes, ears, and an intangible fire from the flat surface. When orange traffic cones force the bus over an asphalt ridge into a single lane, Kambui's graying dreadlocks sweep the page, but his hand never wavers. He puts the last touches on the portrait of Malcolm X just as we reach Tallahassee.

Kambui and I are the last people off the bus, so we exchange a few awkward words before we go. How do you do it? I ask. He looks up, almost. Do what? he says. Make these incredible drawings while the bus rolls and rattles along? Practice, I guess, the artist replies, in a voice two degrees quieter than soft-spoken. You get to different levels. I got a few levels to go. He shows me where he's signed each of his sketches. And that seems to be that.

In the depot snack bar, an Anglo guy with a ten-dollar bill in his hand inquires, How much is the chicken plate? Six dollars, the bored cashier tells him. How much is a hot dog? he wants to know. Two ninety-nine. What if I get the chicken with no coleslaw on the side? he asks. We're out of coleslaw. Well, what can I get instead? No substitutions, she says. How much will you give me off, then? he asks. Can't give nothing off, the cashier responds, it just be like that. You want the hot dog? He walks out with nothing.

Once I settle on a microwave burrito as the lesser of several evils on offer in the cafeteria line, my path crosses Kambui's again. He wants to know if I'm maybe interested in buying a sketch. A stack of drawings emerges from his duster. Besides the latest ten-by-twelve rendering of Malcolm X, there's Jimi Hendrix, Bob Marley, and a host of other black leaders. I ask Kambui how much he wants for one and he says five dollars. Four dollars would be fine, he adds, if that's all you got. Four dollars for a drawing by a man who has the kind of talent you can't go to school for.

Are those Buffalo Soldiers? I ask, noticing the small figures on horseback that race through Bob Marley's hair. That was the idea I was working with, yeah, Kambui says, meeting my eyes for the first time. You know that song? Kambui sings a few bars: "Stolen from Africa, brought to America." That's where I jump in: "Fighting on arrival, fighting for survival." I tell him how I used to work near Fort Huachuca in Arizona, where a lot of Buffalo Soldiers were stationed. When Kambui finds out I'm on my way to Montgomery to check out the new Rosa Parks Museum, he lights up. I wish you stayed in Tallahassee, he says, diving across the color line and coming up a bit surprised. I ain't got no problem with you!

There are people who tear through your life like a meteor and in the flash of connection you could swear you'll see them again, even though you know you probably won't. At the head of the line for the Alabama bus I turn around, both hands full, and nod goodbye to Kambui with my chin. He waves. He's been looking for me.

The practice of taking your politics onto the bus and taking the bus to a place where you can demonstrate your politics has a long and honorable history. Montgomery, Alabama, was not only the site of the 1955 Montgomery Bus Boycott that sparked the civil rights movement, but also a key destination for Freedom Riders who traveled by bus through the South to demand transportation equality. As Americans of many colors are fond of remarking, more than half a century after Rosa Parks refused to move to the back of the bus, a lot has changed. If you can scrape together the money for a ticket, you can sit wherever you want.

For the most part, the back remains the liveliest part of the bus and passengers sort themselves out accordingly. If you want to kick back with other black and brown folk or you want to escape the driver's scrutiny, the back is where it's at. If you're a church lady traveling with your little grandson and you'd rather he wait a few years to find out about the world, you'd best stay up front.

But change is not always an equalizer. In a speech at the University of California at Berkeley in 1963, Malcolm X put it this way: "Whenever you get on the bus or the subway or the streetcar and you have to use a token, that token is not the real thing but it is the substitute for the real thing. And wherever you have a token, you have a substitute. And wherever you have token integration, you don't have anything but a substitute for integration. There's no real integration anywhere in North America, North, South, East or West."[1] Certainly not when it comes to poverty.

Half a century after Rosa Parks refused that racist order to get back, a complicated mix of credit, inflation, lack of health insurance, low-paying jobs, neoliberal promises, and debt was making it harder and harder for poor people across the country to cope. Poverty stood ready to embrace even the middle classes, with a fervor that integrationists never would display. The statistical face of poverty in the United States might have been white, but that was primarily because white people still made up a majority of the population. Look at the numbers proportionally and the "other side" of the class divide shifted toward sepia, indigo, tan. Some of the very ones that the civil rights and La Raza movements had helped "move on up" were skidding toward a moment of reckoning.

Dothan, Alabama, is filled with original editions of the rambling wooden houses that inspired Celebration. To get to the center of town, you have to travel streets lined with billboards that offer loans against your next paycheck, loans in exchange for the title to your automobile, and express loans up to six hundred dollars secured by something akin to your firstborn child. People do what they can to help each other out. At the Dothan bus terminal, someone has scrawled "Free Clothes" on a sheet of construction paper and taped it to the plate-glass window above a rack made from a piece of old pipe. Shirts, mufflers, and jackets left behind by sleepy passengers flutter in the wind every time the door opens, there for the taking.

As we head to the northern part of the state, we step off into another climate zone. At 10:30 p.m. Montgomery is freezing. A pony-tailed white kid shivers at the gate. His vacation ended abruptly when his so-called best friend stole all his money, along with his Martin guitar. I packed for the tropics, he whines. Well, says the guy standing next to him, you are definitely headed in the wrong direction. At least you almost got a vacation! I fight my way through the glare of headlights along the five-lane highway that fronts the station until I find a one-star motel with discount rates. The family that owns the place has worked hard to produce touches of home. Handmade flowers decorate the lobby. In my room the door of the mini-refrigerator insists on swinging open, but it's nothing that can't be fixed with a trash can used as a wedge.

When morning comes I tackle the puzzle of how to get to

Montgomery. I'm *in* Montgomery, yes, but not the part that
any visitor would come to see. Of late the trend has been to
relocate bus terminals away from city centers to the no-man's-
land off expressways on the city's outskirts. This arrangement
is convenient for bus companies that need to stay on schedule, damned inconvenient for already struggling people who
have to pay to get a taxi into town.

A taxi it is, then. Before I seek out the museum, so new
that cab drivers don't yet know its location, I stop by the Dexter Avenue Baptist Church. That's where Dr. Martin Luther
King worked with the Montgomery Improvement Association to organize the bus boycott. Everything about the
church looks up, from the red brick walls that ascend the hill,
to the neatly painted stairway that rises to meet the front en-
trance, to the slatted windows in the white belfry. In the
church basement women from the congregation keep watch
over a collection of awards and memorabilia. Yet there is
something isolated about this onetime heart of a community. Courts and legislative offices surround the modest brick
building, including some of the very institutions of state that
tried to stifle the boycott.

Among the documents on display over at the Rosa Parks
Museum are memos from the mayor's office that proposed
various schemes to break the boycott. On the walls hang
grisly newspaper accounts of the bombing of Dr. King's residence at the parsonage, an attack by segregationists that
could easily have taken the lives of his family. A reproduction of Section 10 of the Montgomery City Code ("Separation of races—Required") grants bus operators the power "to
assign passengers seats on the vehicles under their charge in
such manner as to separate the white people from the negroes, where there are both white and negroes on the same
car; provided, however, that negro nurses having in charge

white children or sick or infirm white persons, may be assigned seats among white people." Section 11 continues, "Any
employee in charge of a bus operated in the city shall have the
powers of a police officer of the city while in actual charge of
any bus, for the purpose of carrying out the provisions of the
preceding section." The original police report of Rosa Parks's
arrest is there as well, indifferently typed onto a sheet of two-
hole-punched paper.

The most engaging exhibit is a room-length cutaway of a
Montgomery city bus. After a caretaker shuts the door behind me, the lights dim and the iconic scene of Ms. Parks's
stand is reenacted on tape. The slight sense of claustropho-
bia produced by the layout and the closed doors underscores
the threats emanating from the confined quarters of the bus,
as lamps silhouette figures in the various bus windows. It's
low tech but extremely effective.

I have one more mission before I head back. Somewhere
in town is the old Greyhound bus station. Although there
have been rumors that it may be turned into a museum to
honor the Freedom Riders, it's not listed in the phone directory and no one I approach on the street seems to remember
where it is. I resort to the tourist information counter at the
old train station, where a white woman in a fur coat who
hails from Selma doesn't even try to pinpoint it on the map.
She calls over an African American man about my age who
is pushing a broom across the floor. He would have been a
child during the freedom rides, a glimmer in his mama's eye
at the time of the boycott. He thinks he remembers the station, though, and gives me perfect directions.

The Freedom Rides tried to do for overland transport
what the boycott accomplished for city transportation.
There's almost nothing left to indicate the purpose of the
low-slung beige depot when I find it, just a rusting anchor for

what must have been the marquee and a historical plaque out front. Anyone who troubles to read the plaque will learn that when the Freedom Riders arrived in Montgomery on May 20, 1961, "their police escort disappeared, and an angry mob of over 200 Klan supporters attacked and injured them at the terminal." John Lewis, one of the Student Nonviolent Coordinating Committee (SNCC) members who led the ride, and later a U.S. congressman, described the bus they boarded as a symbol of freedom, the "freedom to travel as first-class American citizens."[2] Like the Dexter Avenue Baptist Church, the old Greyhound terminal, too, rests in the shadow of the state. Letters on the curved wall of the judiciary building at its back spell out "justice."

Freedom to travel is all well and good, but forty-four years after the Freedom Rides, it still doesn't come free. "When low-income people have completely run out of money, they just do not go places," writes Eric Mann in a collection called *Highway Robbery: Transportation Racism and New Routes to Equity.* "As such, their lives are reduced to 'home to work,' and they are denied the right to go to church, to visit family or friends, to attend cultural and educational programs, or even to look for better jobs."[3]

Back at my motel in the sprawling wasteland, I scrounge up dinner at a Taco Bell, where I order the "healthy" alternative, a taco salad. Not a bad source of nutrition if you load it up with jalapeño peppers, unless of course you eat the deep-fried shell, which is the tastiest part. An interracial couple sits playing rummy at one of the plastic tables, transforming their visit to the fast-food joint into an old-fashioned lingering after-dinner affair.

On the well-worn path beside the highway, I pass an African American man in battle fatigues. Just as he begins to drift out of range, he turns around to spare-change me. Do you have two dollars so I can buy a sandwich? he pleads. I need to eat! I just got back from Iraq.

When the snow parts on the ancient TV in my motel room, I discover that while I was on the Freedom Riders' trail I missed a gathering at the Jefferson Davis House. Apparently people "interested in the Confederacy" have come to Montgomery from miles away to celebrate Robert E. Lee's birthday. However, the reporter continues breathlessly, the event was marred by the theft of a "priceless painting" from the home. As the camera pulls back to cover this event to which everyone was at liberty to come, the faces shine white.

I wake up early and hike over to the depot to make the morning bus for Mobile. Inside the Travelers Grill, an arthritic black woman whose every move requires a cane is searching for water. You say twenty-five cents? Just for the cup? We also give you the ice, the young African American counter attendant replies respectfully. The ice is free. What if I leave the ice? she asks. Still twenty-five cents, he replies. Like the white man in the Tallahassee snack bar, she hobbles back out to the lobby, empty-handed.

This, then, is capitalism's solution to the segregated water fountain. There's no discrimination at the modern Montgomery terminal. In fact, there are no fountains at all!

Space is at a premium in the lobby, so the thirsty woman sits down at a table with a middle-aged stranger. This white man bursts into a story about all the trouble he's having with the company where he drives a truck. They don't pay him on time. They make him work hours he doesn't get paid for. He has no control over what they want him to haul. If it's toxic, so be it, he has to load it on the truck. Right now the company owes him three hundred dollars.

Three hundred dollars! the thirsty woman exclaims. That's

a lot of money! But if you don't fight for your rights, she adds, stamping her cane for emphasis, then that's it. Talking ain't doing you no good.

Take a Deep Breath

There's one stop where we all get off in the same place. That's death. As to the timing, no one can say. But there's plenty that can be said about the ways that living cash poor can lead to an unnecessarily early grave.

In 2003 the *New York Times* commissioned a series on class differences in the United States, later published as a book called *Class Matters*. One reporter, Janny Scott, followed three people who had heart attacks about the same time but who were very differently situated. The first, an architect who worked in midtown Manhattan, received instant angioplasty and excellent follow-up care. The second, a worker with a steady job at a utility company, ended up in a hospital that served some of Brooklyn's poorest neighborhoods. Doctors there could not perform angioplasty. The third, an immigrant who worked as a housekeeper, spent so many hours waiting for doctors and traveling to appointments by bus and train that the very process of seeking medical care put her system under stress. Her disability payments amounted to only half her low weekly salary and she soon reached the limits of the medication benefits afforded by her union health plan. Guess who was faring the best a year on? Then imagine how events unfold when the same constriction of blood vessels hits one of the 45 million people in the United States without any health care coverage at all.[4]

Like heart attacks, hurricanes don't discriminate on the face of it. The most powerful ones are equal-opportunity destroyers, gobbling up tarpaper shacks and three-floor Victorian mansions alike. It takes a combination of inequitably distributed wealth, bad public policy, and markets that recognize only profits to load the heaviest burdens of "natural" disasters onto those least equipped to bear them.

On this fine day in January, it's hard to imagine that only seven months from now, a massive hurricane called Katrina will tear through Mobile, decimate New Orleans, lay waste to housing in the area's Native American communities, and wipe the Biloxi, Mississippi, beachfront off the map. Who would have thought that authorities with so many resources at their disposal would leave people trapped in attics as the waters rose, then bar citizens from coming to their aid? Who would have thought that some officials would blame the residents themselves for their fate? Apparently it never occurred to them that a person could live so close to the edge that he would lack the money for transportation to leave the city, much less pay for a room at a hotel. Apparently it never occurred to them that the prisoners in orange jumpsuits who clung to girders to escape the waters were human beings in the state's care and thus their responsibility to evacuate.

In retrospect I will be haunted by the faces of my fellow passengers, many of whom are heading by bus to take up what they think will be ordinary lives in the Bayou's most beautiful city. In retrospect, the omens were there. All along the road from Montgomery to Mobile trees have snapped, torn away at the roots, and bent themselves into improbable shapes. Like the blue tarps scattered across roofs under repair in Orlando, these twisted saplings bear the signature of the last little storm.

Hurricanes are just a fact of life in these parts, comments the preacher riding next to me. We get used to it. I suppose we shouldn't. Someday the big one's gonna come.

The prophet-cum-preacher's whitening hair peeks out from beneath a cap embroidered with the name "Messiah Messengers®." He pulls out a business card, which identifies him as a pastor in the Full Gospel/Apostolic Church, Th.B., M.B.S., Ph.D., D.D. If you ever get to New Orleans and you need a place to stay, he says, call me. I'll drive out from the church and pick you up. We got enough folk living on the streets. He extends the same offer to everyone who boards. The motto on his card is taken from the Book of Jeremiah: "There is nothing too hard for thee."

The limited-service bus stop at Atmore, Alabama, turns out to be a Texaco Station run by the Poarch Band of Creek Indians. Following passage of the Indian Removal Act of 1830, the U.S. government marched most Muscogees to Oklahoma at bayonet point. With them went the ceremonial fires. The Poarch settlement here coalesced from some of the Muscogee families who stayed behind and managed to retain their lands near the Alabama River.

While the bus waits for passengers to materialize, a red Bamoco Disaster Response truck pulls up, but it's not on a mission on this cloudless morning. The driver is just searching for a place to unwrap his sandwich.

As we pull back onto the road, an adventuring man in his twenties named Antoine worries about how to tell a woman's age. He tries to keep his voice down because he knows the preacher is listening. Those young ones are the ones that spell trouble, he explains to the lady sitting next to him. I try to tell. Can you tell? This girl, she looked twenty-four, I swear. The way she held herself. That girl was fourteen! I ain't going to lie to you. And her father was a sheriff!

I told him I didn't know, Antoine continues. I didn't! Luckily her parents was cool with it. I would be in jail today, otherwise.

Antoine is working his way up to hitting on his seatmate, who has already made it clear that she has a daughter his age. "I don't mind" is his response. Tell me if I'm out of line, Antoine says, but know that I am persistent. I understand that no means no. I do. A woman might tell me no, but I persist. I like to play cat and mouse. I like the chase. You see, the mouse, it naturally runs when it sees the cat. But if the cat persists, eventually . . . Antoine laughs. So I know you told me no, he says. I do. But I might try again. That's just how I am. He gives the lady, who's listening now, his finest gap-toothed smile. Antoine, too, is headed for the coast.

We're on a long road that slopes down to the sea, where oil rigs, container ships, and Navy Seabees work the Gulf. Billboards urge us to get checked for colon cancer and to visit "America's Battleship," the USS *Alabama*. In the right lane a logging truck tailgates a cement mixer. The side of the road is littered with crosses where strangers have died in traffic accidents, but this we perceive as their particular misfortune.

Across the aisle Jamaal counsels a woman who wants to relocate to Mississippi that she needs to get herself situated first. Otherwise she'll come down here and get lost. Jobs, he says, are hard to come by. Not just in Mississippi, but in Louisiana, too. Without family, friends, and some planning, it will be hard for her to get hooked up.

Jamaal says he doesn't know what would have happened to him without his cousin. After he got put in the foster home, he got expelled from school for fighting. His cousin is the one who got the school to send him a tutor so he could get his papers. The school wanted to get rid of him so bad they graduated him a month early. But then he found out that to go to college he'd still need a GED, because they had tracked him into vocational education classes. These days, he says, he tries not to fight. He tries to find another way. Sometimes that means letting things work on his nerves until he almost can't stand it.

Jamaal believes in the importance of planning. Whenever he sees men getting ready to go to the clubs where he lives in New Orleans, he makes sure they take condoms with them. Because males and females, he says, once they get started, they get caught up and whatnot. They're not going to take care of it then. I don't mean everyone, he says, but your average males and females. So Jamaal buys condoms in bulk at the pharmacy, then sells them to the men he knows at cost. Sometimes somebody got to step in, Jamaal explains. People need that little push. There's a safe way to do everything.

Like building a levee, I would think later.

A sign welcomes us to Biloxi, Playground of the South. These white sand beaches have hosted a resort town in one form or another since the mid-nineteenth century. A second sign welcomes us to Biloxi, Home of Keesler Air Force Base. Biloxi is shrimp, crawfish, and festivals, says the driver. Biloxi is where they send new recruits to boot camp, says a rider. Biloxi is the one place in Mississippi that I would like to come back and spend some time in, says a man who was born here. Biloxi ain't nothing but a strip of casinos on the beach, says the woman ahead of me in disgust as we follow a concrete causeway into town. It's pretty, says a little girl with pigtails as we catch the first glint of sunlight off the bay.

On the small green near the bus station, protesters have erected a plywood sign. "Living the Lie," it says. To get the point, we have to wait until the bus turns the corner so we can read the other side: "No amount of yellow ribbons and flag waving justifies one dead American in Iraq."

The timing of the sign's appearance becomes clearer after I check into the last in a string of budget motels. On an overstuffed sofa in the lobby, the matriarch of the family that runs the place applauds as she watches George Bush make his way down Pennsylvania Avenue. It's Inauguration Day. At the break, the television station cuts to a group of New Orleans activists who have staged a jazz funeral, complete with brass band and a horse-drawn hearse containing a copy of the Patriot Act. Like Jamaal, the activists believe in planning. Their strategy is to mount a defense of civil liberties by burning the Patriot Act and scattering the ashes in the Mississippi River.

Outside the close quarters of the lobby, the beach is chilly and deserted. I walk past the pink-and-turquoise façade of Sharkshead Souvenir City, where shoppers have to negotiate the toothy jaws of a one-story-high Great White Shark before they can purchase their Mardi Gras sweatshirts, flip-flops, and support-our-troops magnets. I walk until I reach an unoccupied stretch of sand. On one side of me, a heron wades in the reeds. On the other, Humvees and Ford Explorers stream by.

I take a deep breath. My body enters the stream. This windswept spot offers one of the best places to do *qigong* that a person is likely to find on a bus trip. The heron watches as I coil into Single Whip, Flowing Motion, Wave Hands Like Clouds. All things passing.

In seven months' time, the hotel where I'm staying will be gone. Houses near the beachfront, turned into driftwood. Biloxi's casinos, unmoored. Sharkshead Souvenir City, obliterated. The poorest districts of New Orleans, submerged. Half the storefront churches in Orleans Parish, demolished. The Tunica-Biloxi tribe will open its convention center to refugees. Acupuncturists Without Borders will offer free treatment to survivors. The United Houma Nation will create a relief center to assist the eight thousand tribal members affected by the hurricane. Common Ground Collective will found a health clinic and organize residents in the Algiers neighborhood of New Orleans to clean up debris. The president will fly in and out of the city to make a television address.

I never found out what happened to Antoine, to the preacher, to the family that ran the hotel, or to Jamaal. The media did cover what happened to the Greyhound station in New Orleans. After the storm surge flooded local jails, authorities transformed the bus station into an impromptu prison camp. They trucked in portable toilets, strung chain-link fencing around the docks to create holding pens, and requisitioned the gift shop for the lawyers. When they finally opened the highways and reestablished train service, inter-city buses to New Orleans still did not run. The poorer you were, the harder it was to get out. The poorer you were, the harder it was to get back home.

There's one stop on the route where we all get off in the same place. That's death. But for some of us, it won't come on the day we land in an open-air jail or an underequipped hospital or a tax-starved neighborhood with a badly main-tained levee. And that's the difference.

Vietnam Thirty Plus

Bo lifts up his arm and sniffs. Scrunches up his face. I need a shower! he shouts. To the people farther up in the coach who turn around, he explains how it is: I feel like that man in the commercial. The one who raises his arm and every-body around him passes out. This whole bus could pass out! They ought to have showers. Or just rig up a hose at the rest stop. Anybody been on the bus for more than one day, take him out and hose him off!

With his red nylon do-rag, twenty-four-carat smile, and Atlanta Braves jersey unbuttoned down the front, Bo cuts a memorable figure. He's been on the bus since Texas. If he makes it to Florida, which at the moment seems like a mythical prospect, he'll start a new job in advertising that his mother helped him get. Later I find out that "advertising" means making cold calls to solicit classified ads for a newspaper.

Most people tend to take me for African American, Bo explains. Bet you thought that, too. They don't realize I'm Creole. Even where I come up in St. Louis, people call us "country." Maybe because my family still holds to their Creole ways. Eating rice and beans, rice and beans up there in the city! Most of my family is yellow. I got one aunt in Hawaii, born over there. She's from the beautiful side of the family. Good hair and those green eyes. I want to visit her someday if I can get the money. I'm the darkest one. They say I take after my grandfather.

Bo says his mother doesn't like it when he loafs. I tease him: What mother does? I tried to tell her I want to travel, he says, see things while I'm young. She doesn't understand that I'm a responsible person. I don't even drink. So she got me the job. I guess I'm too much like her. Bull-headed. That's why we don't get along.

Among the people who turn around to listen to Bo's lament is Lanh. You could think of Lanh as just another Vietnamese guy with spiky red-tipped hair, a form-fitting black leather jacket, and a cigarette habit. (He's from California, explained the old white lady who lit up with us outside the Biloxi station, nodding knowingly.) Or you could think of him as a man who has traveled so long he has almost merged with the road.

Like Bo, Lanh is traveling to Florida for work his family

has arranged for him. He'll be painting nails, as he puts it, while he lives in quarters provided by his boss. But the rest of Lanh's journey trumps anything the bus has to offer. He has been in this country seven years. Before that, he spent a lifetime in a refugee camp in Thailand. (Waiting, waiting, waiting? I conjecture. Yes! he replies, eyes alight with the unexpected pleasure of understanding.) Before that, there was the leaky boat on which his family staked their lives when they fled Vietnam.

Lanh and I start talking because the announcements coming over the microphone at the various stations on the route are hard for him to understand. Thirty-minute break until eleven o'clock or break until eleven-thirty? he asks me in confusion. I explain that we need to be back on the bus by eleven o'clock. I follow you, he says.

When Lanh sits, his left leg twists in such an improbable way that he must be wearing an artificial limb. Perhaps he lost a leg to one of the 300,000 tons of explosives left behind in Vietnam when the fighting officially ended. But we don't know each other well enough to have that conversation, even on the strength of anonymity. Amidst the din of the camp, Lanh says he grew up with a particular kind of silence. His parents didn't like to talk about their experiences during the war.

When Bo announces to the entire bus that he's thinking about joining the air force like his Moms did back in the day, Lanh just listens. If I join up, Bo explains, I can see more things. From his bag he extracts a multicolored notebook that he made himself from construction paper. Someone has written "Life Science" on the cover in magic marker. What do you use that for? I ask, curious. Bo shows me some of his notes and sketches. There's a poem he's written. A drawing of an insect I've never seen before. The penciled contours of what looks to be a bus station ceiling. A paragraph of reflections on the neighborhood where he grew up. I guess I'm just a nerd, he confesses. I like to learn things.

Bo is indeed a man of questions. On the trail of a contradiction, he won't quit. We discover as much when the driver suddenly pulls the bus over to the side of the road and comes clear down the aisle to announce in excessively formal diction that he knows somebody is smoking in the bathroom. Smoking will not be tolerated, he announces. I'm not going to warn you a second time. If I catch you, you will be put off this bus.

Understand that passengers don't usually rat out other passengers for breaking the company rules. We all know that this latest lecture pertains to the hard-living chain-smoking white veteran seated just ahead of us who sips greedily from a bottle of liquor-laced Pepsi. His curly gray hair shows streaks of its original blonde. I don't smell no smoke, people mutter just loud enough to provide The Vet with covering fire. I don't like this driver, either, they whisper to one another. He's rude! That's when Bo makes his contribution. The sign up there says "Safe–Reliable–Courteous," he points out to the driver. Let's see some courteous now!

After that The Vet decides to introduce himself to Bo. He wants to caution him against joining the air force. 'Nam, he says, was a helluva place for a person to get stuck in. Not much of an adventure for the ones who didn't make it back.

When you set out, The Vet reminisces, they issued you an eighty-pound rucksack. Reconnaissance mission, you know. Then I was young, I could lift eighty pounds. They don't tell you what to do when those eighty pounds of supplies run out and you're sixty miles from where you need to get back to. In Vietnam we cut off tree bark and sucked on it. Ate rats to survive.

Lanh listens avidly to the conversation, his leg still tucked into that impossible position. He almost speaks but thinks better of it.

When The Vet gets to the part about the tree bark, Bo nods. My uncles told me stories like that, he says. They had to eat cockroaches, too.

All the slurring disappears from the older man's voice as he repeats his advice: Don't go. I like you, he explains to Bo. You're friendly. That's why I tell you all this. Be a shame for you to die young.

I always talk but I'm not always friendly, warns Bo with that winning smile. The Vet turns around then and Bo turns to face the window so the tag on his do-rag shows. Made in Vietnam, it says.

Snap! Judgments

From Mobile to Pensacola I move back a seat so Bo can lie down to get some shut-eye. After Pensacola, though, we are really in for a ride. A huge influx of passengers streams through the folding door at the front; the back of the bus is bursting at the seams. We're sitting in the toilet! laughs a grandmotherly Latina as she finally finds a place. Nice while it lasted, sighs the kind-faced woman across from me as she pulls her little girl out of the aisle to safety. The two are on their way to a funeral in South Carolina.

The last seat is taken by a young man who draws attention because he's speaking a language most of us haven't heard before. What's that? asks Bo, who struggles to get upright. It's Portuguese, the newcomer explains. I been in Brazil. My father's African American and my mother's Brazilian. I can speak Portuguese, Spanish, and Arabic. Picked up some Arabic in Saudi Arabia when my father went there to work. Didn't think I'd get back here. We got caught in that first Gulf War.

Bilingual, huh, says Bo. I respect that. It's like you got your own code. Guess you can say whatever you want about the rest of us on this bus. We'll never know! He laughs. Me, I got enough trouble with English!

The little girl starts pestering Brazil about what South America is like. Are there lots of snakes like you see on TV? How big are they? Bo testifies that he saw one snake on a documentary that was three feet long. Oh, that's a baby, says Brazil. But it's not like there are snakes on every street corner. Maybe if you went from here to way over there by those bushes, you could find some, he says, pointing to the scrappy forest that lines the highway. But that's not what you'd do. You'd follow the road like we are now, right into the next town, and then you wouldn't have to deal with no snake.

I'll tell you what they do have, Brazil continues. They got the best carnival in the world. New Orleans and Mobile can't touch it. What about Amazons? Bo wants to know. Amazons?!? Brazil snorts. You know, Bo says, those hard-ass women who can fight. Oh, says Brazil, you must be thinking about the river. The Amazon River. But some of those women from the Indian villages can fight pretty good. They're really talented. You definitely wouldn't want to mess with them.

After a little give-and-take about capoeira, the Brazilian martial art that slaves created to resist oppression and generally have a good time, the topic drifts toward the upcoming Super Bowl. Who do you like? Aw, I thought we were gonna hear more about Brazil! objects the funeral-bound woman with the kind face at the first mention of football. I don't know nothing about sports!

That's because you don't have testosterone, Brazil explains in all seriousness. Sports is a testosterone thing. Bo tells Brazil he better check that. Look at her! he says, pointing to my Chicago Bears T-shirt. *She* likes sports! As is his way, he savors the contradiction. Everybody stops for that infinitesimal second that says Brazil's theory has been blown out of the water, most definitely.

Now we're talking sports, but we're also talking politics. What do you think about the money those players get? They make more in a day than us poor folks make in a year! So the funeral-bound woman has something to say about sports after all.

I don't mind if they make that kind of money, long as they give some back, says Bo, rubbing his sleepy eyes. Look how some of them helped people after the tsunami. Look how some of them help the youth, the minority youth. There's a lot of poor white ones need help, too.

Same with musicians. You don't like Puff Daddy, Bo says to Brazil, but I'll tell you what: Puff Daddy gave money for Africa. He hooked up with Sister Souljah to run that place of his [Daddy's House Social Programs]. He wants to build confidence. How can you not like that?

P. Diddy only gives money to the community when he's in trouble with the law, Brazil objects. He does it to make himself look good.

But he *does* it, says Bo. Same with R. Kelly. Let them make their money. What, you'd rather have them working for Disney for $6.50 an hour like her sister? he adds, pointing at me again. That's slave wages! This ain't no slavery times. I would never work for that. Can't pay no bills with that.

No indeed, I think to myself. Six-fifty per hour works out to $13,520 per year. Where was $13,520 going to land a person in a major North American city when rent averages over $1,000 per month?

Bo persists. What I'm trying to say is, we need people in a position to build the community. You say being in Saudi Arabia during the war was the worst years of your life, right? Well, there's a war on here. Where I come up, in St. Louis, that's a war zone, pure and simple.

How about Detroit? Brazil responds. I hear things are bad in Detroit. Bo agrees. St. Louis and Detroit have a lot in common. They're neck and neck. He knows the homicide figures for each town and states them. That's a war, he insists. Anybody try to do something about that, I respect.

Tell me about it, says Brazil. Before I left, I got stopped in Harlem for wearing red. You name me a color, says Bo, I can tell you a gang, associate it to a gang. But when they challenge you, you have to know how to answer them. I tell them I ain't representing nothing by it. Just wearing what I want to wear. A person's got to wear clothes! But like I told you: That's a war zone, pure and simple. Anybody try to do something about that, I respect.

And what would it mean, in the broadest sense, to do something about it? In his book, *Street Wars: Gangs and the Future of Violence,* Tom Hayden requests middle-class readers to ask themselves a simple question: "If every homeboy and homegirl removed their tattoos, stripped off their jewelry, apologized to police and parents, made reparations to their victims, and showed up for work, would this country be ready to hire them at decent wages, accept them as equals, and include them as citizens with full rights to vote, run for office, and serve on juries? Or does the perpetual war on gangs reflect what we really want?"[5] Bo likes his tattoos, though he doesn't roll with any gang. And he thinks any fool knows the answer.

Let's talk about something else, the funeral-bound woman suggests. Something positive. Puff Daddy, he's positive, Bo maintains. Something else, the woman repeats firmly. Okay, says Brazil. What's up with all these girls being named Shanequa, Shanunu...? Why can't their parents be more creative?

No, you're wrong, man, says Bo. Why are you always so quick to judge? That *is* creative. Think about it. Each of those names alone has fourteen different ways to spell it. This world being what it is, you got to think to survive.

Lovebug

You talking about St. Louis, I got a St. Louis story for you, says one of the newcomers. Tell your little girl to shut her ears, though, he adds, turning to the funeral-bound woman. This story is for adults only.

All right, then. One time when I was on the bus to Chicago, you won't believe what happened. I'll tell you, but you won't believe it.

I thought this was going to be a St. Louis story, interrupts the funeral-bound woman.

Wait, he says. Wait.

These ones in the back of the bus, he says, they were going at it. Usually you got some that will sneak a smoke, but these two were *doing it* right there! You know what I mean. The way it got out, this grandmother was taking her grandson to the bathroom and she saw. She dragged her little grandson back toward the front by his arm, just about pulled it out of the socket, stuck him back in his seat, and went up to the driver.

"You got to pull this bus over," she says. "Why? What's the matter?" the driver asks. "I ain't gonna tell you. Go back and see for yourself." So the driver pulls the bus over and goes to the back. The whole bus is turning around now, looking around, and them two are *still* at it! Even the driver doesn't know what to say. Finally he says, "Y'all got to get off." So to speak! And he puts them off in St. Louis, bags and all, right in front of a grocery store.

How did they ever manage it? the funeral-bound woman asks. There's not much room back there!

That's what I said! the newcomer agrees. And the bad thing is, I don't think they even knew each other before they got on the bus. Because she was riding way before he got on.

Oh my goodness! That's just wrong!

Mm-hmm. Mm-hmm.

Now I believe in courting a woman, declares Brazil. I took my girlfriend to a nice dinner in New York at the Olive Garden. A hundred and twenty dollars, bring me your best wine. We split a bottle of Sutter Home. Then a ride in a horse-drawn carriage past Rockefeller Center, with that velvet blanket pulled up. Spare no expense. Not if you really love somebody.

She said she liked it, Brazil continues, but it turned out she liked different things. Dancing. See, I don't like clubs. You spend all that time getting ready to go out, all that noise and tension. I'd rather sit home, watch a good movie.

Uh-uh, not me, says Bo. Maybe I'm a little bit roughneck, but I rather go to the clubs. Get outside the house. Go to a museum, learn something. Like I said, I ain't *had* a real relationship, but if I did, I'd be looking for a woman like that!

Wouldn't you rather get one of those really soft blankets and curl up on the couch? Brazil asks. What do you call those? He looks around, but no one can help him find the word. You know, Brazil prompts, those ones that cost around three hundred dollars. Three hundred dollars, the funeral-bound woman exclaims, and you use that to cover up! I'd put that on my wall.

Well, Brazil continues, liking different things wasn't the only problem. My woman wouldn't get a job. Just kept living off me. She keeps saying she will but she never does. Now she's disappeared on me again. I heard she was down here in Florida so I came to try to find her. But I'm not in love with her no more.

Ooh, says Bo, I don't ever want to be no gigolo. But that ain't right. You work. She should work.

On this point there's general agreement. Mm-hmm. Mm-hmm.

I know how you can get her back, Bo offers. Make a whole lot of money! That'll get this one back for sure. Brazil explains that he can't. He's already spent all his money on her. Gone into debt, too. That's why she moved on.

The way I see it, Brazil adds, that girl just lost me three thousand dollars. How'd she do that? the funeral-bound woman wants to know. That's how much it cost for my plane ticket, Brazil explains. I went all the way to South America to meet her and she never even showed up.

Three thousand bucks! Bo doesn't understand how that can be. Where's she at, he asks, the end of the earth? I met a guy from Thailand and it only cost him twelve hundred dollars to get there.

Last-minute tickets, Brazil explains. That's how they do you. I had to borrow it. Gonna take me forever to pay it back.

The next rest stop offers bottled water for $1.49 and a bit of consolation for the lovelorn. Outside the bus a group of us are hanging around waiting for the driver when a fly dive-bombs Bo. That's a lovebug! says one of the passengers. Almanacs describe the lovebug variously as a pest and as a nuisance to motorists in the South, but for us it's an invitation to a game.

We pull back into a circle. Hey, look at you, you got the lovebug! The little fly lands on one rider after another, then bounces off a man who diagnoses himself as "just heartless, I guess!" After that a white guy in a muscle shirt offers to step on the bug. Ooh, observes the funeral-bound woman, you *really* heartless! Look at him! Step on it and grind it, too! Well, the man admits, I've never been lucky in love.

Brazil has to change buses here, but before he goes, he treats the circle to a hip-hop-inspired electronica performance, using his voice to create the lyrics, all the instruments, and the mike. He finishes to a round of applause, but there's one more chorus left:

> Bo: You still in love with her, huh?
> Brazil: No, I'm not.
> Bo: Yes, you is.
> Brazil: No, I'm not.
> Bo: Yes, you is.
> Brazil: Can you see into another person's heart?
> Bo: I can see you just spent three thousand dollars!

Another Get-Poor-Quick Scheme

The Vet is still riding. Still drinking, too. I'm a shrimper, he says to me by way of introduction. A damn good shrimper. But my brother, he's not so good. He sunk my boat. I'm going to Florida to see if I can raise it. Only I'm broke.

None of the rest of us knows what it costs to raise a boat, but it must cost real money. As The Vet gets more emotional, thinking about what he's lost, his words start to blur. Shee, I'm gonna come into shum money. From my cuzza. My cousin, he's rich. I'm going to shtee...steal it from him.

This declaration evokes nervous giggles and averted eyes in a way that the earlier conversation about sex would never have done. The Vet shakes his head as though to clear it. Shee, I'm what you call a functional alcoholic. I drink, but I function. Damn good on a shrimp boat. Damn good.

Then he goes back to comparing notes with the white guy in fatigues sitting next to him on the best cities in which to be homeless. Honolulu emerges as the winner, hands down, but it's too hard to get there.

When it comes to prosperity, the line between dreaming and scheming can be a fine one. In this regard the very poor and the very rich have a lot in common. Where they generally part ways is in the penalty if they're caught. Although there have been a few high-profile exceptions, such as the fraud conviction of officers associated with the bankrupt energy corporation Enron, North American jails are not peopled in the main by executives.

What's also clear is how hard it is for such dream-schemes to work on the margins of the economy. Forget about the drinking problem. Forget about stealing. Forget about the cousin. Suppose you want to run your own shrimp boat, but you've lost at life's little game of roulette and the road has become your home. (It doesn't have to be a shrimp boat, of course. Many are the times a rider with a creative bent has taken me aside to tell me that things are going to change because she just got the papers to patent her idea which, for reasons of security, she can't tell me. But let's stick with the shrimp boat for the sake of argument.) What are your options?

Well, you could hire onto a boat and work your way up. However, that approach would require an upward mobility ladder in a field already shown to be swarming with snakes, plus wages sufficient to allow for savings, plus a way to cover up the gap. By the gap, I mean the one Barbara Ehrenreich has in mind when she writes about her experience looking for employment with an "incomplete" resume:

> One thing I've learned, though: a Gap of any kind, for any purpose—child raising, caring for an elderly parent, recovering from an illness, or even consulting—is unforgivable. If you haven't spent every moment of your life making money for somebody else, you can forget about getting a job.[6]

As for wages, this is America, where real wages for low-income workers have declined during recent periods of "economic growth," the personal savings rate turned negative in 2005, and policy makers continue to talk themselves silly trying to figure out why.

Alternatively, you could try borrowing to make payments on that boat. But even in the frothiest economy built atop low-documentation loans, someone who lacks an address to receive papers is unlikely to be trusted by a banker. That leaves you the option of arranging a loan through the informal economy, which generally commands a higher price that will disadvantage a business and expose the borrower to all manner of unmannerly modes of collection.

If you somehow get your entrepreneurial dream-scheme off the ground, it can just as easily further impoverish you as improve your prospects. The problems are intrinsic to the way the economy runs and the way you are situated, even if you are a motivated, practical person with good financial sense. As for the skinny white kid in Pensacola wearing the motorcycle T-shirt who's planning to start a radio station that plays only the music he likes with no advertising, you can imagine what will happen to him.

The most devious get-rich-quick schemes are hatched not by people who need the money, but by people who have realized that money is to be made off the backs of those who are already financially struggling. If you don't have the ready cash to buy your kids a desk where they can do their homework, don't worry. Your local rent-to-own shop has a payment plan for you. And what a plan! You could end up paying three or four times what the desk is worth, assuming the repossessors don't cart it off first. If you don't have the cash for a prepaid phone card, much less a mobile phone, don't despair. Take a look at the envelope that shelters your bus ticket. The celebrity Mr. T, pictured with five thick gold chains around his neck, has a bright idea: Call collect. "I pity the fool who don't use 1-800-COLLECT," runs his pitch, above the slogan "Save a Buck or Two." Let somebody else pay, at a relatively exorbitant rate. Of course, she may turn out to be your mother.

A similar financial strategy governs the siphoning of money from poor communities through overpriced barrio stores, predatory lending, and fees tacked onto money transfers. (Western Union, which even the business magazine *Forbes* perceives as targeting poor and undocumented immigrants, also regularly advertises on bus ticket envelopes.) Some money transfer services charge the equivalent of a day's wages for transactions that cost less than ten dollars to process. If a woman has to go to a check-cashing outlet because she has no bank account, right here in the state of Florida she can have 4 percent of already survival-level wages deducted for the privilege of accessing her own paycheck. Subprime loans marketed to the poor typically carry interest rates that exceed both the going market rate and the borrower's ability to pay. Yet studies by independent rating agencies such as Standard & Poor's have shown that more than half of borrowers sold subprime loans would have qualified for A or A- prime-quality loans at rates they could have better afforded.[7] These are old tactics, but no less diminishing on the replay.

If the poor are always with you, it is mainly because they are made so. What enriches one tends to impoverish another in an economy that generates more and more inequality. Speaking of the contemporary form of corporate profits, Beth Shulman, the author of *The Betrayal of Work,* concludes that "whatever one thought of America's welfare poor, few people were making money off them. The same cannot be said of our new working poor."[8] Miserly paychecks, workplace injuries, two families to a room, extra hours of uncompensated labor, malnourished children, utilities shut off, full-time jobs without health plans, meals skipped to make ends meet. It's a nineteenth-century story dressed up in twenty-first-century progress. Bob Butler, a knife sharpener interviewed by Shulman who worked at a poultry plant in Albertville, Alabama, put it another way: "You'd be surprised what that one little piece of chicken you're going to eat this Sunday has cost these people."[9]

Arguably more devious still are the schemes that are not schemes at all, but the effects of economic developments and social policies that hit poor people harder than most. The so-called wave of liquidity that swept the globe while I was riding the bus, for example, gave rise to inflation in many parts of the world. Asset inflation sent first stocks and then house prices soaring in the United States. That form of inflation generally leads to widening inequality, because it benefits owners of the assets in question at a time when many people don't own much to speak of. If labor is your main asset, you're likely to experience asset stripping under such conditions, because once an increasing money supply translates into higher prices in the stores, wages seldom if ever keep up with it. "One good thing about inflation," observes a character in the comic strip *Feather* wryly, "is that the money you don't have isn't worth as much as it used to be."[10]

If labor is your main asset, though, better not get sick. Illness is currently one of the leading contributors to household bankruptcy in the United States. It can bust you down to poverty in a heartbeat. Many people in the United States will tell you that this is due to "the high cost of health care," but many other countries take better care of their residents' health with fewer resources. Employers also tend to be far less tolerant of lateness and absences by low-income than professional employees, however diligently or cavalierly each may work. When you run a floor polisher or clean hotel rooms for a living, your daughter's chicken pox can lose you your job.

It's not hard to understand how a person could end up without a roof over his head under these circumstances. Even shrimpers who own their own rigs have been "slipping away" due to a combination of rising diesel prices, rising ice prices, and low-priced imported shrimp, according to Mike Brainard of the Mississippi Department of Marine Resources.[11] In the best of all possible neoliberal worlds, if The Vet had managed to get his hands on a boat, Hurricane Katrina probably would have put paid to his dream. Commercial shrimp licenses to local fishermen were down by 50 percent a year after the storm, with only a few processing plants open to buy the catch. Federal disaster relief legislation never appropriated money to rebuild the harbors.

At our rest stop in Pensacola, a toddler races around the convenience store picking up little cellophane packets of cookies, candies, and biscuits. I want that, I want that, I want that, chants the three-year-old. Mothers are often more practiced than politicians at the timely intervention. Put that back, we can't afford it, his mama says as he reaches for a plastic Spider-Man. You need a new shirt and that costs money. When her little man starts to beg and whine, she puts her foot down. Clothes is more important than games, she explains. You can't wear games. And you can't run around naked.

But all the personal fiscal discipline in the world cannot pull something like affordable housing out of a hat. For that kind of magic, people need to pull together. After Katrina hit, even Mr. T would lay off the bling, reasoning that "it would be a sin against my God for me to wear all that gold again because I spend a lot of time with the less fortunate . . . If you're not going to go down there [to the Gulf] with a check and a hammer and a nail to help the people, don't go down there."[12]

Of course, many people were having a hard time paying the rent here, down there, and everywhere long before the wind whipped up. The reasons were not idiosyncratic and could not be ameliorated by charity or good intentions. Housing in the United States had never before taken such a big bite out of household budgets. The government, which could have done more to assist low-income families, had a hand in creating disparities. In 2001 a minor scandal rocked Washington when it was revealed that 44 percent of Internal Revenue Service audits targeted poor taxpayers who claimed the Earned Income Tax Credit.[13] In the year Katrina hit, federal tax breaks and other incentives subsidized homeowners to the tune of $122 billion, while rent payments remained non–tax deductible and new public housing starts ground to a standstill. According to research by the Western Regional Advocacy Project, the rise of mass homelessness has correlated with cuts to federal housing programs.

One day while I was traveling down a long stretch of desert highway, a woman told me a story. When she was living back east, she set aside a little bit of cash every day for her rent. After she collected enough, she put it somewhere in the house in an envelope for safekeeping. Rent was due at the beginning of the month.

March 1 came and went. No matter how hard the woman looked, she couldn't find the envelope. Friends, neighbors, and relatives banded together to turn the house upside down looking for the money, but it was nowhere to be found.

The woman was in despair. Where could she go for a loan? Her credit score had plummeted since the time the utility company cut off her electricity after she missed work because her car broke down. She didn't think she had enough of value to pawn to make a difference. Then one of the searchers ordered a pizza, conferred with the others, and announced that her hastily assembled collective of well-wishers had decided to pitch in to help her family make rent. I'll never forget it, she said.

This is a kind of solidarity both touching and effective, in its circumscribed way. For it to work, people have to be rooted enough to have created some sense of community. That can be difficult at a time when so many people relocate in pursuit of employment. Even then, if the same woman had had problems paying the rent come April, it was unlikely that her well-wishers could have ponied up the cash for a second month in a row.

That's why so many grassroots organizations have worked to change the conditions that put people in the position of living paycheck to paycheck in the first place. (Or scraping by with no paycheck at all.) Broad-based coalitions like the one described by the late Senator Paul Wellstone in his book *How the Rural Poor Got Power* campaign for livable wages, train mothers to deal with bureaucracies, field candidates for the local housing authority, and fight repressive initiatives such as the Department of Housing and Urban Development's proposal to institute a homeless tracking system. It's not easy. As Robert Coles put it in his introduction to Wellstone's book, the work builds on "small victories amid continual resistance and frequent setbacks."[14]

Three months after the search, the woman who lost her rent money reached for something on top of the old coal bin in her basement and found the envelope, covered with coal dust. I wonder whose pockets that money is lining now.

The Borrowed Time Club

The year I turned seven, my Grandma Erna and her older sister Elsie became card-carrying members of the Borrowed Time Club. Every week they met with other seniors to play cards and trade gossip in the basements of churches and VFW halls that were themselves borrowed for the occasion. Their youngest sister, Irene, though retired, would have nothing to do with it. She found the news thrown down with the pinochle hands disturbing. Too much of it centered on recent finds in the obituaries.

Did you hear about Rose?

Yes, and in her nightgown, too!

Poor woman. It's a shame.

Well, we should have seen it coming. She's had cancer for years.

Not for my aunt Irene the macabre humor of a club whose very name insisted on drawing attention to the end of the line. Call it irrational exuberance. She was never one to step willingly off the coach.

Borrowed time is precisely what the United States has been spending. In the obvious, most monetized sense, the nation's wealth has rested on an ever-expanding edifice of credit and debt whose soundness is open to debate. In the obvious, most intimate sense, the nation's wealth rests in its people, who have been living poor and living poorer, unless they belong to the tiny elite.

By 2005 the official poverty rate had risen for four years in a row. When it came to living conditions, the headlines had not changed much since I started taking the bus. If anything, they had become more worrisome: "Statistics Aside, Many Feel Pinch of Daily Costs." "Mayors Say Requests for Food and Shelter Are Up." "Area Housing Boom Drives Out Mobile Homes." "Looking for Help: Study Finds Big Need for Extended Jobless Benefits." "As Bills Mount, Debts on Homes Rise for Elderly." "Retirement Turns into a Rest Stop as Benefits Dwindle." "More U.S. Families Hungry or Too Poor to Eat." "Las Vegas Makes It Illegal to Feed Homeless in Parks." "Did Willfully and Unlawfully Provide Food."

Seniors were gambling against a future by taking loans against their houses. Workers were borrowing from their health to take second and third jobs. Parents were borrowing from their children by despoiling the land in the name of employment. Leaders were borrowing from who knows where to fund an exorbitantly priced war. Borrowers caught up in a mortgage lending panic were beginning to find out what happens when life forecloses on debts accrued. Governments were trading on the patience of their constituents as they failed to reverse rising inequality.

On the bus people have their own forms of augury. Rather than believe what you read in the papers, one driver suggested, anybody who wants to understand finance should visit the Embarcadero in San Francisco. At one end of Market Street, he explained, there's a business center. You've got your office workers, street entertainers, great jazz. Go a little further down and you've got your druggies, your homeless. (Guess that's what happens to business people when they fail! he laughed.) Travel the length of Market Street and you've got a barometer of the economy. The politicians may tell you times are good, but why not go down there and judge for yourself?

Near Ocala, Florida, next to a rundown trailer park, we pass a tavern that used to be called Amanda's. Weathered plywood hangs from the windows like drunken shutters. In this country you know things are tough, The Vet observes, when even the bars can't make it.

Sandra's read on the state of the nation overtakes us in Marianna, Florida, a place so small that a citified rider describes it as "nowhere in the middle of nowhere." But of course everybody's nowhere is somewhere to somebody else. Sandra and her husband live out in the country on their own "eighty-eight" (that's eighty-eight acres, for the uninitiated). They keep hunting dogs for protection, although Sandra doesn't really like hunting unless it's done because a person needs to eat. These days, she says, too often that's not the way it's done.

One morning Sandra walked down to the end of her road to find three deer propped up against the gate in different poses. Three dead deer sitting in a row. One had its hooves over its mouth. One had its hooves over its ears. The last one had its hooves over its eyes. See no evil, hear no evil, is that what you call it? Somebody's idea of a joke, she says. Now what kind of person does that?

And do you know what the worst thing is? Sandra asks the rest of us. Whoever killed those deer didn't use one shred of meat. What with all these people going hungry!

Hear no evil. Speak no evil. If statistics alone could do the job of redressing indifference and inequality, we'd all have joined hands and be singing the third chorus of "Kumbayah" by now. It's well established that in 2003 there were almost a million black children living in households in the United States with after-tax earnings less than half the paltry government-established poverty rate. A million. These are numbers for children, mind you, the ones with no boots yet to fill, much less bootstraps to pull themselves up by. Under these circumstances, does it make any sense to hope for the best and just keep on riding?

Check around you in the overhead racks for anything you may have forgotten. A sense of responsibility, perhaps. A floor under wages that keeps pace with inflation. Release from the workhouse economy. Protections for collective bargaining. Freedom to move. Freedom to grasp the landscape of grass and sky in a box of beads. Freedom to notice the amethyst in the wings of the songbird when it lights on the dumpster. A kind of wisdom that will always trump money when it comes to a better life. The debt that all bootstraps owe to the tanner, the cobbler, and the cow. Who really travels alone?

A person never gets used to bad treatment. Nor should she. But in the telling of the stories, in the determination that something must be done, in the moments of solidarity forged with Bo and Marcelina, Too-Tired and The Taker, Dolores and Kambui, there's something else that happens then. Call it *sastimos*. Well-being. Happiness. If you try to hang on to it, it dissolves. To find it, you have to pass through.

You got a long ways to go? Always. How far you riding? To the end.

On his first foray into New York City, the white boy sitting across from me complained, Where is it? I don't see it! See what? asked his friend. The Statue of Liberty, replied the first, where's it at? The two peered out the rain-streaked bus windows as if their lives depended on it, and perhaps they did.

It's got to be around here somewhere, his friend admonished. Keep looking. Anyway, it's not the Statue of "Liberty." Why do you call it that? It's the Statue of Trade!

Really? exclaimed the first child, green eyes widening. When did they change it? They didn't change it, stupid, insisted his friend, with a confidence born of youth and a bit more opportunity than most. It's always been that way!

How fitting that Lady Liberty should appear draped in capital to a generation raised on economic bubbles. Time is short. When people get arrested for giving sandwiches to the needy in a public park, there's a famine in the land of a kind that can't be solved with food. But what will it take to see it?

Acknowledgments

There are debts that cannot be counted and among them are the many intangibles that contribute to the writing of a book. This project was a lifetime in the making, seven years in the traveling, and four years in the crafting of a page. For sustenance of all kinds over the course of it, thanks go to my parents, Darlene Weingand and Wayne Weston; my sisters Lynda Foster, Judi Weston, and Jeanne Lisse; and the memory of my Grandma Erna and her sisters Elsie and Irene, who raised me to become what I would. My great-grandfather, Anton Werstovshek, and his son Ervin taught me something about the road in their quiet way, but much of my understanding of travel as a path to camaraderie and learning rather than colonization comes from my father. *Nashti zhas vorta po drom o bango.* You can't walk straight on a bent road.

So many friends have helped as well, many of whom are also family. It was as a guest under Anjali Arondekar's roof that I woke up from the dream that told me how to go about framing this project. It was as a guest in Stacy Makishi and Vick Ryder's calming yellow room at the top of the stairs that I happened upon the prologue. While I was on the road, Kumkum Sangari, the Fosters, Lisa Márquez, Naren Subramanian, Marie Chavez, and Anindyo Roy all offered me a place to restore my spirits and my sleep besides. As I began to draft the first chapters, Sheba Chhachhi and Major General S. S. Chhachhi opened their home to me and my wife with a generosity we will long remember.

For someone already blessed with many *hermanas,* Lisa Márquez and Salem Mekuria have been a gift, always knowing the right thing to say, always at my side. Anindyo Roy, Tressa Berman, Neloufer de Mel, Manny Avalos, Kumkum Sangari, Lisa Rofel, Vince Brown, Ajantha Subramanian, Steven Kossak, Yael Navaro-Yashin, Anjali Arondekar, Robert Crusz, Young-Ae Park, Akhil Gupta, Purnima Mankekar, Lamont Thomas, Llew Smith, Kathy Coll, Lucy Burns, Sue Kahn, Rhian Cull, Elena Tajima Creef, Mini Menon, and the late Begoña Aretxaga provided just the right kind of support and critique: enough to keep me on track without derailing me. The same can be said for my editor at Beacon, Gayatri Patnaik, who keeps faith with the art of editing at a time when the winds of the economy blow hard against it. I'm also grateful to my copyeditor, Rosalie Wieder, for improving the manuscript with her light yet deft touch.

Rosie the Rescue Dog is a character as real as any in the book. The tremendous debt I owe to her and her owner, Susan Cahn, should be obvious to anyone who has read the second part of the book. Mel Schottenstein helped me with background research out of a belief in the importance of the topic and the goodness of her heart. Bob Garraway kept me real and raised my spirits every time I ran into him on the block. There would be many poorer rats in this world if it weren't for souls like him.

It is said that students sometimes make the best instructors. I have been privileged while working on this project to have mentored several students who have encouraged me enormously, even as they thought I was encouraging them. Special thanks here go to Lyndon Kamaal Gill and Lilith Mahmud.

To my teachers, on and off the road, this book probably owes the most. First and foremost come the many riders who bothered to talk to a wandering scribbler. Throughout the writing I have circled back to the insightful words of Mengro and Lele, moderators of the now defunct Internet list Allgypsies, which welcomed all Roma, old and new. Grandmaster Bow Sim Mark, Dr. Yang Jwing-Ming, Jean Lukitsh, Roger Jahnke, and Juan Galva taught me the rudiments of *qigong* and tai chi, which feed me as much as words. It was Roger who suggested that I write my practice of *qigong* into the book. Amjee Keyzom Bhutti, founder of Tibet Elderly Help, has inspired me to look beyond the material world in the course of understanding its importance. Somewhere toward the back of the bus sits my second-grade teacher, Mrs. Eileen Kolf, for she is the one who got me thinking that maybe, just maybe, a child without money or connections could write.

No journey I take can come to an end without offering *ishq* and appreciation to my traveling companion in this life, Geeta Patel. Although we've never ridden the bus together, you have been the guardian of time, clarity, and the open door.

Author's Note

Anyone who writes about what it means to live without ready access to cash knows how hard it is to break with genre conventions and refuse to play the voyeur. How many volumes have been written in which well-meaning elites go slumming in order to regale a middle-class readership with stories of hardship? How many volumes have been written in which mean-spirited commentators blame the poor for "their" troubles? I am sure I have unwittingly fallen into such conventions at times, but my goal has been to disrupt them.

I have changed the names of people I met on the road, with the exception of friends who gave permission to do otherwise. In a few (very few) cases, I have also created composite characters and/or altered the time and location where an event occurred. Most of these instances involve bus drivers, who can easily be traced to particular routes and after all have a job to protect. Such changes were introduced at my discretion, not at the request of those with whom I traveled, since people outside the publishing trade may not always realize the long reach of a page.

The book's format attempts to reclaim for intimacy what anthropologists call the ethnographic present. The present tense fell into disrepute for its use during the colonial period to misrepresent "cultures," especially indigenous cultures, as timeless or stuck in the past. To revive the present tense in the midst of punditry about a mysterious "culture of poverty" that has trapped generations in lives of misery (what nonsense!) is a tricky proposition at best. By emphasizing the huge part that political economy and neoliberal policies have played in catapulting increasing numbers of people into material distress, I hope to have avoided any such reductionism. By emphasizing the artistry involved in living poor, I hope to have rendered people who have experienced the downside of globalization as far more than victims. By interweaving the now of my journeys with intimations of what was yet to come and reflections that look back from the time of the book's writing, I hope to have conveyed something of the poignant way that life unfolds in a dance with interpretation.

Readers will also have noticed that the dialogue in the book lacks quotation marks. This is a literary device, put into service here to mark the fact that I make no claims to mechanical reproduction of any of the exchanges. I traveled with no tape recorder; it would have disrupted the flow of life on the road. Instead I cultivated the time-honored arts of memory, training myself to memorize conversations and put them to paper at the first opportunity. (The first opportunity being, in many cases, a rest break. The first medium being, in many cases, a brown paper bag or a length of toilet tissue.) All the events narrated here occurred in life, or perhaps I should say, in life as I have understood it.

I have done my best to honor the spirit and the sensibilities of those who trusted me, as well as those who understandably remained skeptical of my ambitions. May compassion grow, justice flourish, and inequalities lessen.

Notes

It's a Poor Rat That's Got But One Hole:
An Introduction to Living Poor in a Rich Country

1. Associated Press, "Study Says White Families' Wealth Advantage."
2. "Ever Higher Society . . ."
3. Leonhardt, "U.S. Poverty Rate Was Up."
4. UNICEF, *League Table of Child Poverty.*
5. Francis, "It's Better to Be Poor."
6. For a graphic illustration of these trends, see the chart titled "1979 to 1998—Real Family Income Growth by Quintile and for Top 1%" in Collins and Yeskel, *Economic Apartheid in America,* 42; Henwood, *After the New Economy.*
7. "Ever Higher Society," 2.
8. For a sense of the public relations wars over the class composition of bus ridership, see Kevin Merida's "Traveling with Uncertainty" and Jodi Wilgoren's "A Nation Challenged: Bus Travel," along with the riposte by Craig Lentzsch, then CEO of Greyhound Lines, published as a letter to the editor in the *New York Times* under the headline "Staying Safe on the Bus."

1. When the Desert Fails to Bloom:
Albuquerque to Missoula via Vegas

1. Tarlo, *Unsettling Memories,* 16.
2. Cole, *No Equal Justice,* 16.
3. Ibid., 19.
4. Kutalik, "Dockside Wildcats Halt Freight Traffic."
5. Conlin and Bernstein, "Working . . . and Poor," 58.

6. Brennan, *Globalization and Its Terrors.*
7. Shipler, *The Working Poor,* 26.

II. *Leaving the City of Cranes:*
Boston to Milwaukee in Two Alimentary Acts

1. Fullilove, *Root Shock.*
2. Freeman and Rogers, *What Workers Want,* 14.
3. Patel, "Risky Subjects."
4. Williams, "Government Economic Reports."
5. Fox, *It Was Probably Something You Ate,* 201.
6. Schlosser, *Fast Food Nation.*
7. Institute for Women's Policy Research, "Gender Wage Ratio," 1.
8. Boushey et al., *Hardships in America,* 42.
9. Economic Policy Institute, "Economic Snapshots."
10. UNICEF, *League Table of Child Poverty,* 11.
11. Bahney, "Bank of Mom and Dad."
12. Dodson, *Don't Call Us.*
13. Uchitelle, *Disposable American,* 64.
14. Ibid., 205.

III. *Going Coastal: Five Hundred Years of the Poverty Draft,*
New York to St. Augustine

1. Although the bill did not pass, Rangel reintroduced it in 2007. In a message posted on his website, he explained that he proposed to reinstate the draft because "if Americans are to be placed in harm's way, all of us, from every income group and position in society, must share the burden of war" (http://rangel.house.gov).
2. Henwood, "Boom for Whom?"
3. In recent years historians such as Vaughnette Goode-Walker and anthropologists such as Deborah L. Mack have worked to develop counternarratives to this sort of presentation by highlighting Savannah's African and African American legacies, including those that affected everyday life and craftsmanship at the Owens-Thomas house.

IV. *The Fine Arts of Moving in Circles:*
El Monte to Bishop and Back

1. "Ever Higher Society," 4.
2. Baldwin, *No Name in the Street,* 64.
3. McWilliams, *Factories in the Field,* 26.
4. Pace, "More Blacks Live with Pollution."
5. "Beyond Right and Left."

V. *Living on Debts and Promises:*
Montgomery after the Boycott, New Orleans before the Storm

1. An audio version of the speech is available online at www.lib.berkeley.edu/MRC/audiofiles.html.
2. Lewis, "Foreward," viii.
3. Mann, "Los Angeles Bus Riders," 41.
4. The figure of 45 million is based on U.S. Census Bureau statistics for 2003, as reported in Freudenheim, "Record Level of Americans."
5. Hayden, *Street Wars,* 309. To put Bo's comments in a multiregional perspective, Hayden writes that "in Los Angeles alone, over 11,000 young men died in gang wars between 1980 and 2000" (*Street Wars,* 90).
6. Ehrenreich, *Bait and Switch,* 169.
7. Bradley, "Predatory Lending."
8. Shulman, *Betrayal of Work,* 4–5.
9. Ibid., 23.
10. Ryan, *Feather.*
11. "Shrimp Farms," 31.
12. Associated Press, "Mr. T's Makeover."
13. Prakash, "IRS Audits."
14. Wellstone, *How the Rural Poor,* xii.

Read On . . .

Agyeman, Julian, Robert D. Bullard, and Bob Evans, eds. 2003. *Just Sustainabilities: Development in an Unequal World*. Cambridge, MA: MIT Press.

Allison, Dorothy. 1994. *Skin: Talking About Sex, Class, and Literature*. Ithaca, NY: Firebrand Books.

Anderson, Sarah, and John Cavanagh. With Thea Lee. 2000. *Field Guide to the Global Economy*. New York: New Press.

Archibold, Randal C. 2006. "Las Vegas Makes It Illegal to Feed Homeless in Parks." *New York Times* (July 28).

Arsenault, Raymond. 2006. *Freedom Riders: 1961 and the Struggle for Racial Justice*. New York: Oxford University Press.

Associated Press. 2006. "Mr. T's Makeover: The Gold Is Gone: Says He Realized after Katrina It Would Be a 'Sin' to Wear His Jewelry" (July 14). www.msnbc.msn.com/id/13857252/.

———. 2004. "Study Says White Families' Wealth Advantage Has Grown." *New York Times* (October 18).

———. 2003. "More U.S. Families Hungry or Too Poor to Eat, Study Says." (November 2).

Bahney, Anna. 2006. "The Bank of Mom and Dad." *New York Times* (April 20).

Baldwin, James. 1972. *No Name in the Street*. New York: Laurel/Dell.

Bayot, Jennifer. 2004. "As Bills Mount, Debts on Homes Rise for Elderly." *New York Times* (July 3).

Becker, Elizabeth. 2002. "Mayors Say Requests for Food and Shelter Are Up." *New York Times* (Dec. 18).

Bernstein, Jared, Chauna Brocht, and Maggie Spade-Aguilar. 2000. *How Much Is Enough? Basic Family Budgets for Working Families*. Washington, DC: Economic Policy Institute.

"Beyond Right and Left, the Spiritual Center." 2003. *Indian Country Today* (July 9):A4.

Blau, Joel. 2001. *Illusions of Prosperity: America's Working Families in an Age of Economic Insecurity.* New York: Oxford University Press.

Boushey, Heather, Chauna Brocht, Bethney Gundersen, and Jared Bernstein. 2001. *Hardships in America: The Real Story of Working Families.* Washington, DC: Economic Policy Institute.

Bradley, Jeanette. 2000. "Predatory Lending: Banks Trick Poor into Expensive Loans." *Dollars and Sense* (January/February):12–14, 37.

Brennan, Teresa. 2003. *Globalization and Its Terrors: Daily Life in the West.* New York: Routledge.

Bullard, Robert D. 2000. *Dumping in Dixie: Race, Class, and Environmental Quality.* Boulder, CO: Westview Press.

Bullard, Robert D., Glenn S. Johnson, and Angel O. Torres, eds. 2004. *Highway Robbery: Transportation Racism and New Routes to Equity.* Cambridge, MA: South End Press.

Bureau of Labor Statistics. 2006–07. *Occupational Outlook Handbook.* Washington, DC: Office of Occupational Statistics and Employment Projections.

"Bush's Harvest of Shame: One Million Black Children in Extreme Poverty." 2003. *The Black Commentator,* http://blackcommentator .com/41/41_cover_pr.html.

Chapman, Jeff, and Michael Ettlinger. 2004. "The Who and Why of the Minimum Wage." *EPI Issue Brief* 201 (August 6):1–7.

Childers, Mary. 2006. *Welfare Brat.* New York: St. Martin's Press.

Cliff, Michelle. 2004. *Free Enterprise.* San Francisco: City Lights.

Cole, David. 1999. *No Equal Justice: Race and Class in the American Criminal Justice System.* New York: New Press.

Collins, Chuck, and Felice Yeskel. With United for a Fair Economy. 2000. *Economic Apartheid in America: A Primer on Economic Inequality and Insecurity.* New York: New Press.

Conlin, Michelle, and Aaron Bernstein. 2004. "Working... and Poor." *Business Week* (May 31):58–68.

Davis, Angela. 2003. *Are Prisons Obsolete?* New York: Open Media/Seven Stories.

Davis, Mike. 1999. *Prisoners of the American Dream: Politics and Economy in the History of the U.S. Working Class.* London: Verso.

Depastino, Todd. 2005. *Citizen Hobo: How a Century of Homelessness Shaped America.* Chicago: University of Chicago Press.

Dhar, Lopamudra Banerjee. 2003. "A Clear Case of Racism: In New York, Bus Depots Are Located in Areas Where Coloured People Live." *Down to Earth* (November 30):44.

Dodson, Lisa. 1999. *Don't Call Us Out of Name: The Untold Lives of Women and Girls in Poor America*. Boston: Beacon Press.

"Doggone Shame: Greyhound Fails Test of ADA Compliance." 2006. www.mcil.org/mcil/adapt/greydog5.htm.

Duneier, Mitchell. 1992. *Slim's Table: Race, Respectability, and Masculinity*. Chicago: University of Chicago Press.

Economic Policy Institute. 2005. "Economic Snapshots: The Gender Wage Gap Is Real" (September 14). www.epi.org/printer.cfm?id= 2111&content_type=1&nice_name=webfeatures_snapshots_ 20050914.

Ehrenreich, Barbara. 2005. *Bait and Switch: The (Futile) Pursuit of the American Dream*. New York: Metropolitan/Henry Holt.

———. 2001. *Nickel and Dimed: On (Not) Getting By in America*. New York: Metropolitan/Henry Holt.

"Ever Higher Society, Ever Harder to Ascend: Meritocracy in America." 2004. *The Economist* (December 29).

Fox, Nicols. 1999. *It Was Probably Something You Ate: A Practical Guide to Avoiding and Surviving Food-borne Illness*. New York: Penguin.

Francis, David R. 2005. "It's Better to be Poor in Norway than in the US." *Christian Science Monitor* (April 14).

Freeman, Richard B., and Joel Rogers. 1999. *What Workers Want*. Ithaca, NY: ILR Press.

Freudenheim, Milt. 2004. "Record Level of Americans Not Insured on Health." *New York Times* (August 27).

Fullilove, Mindy Thompson. 2005. *Root Shock: How Tearing Up City Neighborhoods Hurts America, and What We Can Do About It*. New York: One World/Ballantine.

Gilliom, John. 2001. *Overseers of the Poor: Surveillance, Resistance, and the Limits of Privacy*. Chicago: University of Chicago Press.

Giroux, Henry A. 1999. *The Mouse That Roared: Disney and the End of Innocence*. New York: Rowman & Littlefield.

"Greyhound Fails Activists' Test of ADA Compliance." 1998. *RESIST Newsletter* (May):3.

Harrington, Michael. 1997 [1962]. *The Other America: Poverty in the United States*. New York: Scribner.

Hayden, Tom. 2004. *Street Wars: Gangs and the Future of Violence.* New York: New Press.

Hays, Sharon. 2003. *Flat Broke with Children: Women in the Age of Welfare Reform.* New York: Oxford University Press.

Henwood, Doug. 2003. *After the New Economy.* New York: New Press.

———. 2000. "Boom for Whom?" *Left Business Observer* 93 (February).

Herivel, Tara, and Paul Wright, eds. 2003. *Prison Nation: The Warehousing of America's Poor.* New York: Routledge.

hooks, bell. 2000. *Where We Stand: Class Matters.* New York: Routledge.

Hudson, Michael, ed. 1996. *Merchants of Misery: How Corporate America Profits from Poverty.* Monroe, ME: Common Courage Press.

Indian Health Service. 1998. "Indian Children and CHIP: Children's Health Insurance Program." www.ihs.gov/MedicalPrograms/HealthCare/consult.asp.

Institute for Women's Policy Research. 2005. "The Gender Wage Ratio: Women's and Men's Earnings" (IWPR Fact Sheet #C350). www.iwpr.org.

Jackson, Carlton. 1984. *Hounds of the Road: A History of the Greyhound Bus Company.* Dubuque, IA: Kendall/Hunt.

Kawachi, Ichiro, and Bruce P. Kennedy. 2006. *The Health of Nations: Why Inequality Is Harmful to Your Health.* New York: New Press.

Kennedy, Michelle. 2005. *Without a Net: Middle Class and Homeless (with Kids) in America.* New York: Viking.

Kozol, Jonathan. 1988. *Rachel and Her Children: Homeless Families in America.* New York: Fawcett Columbine/Ballantine Books.

Kutalik, Chris. 2004. "Dockside Wildcats Halt Freight Traffic: Gas Prices Fuel Port Drivers' Revolt." *Labor Notes* (June).

Leff, Walli F., and Marilyn G. Haft. 1983. *Time Without Work: People Who Are Not Working Tell Their Stories.* Boston: South End Press.

Lentzsch, Craig. 2001. "Staying Safe on the Bus." (November 17):A22.

Leonhardt, David. 2005. "U.S. Poverty Rate Was Up Last Year." *New York Times* (August 31).

———. 2004. "More Americans Were Uninsured and Poor in 2003, Census Finds." *New York Times* (August 27).

Lewis, Diane E. 2002. "Looking for Help: Study Finds Big Need for Extended Jobless Benefits." *Boston Globe* (February 16).

Lewis, John. 2004. "Foreward." In Robert D. Bullard et al., eds., *Highway Robbery,* viii–ix. Cambridge, MA: South End Press.

Liebow, Elliot. 1995. *Tell Them Who I Am: The Lives of Homeless Women.* New York: Penguin.

Lindorff, Dave. 2003. "Dishonorable Discharge: Bush Administration Slashes Veteran's Benefits." *In These Times* (November 26). http://inthesetimes.com/comments.php?id=465_0_2_0_C.

Lubove, Seth. 2004. "On the Backs of the Poor: Illegal Immigrants Don't Dare Open a Bank Account in the U.S. to Wire Money Overseas." *Forbes* (November 15):156–160.

MacLeod, Jay. 1995. *Ain't No Makin' It: Aspirations and Attainment in a Low-Income Neighborhood.* Boulder, CO: Westview Press.

Mahler, Sarah J. 1995. *American Dreaming: Immigrant Life on the Margins.* Princeton, NJ: Princeton University Press.

Mann, Eric. 2004. "Los Angeles Bus Riders Derail the MTA." In Robert D. Bullard et al., eds., *Highway Robbery,* 33–47. Cambridge, MA: South End Press.

May, John P., and Khalid R. Pitts, eds. 2000. *Building Violence: How America's Rush to Incarcerate Creates More Violence.* Thousand Oaks, CA: Sage.

McWilliams, Carey. 1999 [1935]. *Factories in the Field: The Story of Migratory Farm Labor in California.* Berkeley: University of California Press.

Meier, Albert E., and John P. Hoschek. 1975. *Over the Road: A History of Intercity Bus Transportation in the United States.* Upper Montclair, NJ: Motor Bus Society.

Merida, Kevin. 2001. "Traveling with Uncertainty." *Washington Post* (October 13):C1.

Mintz, Sidney W. 1986. *Sweetness and Power: The Place of Sugar in Modern History.* New York: Penguin.

Mishel, Lawrence, Jared Bernstein, and Sylvia Allegretto. 2006. *The State of Working America 2006/2007.* Washington, DC: Economic Policy Institute.

Moore, R. Laurence. 1994. *Selling God: American Religion in the Market-place of Culture.* New York: Oxford University Press.

National Endowment for the Arts. 2004. *Reading at Risk: A Survey of Literary Reading in America.* Research Division Report #46. Washington, DC: National Endowment for the Arts.

Nelson, Margaret K. 2005. *The Social Economy of Single Motherhood: Raising Children in Rural America.* New York: Routledge.

Nestle, Marion. 2003. *Safe Food: Bacteria, Biotechnology, and Bioterrorism.* Berkeley: University of California Press.

Neubeck, Kenneth J., and Noel A. Cazenave. 2001. *Welfare Racism: Playing the Race Card Against America's Poor.* New York: Routledge.

Newman, Katherine S. 2000. *No Shame in My Game: The Working Poor in the Inner City.* New York: Vintage.

———. 1999. *Falling from Grace: Downward Mobility in the Age of Affluence.* Berkeley: University of California Press.

O'Connor, Alice. 2001. *Poverty Knowledge: Social Science, Social Policy, and the Poor in Twentieth-Century U.S. History.* Princeton: Princeton University Press.

Otto, Mary. 2002. "Area Housing Boom Drives Out Mobile Homes." *Washington Post* (December 27).

Pace, David. 2005. "More Blacks Live with Pollution." *Associated Press* (December 14).

Patel, Geeta. 2006. "Risky Subjects: Insurance, Sexuality, and Capital." *Social Text* 24/89 (4):25–65.

Penelope, Julia, ed. 1994. *Out of the Class Closet: Lesbians Speak.* Freedom, CA: Crossing Press.

"The Poor and the Near-Poor Struggle to Stay Afloat." 2006. *International Herald Tribune* (May 10).

Porter, Eduardo, and Mary Williams Walsh. 2005. "Retirement Turns into a Rest Stop as Benefits Dwindle." *New York Times* (February 9).

Prakash, Snigdha. 2001. "IRS Audits." *All Things Considered* (National Public Radio broadcast, February 16).

Prashad, Vijay. 2003. *Keeping Up with the Dow Joneses: Debt, Prison, Workfare.* Cambridge, MA: South End Press.

Ravallion, Martin. 1996. "Issues in Measuring and Modeling Poverty." *Economic Journal* 106:1328–1344.

Reuters. 2007. "US Icon Greyhound Now in British Hands." *Hindustan Times Business & World* (February 10):1.

Riis, Jacob A. 1997 [1890]. *How the Other Half Lives: Studies Among the Tenements of New York.* New York: Penguin Books.

Rimer, Sara. 2001. "Six Die in Greyhound Crash After Driver's Throat Is Slit." *New York Times* (October 4).

Rosaldo, Renato. 1993. *Culture and Truth: The Remaking of Social Analysis.* Boston: Beacon Press.

Rossi, Peter. 1989. *Down and Out in America: The Origins of Homelessness.* Chicago: University of Chicago Press.

Ryan, Sonny. 2006. Feather. *Indian Country Today* (June 21):B3.

Schlosser, Eric. 2002. *Fast Food Nation: The Dark Side of the All-American Meal.* New York: Harper Perennial.

Seabrook, Jeremy. 2003. *The No-Nonsense Guide to World Poverty.* London: New Internationalist/Verso.

Sennett, Richard, and Jonathan Cobb. 1972. *The Hidden Injuries of Class.* New York: Vintage Books/Random House.

Sharff, Jagna Wojcicka. 1998. *King Kong on 4th Street: Families and the Violence of Poverty on the Lower East Side.* Boulder, CO: Westview Press.

Shipler, David K. 2005. *The Working Poor: Invisible in America.* New York: Vintage.

Shorris, Earl. 1997. *New American Blues: A Journey through Poverty to Democracy.* New York: W.W. Norton.

"Shrimp Farms on the Gulf." 2006. *The Economist* (November 25):31–32.

Shulman, Beth. 2003. *The Betrayal of Work: How Low-Wage Jobs Fail 30 Million Americans.* New York: New Press.

Silko, Leslie Marmon. 1997. *Yellow Woman and a Beauty of the Spirit.* New York: Simon & Schuster.

Sklar, Holly, et al. 2002. *Raise the Floor: Wages and Policies That Work for All of Us.* Cambridge, MA: South End Press.

Slessarev, Helene. 1997. *The Betrayal of the Urban Poor.* Philadelphia: Temple University Press.

Steinhauer, Jennifer. 2006. "Statistics Aside, Many Feel Pinch of Daily Costs." *New York Times* (May 6).

Stewart, Kathleen. 1996. *A Space at the Side of the Road: Cultural Poetics in an "Other" America.* Princeton, NJ: Princeton University Press.

Sudbury, Julia. 2005. *Global Lockdown: Race, Gender, and the Prison-Industrial Complex.* New York: Routledge.

Tarlo, Emma. 2003. *Unsettling Memories: Narratives of the Emergency in Delhi.* London: Hurst & Co.

Terkel, Studs. 2000. *Hard Times: An Oral History of the Great Depression.* New York: W. W. Norton.

Tiny, a.k.a. Lisa Gray-Garcia. 2006. *Criminal of Poverty: Growing Up Homeless in America.* San Francisco: City Lights.

Uchitelle, Louis. 2006. *The Disposable American: Layoffs and Their Consequences.* New York: Knopf.

UNICEF. 2000. *A League Table of Child Poverty in Rich Nations* (Innocenti Report Card Issue No. 1). Florence: UNICEF Innocenti Research Centre.

Veseth, Michael. 1990. *Mountains of Debt: Crisis and Change in Renaissance Florence, Victorian Britain, and Postwar America.* New York: Oxford University Press.

Wellstone, Paul. 2003 [1978]. *How the Rural Poor Got Power: Narrative of a Grass-Roots Organizer.* Minneapolis: University of Minnesota Press.

Western Regional Advocacy Project. 2006. "Without Housing: Decades of Federal Housing Cutbacks, Massive Homelessness, and Policy Failures." www.wraphome.org.

Weston, Kath. 2005. "Class Politics and Scavenger Anthropology in Dinesh D'Souza's *The Virtue of Prosperity.*" In Catherine Besteman and Hugh Gusterson, eds., *Why America's Top Pundits Are Wrong: Anthropologists Talk Back,* 154–179. Berkeley: University of California Press.

Wilgoren, Jodi. 2001. "A Nation Challenged: Bus Travel: On the Greyhound Bus, Too, Life Changed After Attacks." *New York Times* (November 10):A1.

Williams, John. 2004. "Government Economic Reports." Series Master Introduction (August 24). www.shadowstats.com/cgibin/sgs/article/id=340.

Wilson, William Julius. 1996. *When Work Disappears: The World of the New Urban Poor.* New York: Vintage Books/Random House.

———. 1987. *The Truly Disadvantaged: The Inner City, the Underclass, and Public Policy.* Chicago: University of Chicago Press.

Wolff, Edward N. 1995. *Top Heavy: The Increasing Inequality of Wealth in America and What Can Be Done About It.* New York: New Press.

Wray, Matt, and Annalee Newitz, eds. 1997. *White Trash: Race and Class in America.* New York: Routledge.